HUMAN RIGHTS AND CULTURAL DIVERSITY

This series publishes ground-breaking work on key topics in the area of global justice and human rights including democracy, gender, poverty, the environment, and just war. Books in the series are of broad interest to theorists working in politics, international relations, philosophy, and related disciplines.

Textbooks in Global Justice and Human Rights
Series Editor: Thom Brooks

www.euppublishing.com/series/sgjhr

HUMAN RIGHTS AND CULTURAL DIVERSITY

Core Issues and Cases

Andrew Fagan

EDINBURGH
University Press

Edinburgh University Press is one of the leading university presses
in the UK. We publish academic books and journals in our selected
subject areas across the humanities and social sciences, combining
cutting-edge scholarship with high editorial and production values to
produce academic works of lasting importance. For more information
visit our website: edinburghuniversitypress.com

Edinburgh University Press Ltd
The Tun – Holyrood Road, 12(2f) Jackson's Entry, Edinburgh EH8 8PJ

Typeset in 11/13 Palatino Light by
Servis Filmsetting Ltd, Stockport, Cheshire,
and printed and bound in Great Britain by
CPI Group (UK) Ltd, Croydon CR0 4YY

A CIP record for this book is available from the British Library

ISBN 978 1 4744 0116 6 (hardback)
ISBN 978 1 4744 0118 0 (paperback)
ISBN 978 1 4744 0117 3 (webready PDF)
ISBN 978 1 4744 0119 7 (epub)

Contents

Acknowledgements

This book has benefited from a great deal of support and advice. For many years, I have had the good fortune of teaching and researching human rights within one of the world's foremost academic human rights centres: the Human Rights Centre at the University of Essex. The Essex human rights community provides a superb environment in which to teach and research human rights. Particular mention must be made of Julian Burger, Fabian Freyenhagen, Paul Hunt, Sheldon Leader, Noam Lubell, Lorna McGregor, Sabine Michalowski, Nigel Rodley, Colin Samson and Ahmed Shaheed, all of whom have either supported this project or directly provided detailed feedback and commentary on various chapters. My understanding of the complexity of specific areas of human rights and cultural diversity has also greatly benefited from the feedback offered by participants at various conferences and symposia at which I presented papers which influenced the final drafting of this book. Particular mention should be made of Mark Bevir and Richard Ashcroft at UC Berkeley, Max Pensky at SUNY, and various participants of a panel discussion at the 2015 Annual Conference of the American Political Science Association, in particular Thomas Dumm and Sarah Song. My series editor, Thom Brooks, has proven to be a very understanding, patient and sympathetic interlocutor during the initial discussions concerning the content of the book and the twists and turns in the subsequent journey towards its completion. I am extremely grateful to Thom. My partner, Julia Firmin, has not only provided invaluable research support and a critical sounding-board but has ultimately tolerated my long mental and physical absences in producing this final manuscript. Thank you, my love. Finally, I dedicate this book to my grandson, Jesse Jake, who is just now beginning to discover his own voice and in whom the human spirit burns brightly indeed. I hope Jesse will learn to value diversity as I have done.

Abbreviations

ASEAN	Association of Southeast Asian Nations
CCPR	Committee for Civil and Political Rights
CEDAW	Convention on the Elimination of All Forms of Discrimination against Women
CKGR	Central Kalahari Game Reserve
CRC	Convention on the Rights of the Child
DEVAW	Declaration on the Elimination of Violence against Women
ECHR	European Convention on Human Rights
ECLAC	Economic Commission for Latin America and the Caribbean
ECtHR	European Court of European Rights
FGM	female genital mutilation
GDP	gross domestic product
HRBA	human rights-based approach to development
HCP	harmful cultural practice
HRC	United Nations Human Rights Council
ICCPR	International Covenant on Civil and Political Rights
ICERD	International Convention on the Elimination of All Forms of Racial Discrimination
ICESCR	International Covenant on Economic, Social and Cultural Rights
IDB	Inter-American Development Bank
IFAD	International Fund for Agricultural Development
IHRL	international human rights law
ILO	International Labour Organization
LGTB	lesbian, gay, transgender and bisexual

OHCHR	Office of the United Nations High Commissioner for Human Rights
OIC	Organisation of Islamic Cooperation
UDHR	Universal Declaration of Human Rights
UN	United Nations
UNDRIP	Declaration on the Rights of Indigenous Peoples
UNESCO	United Nations Organization for Education, Science and Culture
UNPFII	United Nations Permanent Forum on Indigenous Issues
VDPA	Vienna Declaration and Programme of Action

Introduction

This book addresses a series of challenges which have largely defied attempts to secure a lasting and successful resolution to the problems they exemplify. Specifically, these challenges speak to the enduringly troubled relationship between the promotion of human rights and the promotion of cultural diversity. Not so long ago, most contributors to discussions concerning the philosophy and law of human rights sought to ignore the question of culture within human rights generally. All too often, engagement with the cultural dimension of human rights was restricted to a largely futile repetition of the universalists versus relativists 'debate'. Human rights supporters conventionally reasserted their adherence to some form of moral universalism, while those who opposed human rights were dismissed as relativists, or worse still, nihilists. In-between these two intellectual poles there existed a relatively small minority of theorists and practitioners who, although convinced that human rights must be founded upon universally legitimate principles, were nevertheless uneasy over others' dismissal of any consideration of culture within human rights. Thankfully, such days are increasingly a matter for the past. Over the past two decades or so, there has been increasing interest in the subtler and more sophisticated challenges which cultural analysis often raises for the justification and implementation of universal human rights norms. This book aims to make a significant contribution to this body of human rights scholarship. For, while the importance of culture is increasingly acknowledged within human rights circles, many within the human rights community remain uncertain about what the effects of acknowledging the importance of cultural membership may be for the continuing implementation of human rights. This book analyses some of those core areas of uncertainty and seeks to identify a relatively under-explored route towards reconciling the two objectives of respecting universal human rights whilst also acknowledging the value and importance of cultural diversity in humankind's continuing story.

We are all of us influenced, to a greater or lesser extent, by the cultural conditions which surround us. The so-called West is no less imbued with culture than any other region of the world. Culture is not something which only afflicts the 'Other'. A hypothetical 'museum of mankind' should not only contain those 'exotic' exhibits to which far too many of the actual museums of mankind around the world shamefully continue to restrict themselves. One way in which human rights discourse has often failed to engage with actual human beings' lives is its previously uncritical acceptance of the assumption that cultural belonging was a problem which afflicted only 'non-Westerners'. Through recognising the sheer ubiquity of the influence of culture upon all of our ways of being and believing, we are able to set to one side this particularly unhelpful and utterly false assumption. One of the core tasks confronting any fruitful engagement between human rights and cultural diversity is to accept that human rights do not necessarily require of each of us that we renounce our cultural commitments as a precondition for enjoying our human rights, or contributing to academic discussions concerning the basis and scope of human rights in the twenty-first century. I take it then that a principal aim of a book such as this is to reject the objective of dispelling the role of culture in thinking about and implementing human rights in a culturally complex world. Neither human rights philosophy nor law originates in some utterly transcendental realm of allegedly pure reason. Human rights are thus an utterly this-worldly phenomenon, which nevertheless holds the promise of establishing a more humane global order for all. In this light, the proper role for human rights is not to deny the importance of culture, but to maintain and promote the potential for all of us to critically engage with the ways of being and believing which can exert such a profound influence upon many of us. While I shall argue for this in greater detail throughout the book, I conceive of human rights as fundamentally valuable to the extent that they embody a particular type of attitude towards humanity and inhumanity. Human rights provide a tangible vehicle for steering humankind away from our horrendously inhumane impulses and towards that which, in a non-theological sense, serves to redeem us: our potential for humanity. No single culture or civilisation has a monopoly claim to the title of embodying humanity, nor is any single culture or civilisation entirely inhumane or barbaric. To this extent, the challenge of reconciling human rights with cultural diversity is a truly global, universal one.

Chapter 1 begins to establish the normative foundations and content of my attempt at reconciling human rights with cultural diversity. I specify what I take human rights to necessarily consist of and discuss my claim that human rights embody a specific disposition towards the ideal of humanity, even though the strongest impetus for human rights consists of the terrible and continuing symptoms of inhumanity. The chapter considers the importance of the ideals of liberty, equality and dignity in underpinning human rights claims. The chapter also introduces an approach to agency which will recur throughout the rest of the book. Specifically, I contend that international human rights law (IHRL) is increasingly responding to identity-based claims and interests from various communities of people across the globe. However, the response of IHRL to the challenge of identity is, I argue, hamstrung by the enduring influence of forms of philosophising which either have little to say about how human identities are formed and maintained, or explicitly reject any such phenomenal conditions as irrelevant for determining the principles upon which communities of human beings should be regulated. Not the least potentially controversial aspect of this book is, thus, my attempt to demonstrate the importance for human rights of an alternative account of human agency, which seeks to build constitutional principles out of an acknowledgement of the essentially relational character of identity formation.

Having introduced the key components of my own position and subsequent analysis, Chapter 2 then proceeds to show how this alternative vision can enable us all to overcome the largely futile universalist/ relativist debate, which generations of human rights thinkers and practitioners have indulged. I provide a detailed analysis of one relatively recent attempt to overcome conceptual polarisation and discuss, particularly, John Rawls's attempt to square human rights with recognising the existence of many non-liberal societies, whose core commitments often do not comply with core human rights ideals. I ultimately reject the proposed solution which Rawls exemplifies and outline an alternative position which appeals to the ideal of humanity whilst affirming a more nuanced conception of culture than is typically found within contributions to this area of concern. All too often such contributions fail to adequately acknowledge the extent to which specific cultural communities are represented through a complex framework of power and politics, in which allegedly essential traditions and practices are affirmed by those seeking a less censorious accommodation with cultural differences. I argue that one of the core justifications for human rights resides precisely in enabling people to contribute to the collective representations of their own lives and aspirations. Human rights exist, in part, to afford people the opportunity to deliberate upon their own 'fate'.

Chapter 3 narrows the focus of the book to what is an essential element of any attempt to reconcile human rights with cultural diversity: the extent to which a collective right to cultural identity must figure within IHRL. Whilst arguing that human rights cannot unconditionally endorse whatever the powerful within any given community claims to be essential for the community's identity, I nevertheless show the extent to which existing IHRL already recognises rights to cultural identity. I argue that IHRL cannot and indeed does not continue to endorse a so-called colour-blind approach to discrimination and inequality. Ignoring the sources of human rights violations does nothing to prevent such violations. I distinguish between what are typically referred to as ascribed and voluntary forms of cultural belonging and argue that the former are the most important for understanding the entire pull towards identity-based claims and also raise some of the most problematic challenges in determining the scope of any right to cultural identity. Chapter 3 revisits the long-standing discussion concerning the status of collective rights claims, and offers a conditional justification for an understanding of human rights claims which do not always collapse into short-sighted individualist assumptions.

Chapter 4 begins the process of applying the normative vision this book presents to specific and particularly significant identity-based claims. I begin with the rights of women and offer a detailed analysis of the extent to which the call to espouse cultural diversity has often entailed exposing some women and girls to systematic human rights violations. I consider the principal instrument of IHRL for protecting women's rights – the UN Convention on the Elimination of All Forms of Discrimination against Women (CEDAW) – and gauge its strengths and weaknesses. I engage directly with the question of cultural harm and consider and reject one well-established response to the possibility of women becoming trapped within their communities. In outlining an account of the potential for cultural communities to severely harm some women, I draw heavily upon the relational account of agency which figures prominently across this book. In doing so, I acknowledge the importance of some feminist thinking in developing a more sophisticated and robust account of how identity can be formed and deformed.

Chapter 5 engages with another area of so-called identity politics which has often wreaked havoc within and across many communities: national and ethnic identity. I argue against some recent theorists who have proclaimed the death of such forms of identity, and insist that IHRL does and must continue to take seriously the phenomenological reality of many people's lives in which such forms of identity loom large. I show how national and ethnic identity claims have exerted a profound influence upon the entire body of minority rights and ultimately aim to show more constructive grounds upon which national and ethnic identity claims can be better reconciled with the core objectives of IHRL.

Chapter 6 then turns towards the often severe challenges which indigenous peoples have experienced in their attempts to protect their collective ways of being and believing against the encroaching forces of a particular form of modernity. I discuss and explain the relative lack of established IHRL covering the rights of indigenous peoples and consider the extent to which successfully defending the human rights of indigenous peoples requires a critical reflection upon a series of influential assumptions underlying aspects of IHRL.

Chapter 7 is the longest chapter in the book and engages with the question of how human rights may successfully ground and provide for the right of religious freedom. Against those who consider human rights and religion to be, in some essential sense, incompatible bodies of thought and belief, I show how various religions have directly influenced the development of human rights norms. I consider the complex relationships between various world religions and human rights before proceeding to analyse several areas of long-standing concern and controversy concerning the scope of a right to religious freedom.

Chapter 8 marks the conclusion to this book. I restate the core arguments contained within the prior pages and offer several reflections upon what I consider to be some of the most vital implications of my account of human rights for the continuing challenge of reconciling a respect for human rights with a respect for cultural diversity.

This book is intended for a wide readership, which includes professional academics, human rights practitioners, and also undergraduate and postgraduate students engaged in studies which require a knowledge and understanding of the topics covered here. It is also intended for anyone who is as fascinated and troubled by the challenge of diversity as I have been. The book includes various 'study tools' designed to assist readers new to this area of interest. These include suggestions for further reading at the end of each chapter and key questions at the beginning of each chapter. The latter are particularly intended to encourage an active engagement with the material. Student readers, in particular, are thereby encouraged to read each chapter in a way which enables them to answer the chapter's key questions. Ultimately, the life and spirit of any book depends fundamentally upon who reads it and how it is read. My hope is that this book is read widely and constructively, since now having written it, my work is largely done.

1

A Defensible Universalism

Key questions

1. What role, if any, does geography play in the justification of human rights?
2. What are human rights?
3. What is gained by identifying human rights with IHRL? What is lost by doing so?
4. What are some of the key motivations behind the establishment of the modern human rights movement?
5. Why do philosophers typically disagree on what human rights are?
6. Why are liberty, equality and human dignity so important to human rights?
7. What is the 'positive liberty tradition' and what is its significance for human rights?
8. Why is equality so important to human rights?
9. What are the basis and the limitations of the 'indifferent to difference' approach?
10. Why is it necessary to accord any importance to the social context of human agency in defending human rights?

Introduction

This first chapter presents a framework for understanding human rights in the context of cultural diversity. I begin by addressing the need for human rights and argue that human rights are motivated by the terrible and enduring consequences of inhumanity whilst simultaneously testifying to the persevering potential of humanity. I then proceed to enumerate my understanding of the content of human rights and an account of the normative basis of human rights. I identify the content of human rights with its institutional embodiment within international human rights law (IHRL). Despite this appeal to positive law, I argue that IHRL is inherently normative to the extent that it draws upon three core moral ideals: liberty, equality and dignity. I discuss these ideals and offer formulations of each of them. I conclude by arguing that any attempt to formulate a human rights-based response to cultural diversity is bound to acknowledge the social basis and context of human life and agency.

Human rights, melancholia and loyalty to humanity

For any right to be considered a quintessentially *human* right it must be capable of being possessed by all human beings to whom it applies. For example, all human beings are said to possess an absolute human right against torture. All human beings, wherever they happen to be, whether in the valleys of Kandahar in Afghanistan or the streets of Manhattan, possess this right by virtue of being human. State authorities may not justify torturing someone on the grounds that any particular human being is in some sense less human by virtue of behaving in an allegedly inhumane manner. Similarly, a human right to health care cannot be denied on the grounds that some individuals routinely pursue unhealthy lifestyles. An individual's possession of their human rights is not dependent upon their meritorious behaviour. Nor do contingent circumstances, such as geographical location, affect anyone's fundamental claims to the possession of human rights. Finally, the task of justifying human rights does not ultimately depend upon their being endorsed by all human beings. A coherent case for the universality of human rights can be made despite the fact that not everyone views human rights as universally valid. Thus, human rights must be both universally applicable, essentially independent of their recognition within bodies of law, and, to a certain extent, impervious to people's opinion of them.

In terms of their practical efficacy it is obviously desirable that they are widely endorsed by those who would have an interest in them. I shall argue that the most concerted opposition to human rights emanates amongst those who view human rights as posing a systematic threat to continuing inequality and political injustice. It is also desirable that human rights are legally established and implemented, but legal recognition is not a condition of their moral legitimacy. One must therefore distinguish between human rights as grounded within a moral vision and their existence as legal rights, which may, or may not, be adequately respected and protected by those who have incurred a legal duty to do so. To dispense with an appeal to moral argument would render any inclusion of the *human* within human rights largely superfluous and leave us with only collections of legal rights whose existence is dependent upon legal and political contingency. In practice, of course, all human beings' enjoyment of their human rights is largely dependent upon the will and power of contingent authorities to make good their legal commitments. However, we are only able to criticise such inequalities in accessing human rights by appealing to the morality of human rights, which grounds their universal legitimacy.

Moral argumentation is essential to the justification of human rights. However, the indispensable role of moral argument within human rights also provides the source for endless debate and discussion. The interminable character of moral argument offers one of the most compelling reasons why many human rights defenders prefer to ignore morality and focus instead upon the tangible and irrefutable nature of legal rights. While frustration with moral philosophy is often understandable, to dispense with morality is to throw the baby of human rights out with the bathwater of apparently unending intellectual debate.

Setting aside for the moment those who argue that no moral principle can ever be shown to be objectively and universally true, those philosophers who have attempted to identify the distinctly moral foundations of human rights have typically added to the frustration with philosophy by proposing a very diverse and sometimes mutually incompatible range of arguments and justifications. Thus, some philosophers have argued that a genuinely universal set of human attributes and capacities can only really offer a defence of civil and political rights and thus does not extend to all existing IHRL. Such arguments tend to conceptualise equal liberty in terms which restrict the state to largely upholding a limited set of negative rights, which claim to leave individuals free to determine their own commitments and choices but do not actively support the exercise of liberty. Other philosophers have deeply disagreed with this approach to human rights and have insisted that the collection of human attributes and capabilities which human agency consists of entails a commitment to a holistic account of human rights, which includes civil, political, social, economic and, increasingly, cultural rights also. Place any two philosophers in a room and you seem guaranteed to get an argument. This is, of course, problematic when the objective of discussion is precisely to identify a common moral basis for the existence of human rights.

While philosophers of human rights tend to disagree on how human rights can best be argued for, most of these approaches highlight what might be referred to as *laudable* human characteristics, whether it be the capacity for exercising reason or the capacity to commune with the natural environment. If the objective of such arguments is to identify what makes us essentially human in order to ground subsequent claims to the necessary conditions for our agency, then all such approaches are guilty of falsely (or partially) representing humankind.

We are a truly astonishing species. This has been said many times before and in many different ways. We have proven ourselves capable of the most extraordinary intellectual and physical feats. We have constructed civilisations and we have identified the very building blocks of all life. We have also shown ourselves to be capable of the most horrendous acts of brutality and destruction. Generally, philosophers have been reluctant to engage with what might be termed the 'darker side' of humankind, although there are exceptions. Some philosophers simply despair at humankind. For contemporary philosophers such as John Gray (2003) human beings are an essentially rapacious species. The idea of humanity is effectively a myth, which some of us endorse in a futile attempt to avoid having to confront what is left when the deceitful consolations of religion and secular theology fall away: the sheer nihilistic meaninglessness of human existence. Those who have not abandoned all real hope cling to a series of mere illusions that moral progress can be achieved, despite the fact that the very same people are typically incapable of agreeing upon what morality might actually consist of. Much of the rest of humankind blithely continues to inflict largely irreparable harm on one another, non-human animals and the environment in the pursuit of their partial interests. According to another philosopher, renowned for his profoundly melancholic critique of instrumentally rationalised life, 'no universal history leads from savagery to humanitarianism, but there is one leading from the slingshot to the megaton bomb' (Adorno 1973: 320). The despair of the likes of Gray and Adorno echoes Thomas Hobbes's description of life in the state of nature as 'solitary, poore, nasty, brutish and short' ([1651] 1962: 143). It would be tempting to dismiss such melancholic pronouncements as the vocalisations of overly sensitive souls. However, one does not need to be particularly misanthropic to discern humankind's propensity towards violence and destruction. Hobbes was writing in the immediate aftermath of an extremely brutal English Civil War. Adorno fashioned his entire philosophical vision as a direct response to 'Auschwitz', itself a horrific symbol for acts of barbarism and savagery which might once have been considered simply inconceivable. Gray is writing at a time where despite ubiquitous references to human rights, violations of human rights continue to occur on a global and entirely systematic scale. I write these words as, alongside other ongoing human calamities, a refugee crisis is unfolding in Europe and the bodies of three-year-old children are washing up on Mediterranean coasts, while many European states and their populations are attempting to prevent those refugees who do not drown in the sea from entering onto their sovereign soil. It certainly casts into a new light the adage concerning the drowned and the saved.

Some might be tempted to argue that a propensity for causing great harm to others is found only in a very small minority of human beings. Typically, this approach places the blame for inhumanity at the doors of particularly evil and powerful others, who, it is argued, are not representative of humankind. Irrespective of how reassuring is the view that the capacity to inflict terrible harms upon others is the sole preserve of a select and entirely unrepresentative few, it is fundamentally false. As the empirical studies of Stanley Milgram (1974) and more recently Philip Zimbardo (2007) have demonstrated, many of us are actively capable of acts of inhumanity if the situation appears to demand it of us. These insights build upon Hannah's Arendt's (1963) ground-breaking treatise on the so-called banality of evil. Evil-doers are not, when all is said and done, particularly remarkable or unusual. Indeed, one can extend this disturbing line of thinking further to include not just those who cause harm by commission but also those who do so by omission: the multitude of bystanders who fail to act to prevent harm being caused to others. Few amongst us can genuinely claim to be entirely 'not guilty' to that charge. The work of writers such as Arendt, Milgram and Zimbardo serves to demonstrate that it is not only agents of the state that are capable of violating our human rights, and a capacity for causing (by act or omission) great harm is much more widespread than many of us would prefer to imagine.

The only laudable motivation for redirecting attention towards the darker side of humankind is to ensure that one knows what one is up against in seeking to promote and protect the conditions for humanity. Some might be inclined towards a state of cynical resignation, which is incapable of embracing any sense of hope or continuing faith in humanity. On this view, we are all heading towards hell in a handbasket and there will be no collective redemption. The establishment and diffusion of the doctrine of human rights offers one of the strongest responses to those who are inclined towards either giving up on the world, or cynically seeking to profit from humankind's darker side. There would be no real need for human rights if the propensity towards inhumanity did not exist. Human rights grow out of blood-soaked soil. As Michael Perry (a theological supporter of human rights) argues, 'The real world is endlessly fertile in its yield of sobering, wrenching, clarifying contexts for thinking about the idea of human rights' (1998: 4). The modern human rights movement was undoubtedly strongly motivated by an acknowledgement of the need to fashion a new world order, in which norms of international law would serve to limit absolute state sovereignty. No doubt other motives were also at play in the framing of the Universal Declaration of Human Rights (UDHR)[1] but there can be little real doubt that the sheer savagery which characterised the Second World War exerted significant influence upon the moral and political impetus towards the establishment of a universal template for humanity. Auschwitz was a precursor to the UDHR.

The very existence of human rights as a moral doctrine offers testimony for the resilience of those who refuse to give up on the precarious dream of humanity. A commitment to human rights is fundamentally an expression of loyalty with the idea of humanity.[2] Human rights stand as a corrective to the very conditions which, I am arguing, spawned them in the first place: our propensity for causing great harm to others. Human rights provide evidence of what might be simplistically (but never naïvely) referred to as our better side. After all, human rights are something we have constructed. Notwithstanding those who have argued that the morality which human rights rest upon is conceptually in need of a divine being in order to make sense, human rights have been fashioned and revised through the actions of human beings and not gods (see Perry 1998). Human rights are a moral doctrine which, albeit in varying ways, seeks to demonstrate that human beings do have the ability to at least contemplate respecting one another as moral equals. Amongst the many assumptions which human rights rest upon, one of the most important is that it is possible for human beings to live in a state of relative harmony, in stark contrast to the evidence provided by so much of human history and contemporary circumstances. Human rights, which emerge out of systematic savagery, also increasingly provide a language for representing acts of inhumanity. All of which speaks to the power of human rights as an idea. However, the doctrine has become so much more than simply an artefact of some humanist thinkers' hopeful imagination.

As a manifestation of loyalty to the idea of humanity, the animating spirit of human rights has spread across the globe and is embodied in a tangible body of laws, institutions, belief systems and actors. Human rights have become an integral component of international law and politics. The vast majority of campaigns in support of social, political and economic justice appeal directly to the language and iconography of human rights as a means to legitimise and motivate their actions. The content of human rights has extended far beyond the desire to prevent the grossest acts of inhumanity to embrace an ethics of non-discrimination and equality which would extend the principles of human rights into the workplace, the home, the school and a vast range of spaces in which human life is conducted. Even the US State Department has described human rights as one of the key driving forces of globalisation. John Lennon may not have been justified in describing the Beatles as being bigger than Jesus, but human rights most certainly are. The relative success of human rights appears to provide the strongest refutation yet to the vision of humankind as essentially rapacious and destructive.

Humanity is not a myth. It exists and part of the form it takes is embodied in the idea and institutionalisation of human rights. Having said that, human rights are typically most conspicuous when they are being violated. Our continuing propensity towards inhumanity fuels the conditions which, now armed with the language of human rights, we are able to represent as intolerable and inhumane in a particular way. Human rights are inextricably entwined with what might be termed the dialectical character of the pursuit of a truly humane global order: aiming towards a better future but always struggling against the darker side of human possibility and destructive ingenuity.

Some thinkers dispute the claim that human rights are, in a manner of speaking, on the side of the angels. Such critiques typically deny that the doctrine of human rights provides a bulwark against inhumanity in the manner I have claimed above. The constituency of what I shall refer to as *principled critics* of human rights comprises many different authors and perspectives. Some, such as Michael Ignatieff (2001), argue for a far more modest account of human rights than that which I shall defend here. Ignatieff views many human rights principles as containing too much ideological bias, which has the undesirable effect of significantly restricting the potential application of such principles to a more politically diverse and complex world. Others, such as Makau Mutua (2002), present a far more comprehensive repudiation of the emancipatory claims of human rights. For Mutua, the doctrine of human rights amounts to little more than the latest attempt by the 'West' to impose its hegemony upon the 'non-Western' world. On this view, which I shall analyse in far greater detail in Chapter 2, human rights are actually better understood as another manifestation of inhumanity. Unlike the cynical denunciations of human rights expressed by authoritarian leaders in many parts of the world, the criticisms of thinkers such as Ignatieff and Mutua should be taken seriously. Much of the remainder of this book will offer a detailed response to the principled criticism consistently levelled at human rights and their defenders. For the time being I shall offer three brief comments, which offer an initial response to such critiques. The substance of these comments will then be developed further in the next and proceeding chapters.

First, a necessary condition for the universal validity of any moral doctrine is precisely that the norms which comprise that doctrine are not entirely bound to any partial set of beliefs and commitments. Human rights must speak for humanity. Different communities of peoples experience different challenges and threats to their well-being. For example, a community whose principal diet is based on agriculture and grazing animals will be more affected by prolonged drought than a community whose principal foodstuffs are harvested from the sea. Both communities, however, have a fundamental interest in enjoying a human right to an adequate diet.

Second, the institutionalisation of human rights has exacerbated the perception that human rights are political weapons which powerful states wield against weaker states. Such allegations are, I contend, often empirically well founded but they tell us practically nothing about the moral character of human rights norms. The universality of human rights as a set of moral standards applies, in principle and in the first instance, to all states everywhere. All states violate human rights. Some do so in a highly targeted fashion, as was the case in many powerful states' actions as part of the inappropriately named 'war on terror'. In such instances, the violation of human rights is not part of the *raison d'état* of the state but occurs regardless. Another, far more damaging example of many states' violation of human rights can be seen in the growing numbers of entirely destitute human beings living and dying within many extremely wealthy cities within many societies. Enforced destitution is not the object of state economic policy, but it is a largely inevitable consequence of the policies adopted within the key inter-governmental and governmental bodies which attempt to regulate the globalised economy. For other states, widespread violation of human rights is precisely what constitutes the apparent purpose of the governing authorities: such states seem to exist in order to violate the human rights of large sections of their populations. All violations of human rights should be identified and condemned. The institutionalisation of human rights, particularly in the form of the United Nations (UN) system, accords the strongest legal power to criticise and impugn the violation of human rights to states within inter-governmental fora. Given that no state can claim to have entirely clean hands in respect of human rights, it is inevitable that many such condemnations will carry more than a faint hint of hypocrisy. What should and must be critiqued, then, are some aspects of the institutionalisation of human rights and not the doctrine of human rights itself. The name of human rights is routinely abused but this does not mean that all uses of human rights norms are similarly compromised.

Finally, very few, if any, critiques of human rights offer a viable and sufficiently fleshed-out alternative. In the next chapter I will discuss various regional interpretations of human rights, but these typically accept the core principles of human rights, whilst seeking to offer what is defended as a more regionally appropriate complexion. As I argued above, the consequences of inhumanity and our darker side are clear for all to see. Collectively, we have no good reason to endorse conditions in which large numbers of human beings are exposed to the prospect of destitution, systematic discrimination and even violent or premature death. Arguably, the single most important moral consequence of increasing globalisation consists in recognising that we are all implicated in one another's plight. We cannot morally avoid the effects of the suffering of others. There is no realistic prospect of a return to closed-off, de facto sovereign territories. Recreating the model of the gated community will not solve the shared, collective problems which confront us all. Thus, the largest problems which confront humankind are principally global in nature. As such, the ethical frameworks which should guide and direct our responses to these problems must themselves have a global basis and reach. Human rights offer, at the very least, the most firmly established and entrenched expression of the cosmopolitan framework our times require.

The content and basis of human rights

The philosophical literature on human rights is awash with a bewildering range of definitions of human rights, ranging from the very detailed formulation offered by James Nickel (2014, 2006) to the far terser definitions offered by others such as Jack Donnelly (2013) and James Griffin (2008). Philosophers do not agree on what should be counted as a 'human right'. As noted earlier, the argument that many social, economic and cultural rights should be included as human rights has yet to be accepted by all.[3] The practical application of human rights is ill served by such damaging indeterminacy. Thus, my understanding of the content of human rights is principally based upon those rights enumerated within the principal UN human rights covenants and treaties, which together form the central pillar of international human rights law.

Principal IHRL covenants and treaties

- Universal Declaration of Human Rights[4]
- International Covenant on Civil and Political Rights
- International Covenant on Economic, Social and Cultural Rights
- Convention on the Prevention and Punishment of the Crime of Genocide
- International Convention on the Elimination of All Forms of Racial Discrimination
- Convention on the Elimination of All Forms of Discrimination against Women
- Convention against Torture and Other Cruel, Degrading and Inhuman Treatment or Punishment
- Convention on the Rights of the Child
- Convention on the Rights of Persons with Disabilities

This enumeration of human rights does not exhaust the list of core instruments included in the summary provided by the Office of the

High Commissioner for Human Rights. However, the sheer breadth and depth of human rights included in the above list will suffice for the purposes of my subsequent defence of human rights amidst culturally diverse conditions. There are many rights included in some of the above instruments which a lot of people object to. The CEDAW has, for example, attracted particular criticism on the grounds that some of the articles it contains are culturally inappropriate for many. I discuss this further in a later chapter.

Allen Buchanan (2013) has set an unconventional precedent in which a philosophical defence of human rights begins with an appeal to existing IHRL for a determination of the content of human rights. As Buchanan notes, many philosophers propose a normative grounding for human rights which, if implemented, would fall far short of what are already widely recognised as legitimate human rights instruments. For example, James Nickel's (2006) argument that the basis and scope of human rights are essentially set by the requisite conditions for a 'minimally good life' is both conceptually indeterminate and much less ambitious than the existing content of IHRL in its determination of the conditions for human well-being. I share Buchanan's insistence that there are few, if any, good reasons for rolling back human rights instruments in order to comply with the less ambitious aspirations of many other philosophers.[5] However, by basing my determination of the content of human rights upon existing IHRL I do not intend to imply that positive law is essentially devoid of moral substance or that law and morality are two separate spheres of human existence, as many from Hans Kelsen (1967) to Jürgen Habermas (1996) have argued.

Like any other body of law, IHRL exists within a wider field of social, cultural, political and moral signification. Fields of signification impact upon the formulation and application of all law-making. One consequence of this is that existing human rights law is subject to a multitude of differing interpretations concerning its purpose and legitimate content, which the formal law-making bodies and processes cannot legislate for. Robert Cover (1983) refers to this state of affairs as 'jurisgenerativity', an admittedly somewhat cumbersome term which nevertheless underlines why appeals to the law do not mark the boundaries of normative deliberation.[6] Any enumeration of the content of human rights is, therefore, inherently contingent. With this caveat in place, we may now turn to consider the basis of this enumeration of human rights. If IHRL is caught in a field of normative signification, what are the principal elements of its normativity? In keeping with practically every other discussion of the core human rights ideals, I shall focus upon the three moral ideals out of which IHRL develops: liberty, equality and human dignity. Each of these ideals has been conceptualised and interpreted in a variety of differing ways. Each of them is, therefore, conceptually indeterminate. However, taking IHRL as providing the tangible expression of these ideals, I aim to offer formulations of each which are entailed by a commitment to human rights, which will then provide the basis for the analysis of human rights in subsequent chapters.

Liberty

Based upon the number of separate rights which explicitly refer to the application of the liberty ideal, it is fair to say that liberty enjoys the greatest attention within IHRL. Beyond the recurring references made to 'freedom' (synonymous with liberty) as an ideal within numerous preambles to human rights covenants, liberty is central to a vast range of specific human rights. However, different human rights entail different conceptualisations of liberty. There are, at the very least, two different understandings of liberty to be found within IHRL.

The first understanding consists of what Isaiah Berlin (1969) designated as 'negative liberty'. According to Berlin, individuals' enjoyment of negative liberty required the absence of state interference within the so-called private sphere. Negative liberty was essentially marked by non-interference. Berlin defined negative liberty thus: 'I am normally said to be free to the degree that no man or body of men interferes with my activity' (1969: 122). For Berlin, negative liberty consists simply of the absence of constraints upon one's will which, when combined with the principle of non-interference, yields the conclusion: 'the wider the area of non-interference the wider my freedom' (1969: 123). A commitment to negative liberty as a foundation for political authority aims at restricting the potential for the exercise of state power, which like many liberals, Berlin viewed as inherently coercive. While the condition of non-interference figures in many different human rights, conventional wisdom has typically associated negative liberty with the category of civil and political rights (to which one should also add the economic right of property). Many of the most ardent defenders of civil and political rights have appealed directly to the vision of a relatively limited state presupposed by negative liberty.[7] Thus, a right against torture has typically been construed as requiring that the state and its officials simply refrain from torturing people. A right to participate in the political affairs of one's community has also often been interpreted as requiring that political authorities refrain from placing obstacles in the path of citizens' exercise of the right. It does not, therefore, extend to requiring that individuals actively participate in the political affairs of their community. The right does not need to be exercised by individuals in order to be said to be enjoyed by them.

In contrast, the category of economic, social and cultural rights is conventionally far more closely associated with what Berlin referred to as 'positive liberty', or what Carol Gould has recently referred to *approvingly* as the 'positive liberty tradition' (2004: 15). The conceptualisation of positive liberty differs significantly from its negative counterpart. Many of these differences are expressed in Joseph Raz's definition of autonomy as positive liberty. Raz, a leading advocate of the positive liberty tradition, writes:

> if a person is to be maker or author of his own life then he must have the mental abilities to form intentions of a sufficiently complex kind, and plan their execution. These include minimum rationality, the ability to comprehend the means required to realize his goals, the mental faculties necessary to plan actions etc. For a person to enjoy an autonomous life he must actually use these faculties to choose what life to have. There must in other words be adequate options available for him to choose from. Finally, his choice must be free from coercion and manipulation by others; he must be independent. (Raz 1986: 372–3)

The requisite conditions for positive liberty are far more extensive and prescriptive than are those for negative liberty. Where advocates of negative liberty deliberately avoid the inclusion of any concern for the substantial attributes of individual agency (minimum rationality and specific mental abilities) or any references to the character of the environments in which liberty is assured (adequate options), Raz's formulation of autonomy as positive liberty encompasses the key elements of this positive conceptualisation of liberty. Being free, on this approach, requires a great deal more than simply being free from external interference. Being free requires opportunities to exercise one's freedom through purposive deliberation and action. The rights most closely associated with freedom as an 'exercise concept' typically impose correlative positive duties upon the state to establish and protect the conditions for their enjoyment.[8] Most obviously, rights to health, social security, shelter and the like all require more of the state than simply non-interference. For positive liberty rights, obstacles to their being exercised are absolutely to be considered impediments to the effective enjoyment of such rights.

Positive liberty rights form an integral component of existing IHRL and are thus firmly included within my enumeration of the content of human rights. Having said that, a word of caution is in order concerning the risk of unduly fetishising such distinctions. In many instances, the possession and exercise of any given human right will entail furnishing the conditions of both negative and positive liberty. The most obvious example is a right to life. An individual's right to life clearly imposes a duty upon states not to interfere in the individual's private sphere. However, the enjoyment of a right to life will be fundamentally undermined where individuals do not possess a right to receive health care at the very least when confronted by life-threatening disease. There are thus many instances where the conditions for both forms of liberty are mutually supportive. However, many philosophers have harboured (and continue to harbour) concerns over the potential for some understandings of positive liberty to subvert some individuals' deliberation and action. These concerns need to be addressed in order to arrive at a defensible formulation of liberty for the purposes of human rights.

Many advocates of negative liberty consider its essentially formal character to be a distinct advantage over its positive counterpart. The more one stipulates that genuine liberty is dependent upon agents' possession of substantive goods and conditions, the greater the opportunity for some to condemn others' behaviour and commitments as in some senses falling short of the requirements for genuine liberty. The spectre of liberty being used as a mechanism for seeking to legitimise unequal relations between different peoples has reared its head on many an occasion, and is well captured in the distinction Martin Hollis (1999) draws ironically between 'liberals' and 'cannibals'. All too often, accounts of liberty as requiring a sufficiently developed mindset and developed state of civilisation have been used to ideologically legitimise typically colonial powers' subjugation of colonised peoples. The very ideal which is so flagrantly abused by colonialism (and neo-colonialism) has often provided part of the ideological basis for such abuse. A formal conception of liberty, which asks nothing of individuals and places the onus entirely upon states to refrain from interfering in their affairs, might thereby be defended as preventing such abuses of liberty.

A tradition of so-called political liberalism has emerged within contemporary liberal philosophy, which also rejects positive liberty as providing a legitimate foundation for the regulation of diverse societies. Thus, philosophers such as Charles Larmore (1987), John Rawls (1993) and Chandran Kukathas (2003) have argued that the ideal of an autonomous life is not and need not be comprehensively endorsed by all of those citizens who are subject to the jurisdiction of the liberal state. On this view, the moral ideal of a life led autonomously is merely one of a number of reasonable perspectives upon how life might be led within complex societies. Any political morality which was based upon a prioritisation of autonomy in this sense would effectively load the dice of state power towards those for whom autonomy was valuable and against those who, for example, esteemed an unquestioning commitment to some divine being as of primary importance. The alleged partiality of the appeal of an autonomous life is thus seen as fatally undermining the claims which advocates of the positive liberty tradition make on behalf of the foundational status of the ideal. Finally, other philosophers, such as John Gray (1993) and Anthony Langlois (2001), have described the autonomy ideal as an essentially 'Western' construct, which has little purchase within 'non-Western' societies.[9] The inclusion of autonomy within the moral underpinnings of human rights appears to seriously call into question the doctrine's claims to universal validity and its capacity to legislate for diversity.

In response, no one can possibly deny that autonomy has been abused in the name of 'civilising the natives'. However, the mere abuse of an ideal does not suffice to show that it lacks fundamental moral value. After all, the objective of colonial rule was not to provide the conditions by which subjugated peoples might come to freely determine their own lives. The so-called white man's burden was always a very poor alibi for systematic exploitation and the denial of human rights. Indeed, much of what many have condemned in colonialism draws upon the ideal of autonomy as self-determination. The positive liberty tradition and its more substantive criteria for what liberty requires has been consistently drawn upon to uncover the persistence of inequality and exploitation between formally equal parties. This is particularly so in a post-colonial context where the *de jure* sovereignty of former colonies is presented as sufficient evidence of their independence. The very formalism of negative liberty, in significantly restricting the criteria for enjoying liberty, can also, in so doing, obscure recognition of persistent impediments to the enjoyment of liberty. As the saying goes, the destitute person and the millionaire may be equally at liberty to sleep on the street and under the stars, but only one of them is effectively forced to do so.

Whatever its value for more procedural approaches to political morality, negative liberty would provide for only a very diminished form of IHRL. In subsequent chapters, we will see that, despite my insistence that we have no compelling reason to roll back the content of IHRL, a number of contributors to the ongoing debate concerning the implications of cultural diversity for human rights argue in ways which draw upon the thrust of critiques of the positive liberty tradition.[10] Given this, I shall add a couple more elements to my argument that a commitment to human rights entails a commitment to positive liberty.

As both a concept of liberty and the vision of political authority it entails, negative liberty has attracted a great deal of criticism from various directions. For the purposes of human rights, two strands of criticism seem particularly pertinent. The first concerns the implications of placing so much weight upon mere non-interference in determining what liberty consists of. The second focuses upon negative liberty's neglect of the purposive character of human agency. John Gray (1989) argued that Berlin's formulation of negative liberty entailed that an individual's liberty could be increased by a corresponding reduction in the quantity and quality of their desires to act. Negative liberty is, after all, a measure of non-interference in the area(s) in which an individual desires to act. The fewer and less demanding are one's desires to act, the greater the degree of non-interference. The person who desires least might thereby be said to enjoy the most freedom. Gray argued that this meant that it was possible to describe the so-called contented slave as being free, since the slave wants for little beyond what is provided by the 'benevolent' slave-owner: sufficient food, shelter and occasional rest. Gray's line of criticism drew upon an important earlier insight made by Gerald MacCullum (1972). MacCullum argued that the concept of negative liberty was flawed to the extent that it explicitly excluded any concern for what individuals may want to do with their liberty. He wrote:

whenever the freedom of some agent or agents is in question, it is always freedom from some constraint or restriction on, interference with, or barrier to doing, not doing, becoming, or not becoming something. Such freedom is thus always of something (an agent or agents), from something, to do, not do, or not become something: it is always a triadic relation. (MacCullum 1972: 176)

Liberty is thus an ideal whose value lies in its exercise. An exclusive focus upon individuals being free *from* external interference was important, but not the be-all and end-all of defining what genuine liberty consisted of.

Charles Taylor (1985) extended upon this line of criticism by arguing that an exclusive focus upon non-interference entirely ignored the essentially purposive character of human agency. We act within and upon the world and upon each other. We have goals and aspirations. We make plans and devise strategies. Many of us want to grow and develop, perhaps even transform ourselves through concerted action. For each of us, our goals and aspirations will take on differing degrees of significance and importance: some may be relatively trivial, while others may be of profound value and importance for us. An exclusive focus upon negative liberty as non-interference effectively excluded any consideration of the varying degrees of significance of those aspects of our lives which the concept aims to protect from external interference. As Taylor argued, 'freedom is important to us because we are purposive beings. But then there must be distinctions in the significance of different kinds of freedom based on the distinction in the significance of different purposes' (1985: 219). This specific line of criticism is particularly relevant for human rights. After all, the rights contained within IHRL are principally concerned with highly significant aspects of human agency. Many deeply important areas of human life are not covered by human rights; our capacity for loving another, for example, is not supported by an express human right to love. Despite such important exceptions, it is clear that any understanding of liberty that is capable of underpinning and justifying the body of IHRL must be able to pick out the more significant aspects of human agency. Negative liberty, by itself, is unable to do this precisely because it explicitly aims to exclude any such considerations from its understanding of liberty. Existing IHRL, thus, draws upon and reflects a far more substantive account of human agency than advocates of negative liberty allow for.

The necessity of positive liberty for human rights can be illustrated by a brief analysis of one key human right: freedom of expression, which is principally covered by Article 19(2) of the International Covenant on Civil and Political Rights (ICCPR). It also figures in all of the key regional human rights instruments. The capacity and opportunity to freely express oneself cannot be adequately provided for merely by the state's non-interference in the private sphere. First, the capacity for free expression requires individuals' possession of some requisite cognitive faculties. While almost all human beings will possess the hard-wiring for deliberation and speech, the distinct capacity for effective free expression – developing and communicating an opinion or point of view – requires individuals' access to at least a satisfactory education. Second, freedom of expression also requires the existence of a civic culture which is not entirely dominated by a single dogma. Advocates of negative liberty characteristically identify the state as the sole or principal source of authoritarian dogma. But mass communication technologies and mass consumerism can also yield and uphold dogmatic beliefs and prejudices, which can be no less harmful to free expression than state action. Securing sufficient conditions for all individuals to enjoy the opportunity to express themselves freely requires more of the state than simply upholding an equal right to negative liberty.

Remaining with the example of free expression, it is important to note that a condition for exercising the right does not require that all individuals must first engage in a heroic process of critically reflecting upon their beliefs and opinions all of the time. The right is not restricted to only those with a college education. Indeed, this line of reasoning may be extended further to argue that individuals are under no obligation to exercise the right in order to enjoy possession of it. Many of us may prefer to have few opinions about matters of substance. Some of us will prefer to allow others to determine what our political or religious commitments should be. Such conditions do not typically amount to a violation of the right.[11] Arguing that the positive liberty tradition is essential to contemporary IHRL does not create an obligation upon individuals that we must all continuously strive to be autonomous. What is required by positive liberty is that all individuals have sufficient opportunities to develop and express their views and opinions in accordance with the kind of conditions which Joseph Raz identifies as key for autonomy: sufficient mental capacities, available options and independence. It also means that some people's general lack of interest in or even renunciation of the value of autonomy cannot justify their attempts to deny others' access to the core conditions for autonomy. Against those who worry about the overly prescriptive potential of appeals to autonomy as a moral ideal of how life may be best led, autonomy is understood here as a threshold concept and not as what I shall term a heroic ideal.[12]

Equality

We each possess human rights by virtue of being human and, for the purposes of human rights, we may each be considered to be what I shall term 'subjects-of-human rights'. Not everything we do and are is a matter for human rights: many aspects of our lives are not covered by any of the core components of IHRL. However, conceiving of each human being as a subject-of-human rights is central to understanding how it can be that anyone's entitlement to their human rights is not based upon some contingent property of their being or behaviour, but is integral to their subject-hood. While liberty and dignity are vitally important elements of this status, the most important moral ideal in this respect is equality. None of us possesses more or less of this vitally important aspect of subject-hood than does anyone else. As such, equality is a non-negotiable constituent of the entire moral doctrine of human rights. The necessity of equality is recognised in every key human rights instrument, all of which refer to the equal moral status of human beings and the non-derogable (that is, absolute) status of the principle of non-discrimination.

Many advocates of equality have argued that the ideal imposes a fundamentally negative duty upon states in the first instance to accord equal weight to the standing and claims of all of those over whom they exercise jurisdiction. Ronald Dworkin expresses this succinctly when he writes that the equality principle 'requires that the government treat all those in its charge as equals, that is as entitled to its equal concern and respect' (1978: 125). Needless to say, such succinct representations of a profoundly complex and important ideal often obscure just how much devil is in the detail of the terminology. Within political philosophy there is a vast body of literature dedicated to analysing this understanding of equality. Many have argued that human rights developed historically as a response to identity-based forms of discrimination, whether these be based on class, religion, race, ethnicity or gender. Simplifying a very complex debate, some argued that if according value to identity was largely the root cause of inequality and discrimination, then it followed that the most effective cure would be to frame policies and legislation in ways which ignored anyone's identity: that overcoming racism, for example, would best be achieved by adopting a generally colour-blind approach to law and policy-making. Justice required excluding any consideration for those characteristics by which individuals differed from one another in order to ensure all were treated equally. One might say that justice on this approach required being entirely indifferent to difference.[13]

There can be no denying that IHRL has been deeply influenced by this indifference to difference approach. This is most apparent in various interpretations of the basis and content of many civil and political rights in which our possession and exercise of these rights is considered in abstraction from the identities we bear. However, the character of IHRL has significantly changed as is apparent in the development of covenants and instruments which address race, gender, minority status, indigeneity and the like. All of these instruments foreground individuals' concrete identities in their attempts to prevent and combat inequality and discrimination. The perspectives afforded by so-called identity politics and the 'politics of recognition' have become integral components of the formulation of equality within IHRL. All of this reduces to a simple observation: no one has ever suffered discrimination because of their being identified as an abstract bearer of moral and legal worth, which is effectively how individuals are conceived of by the indifferent to difference approach. People are discriminated against *because* of the way others falsely perceive members of oppressed communities to be necessarily inferior or less worthy of respect and consideration. The worst forms of such discrimination base their vilification of others upon appeals to the essential inferiority of others. Racially supremacist ideologies, for example, insist that human beings with a different skin colour can never be 'as good as us' as a consequence of their racial heritage. Less repugnant forms of discrimination allow for the possibility of their becoming 'like us' but insist that doing so is a condition of their claims to equal legal and political status. The first approach has underpinned slavery, genocide and apartheid. The second approach incentivises individuals to abandon their own identities and communities in order to garner the acceptance of members of dominant communities.[14]

IHRL's extension into identity has significantly embraced the equality amidst diversity ethic which has inspired much multicultural thought and action over the past four decades. As referred to above, identity politics and the politics of recognition are essentially based upon the claim that individuals from minority or conventionally subordinated communities are entitled to possess and develop their concrete identities. On this approach, one's entitlement to one's rights is not conditional upon one's renunciation of identity. Indeed, various specific human rights now exist which enable people to enjoy access to core components of their identity, such as rights to language, to religious practice and observance, to collectively owned tracts of tribal land and the like. Rights to cultural identity have emerged and are now well established within IHRL and political discourse. As such, individuals are afforded opportunities to sustain customs, practices and beliefs which, to a varying degree, make them who they are.[15] IHRL has largely accepted that upholding the equality principle precisely requires recognising difference and diversity.

A developing and recurring theme of this book concerns the claim that our moral entitlement to the enjoyment of human rights is not merely dependent upon the actions of states and other power-holders: the protection of human rights is not an entirely top-down process. Our status as subjects-of-human rights is also affected by *our* beliefs, commitments and actions. This is most obviously the case where some individuals' deep-rooted social and cultural prejudices about others have a significant and adverse impact upon the lives of those others. Some people's refusal to recognise others as subjects-of-human rights can reinforce forms of oppression which are deeply resistant to more 'enlightened' legal norms. Although the phenomenon is often less obvious, individuals' enjoyment of human rights can also be undermined by beliefs they have formed about *themselves* and their own worth. Some of us may fail to conceive of ourselves as subjects entitled to the protections afforded by the equality principle as a consequence of affirming formally subordinated roles attributed to us by the cultures we have little option but to identify with. The discrimination in such instances is more often than not *intra*-cultural, rather than inter-cultural in character. Numerous studies and authors have demonstrated and analysed this phenomenon. The precise ethical challenge it creates for a doctrine which is fundamentally based upon the equality ideal is well expressed by Andrew Kernohan when he writes of the plight of women subjected to formally and stringently patriarchal belief systems. He states:

> her beliefs about what is good for her will depend on her beliefs about what she may legitimately expect. If the content of her beliefs about her legitimate expectations is infected with false, inegalitarian social meanings, then her knowledge of her good will be undermined. She can be harmed by her cultural environment even if she does not realise it. (Kernohan 1998: x–xi)

Human rights protection cannot be extended to ways of being and believing which formally and systematically deny that all members of the community are entitled to recognition as subjects-of-human rights.[16]

An adherence to the equality ideal within human rights does not require that all ways of being and believing must become substantively alike. Nor, given the sheer extent of continuing inequalities in 'Western' societies, does it require the global imposition of 'Western' ways of living. It does, however, indicate that human rights are not essentially predicated upon a demand to respect existing identities as such. It is not so much the actual substance of different identities which is worthy of respect but rather people's status as subjects-of-human rights, which may be concretely realised or obstructed by the identities they bear. In turn, this serves to remind us of the importance of a continuing commitment to what might be loosely termed the 'sameness principle' in conceptualising and implementing human rights. Kwame Anthony Appiah expresses the point when he writes:

> our moral modernity consists chiefly of extending the principle of equal respect to those who had previously been outside the compass of sympathy; in that sense, it has consisted in the ability to see similarity where our predecessors saw only difference. The wisdom was hard-won; it should not lightly be set aside. (Appiah 2005: 146)

The equality ideal is binding not just upon states and other significant power-holders but, as I shall argue in greater detail throughout this book, it also has implications for all of us. Basing human rights upon a notion of loyalty to the idea of humanity, as I have done, means that it is not only states who must avoid denying the equal status of all human beings.[17] Communities and even individuals should also be encouraged to overcome those persistent ways of being and believing which posit the inherent inequality of some human beings. This does not entail excessive forms of moral policing or even punishing those who fail to espouse the ideal. It does, however, entail a concerted attempt to transform those conditions in which systematic inequalities continue to wreak the damage they do.

Dignity

The final ideal which human rights appeals to directly is that of human dignity. It differs from liberty and equality in variously important ways. It is less frequently referenced by IHRL than liberty and equality. As such, it is directly referred to in the Preamble and Article 1 of the UDHR. It is also covered by Article 10 of the ICCPR. It is referred to in some other articles as a means for bolstering the specific good included within the article, as is the case with Article 13 of the International Covenant on Economic, Social and Cultural Rights (ICESCR) and its focus upon education. Dignity is also referenced in a number of national constitutions, such as Article 1 of the German Federal Constitution. In addition to dignity featuring less prominently in specific human rights instruments, it differs from liberty and equality in the following, highly significant, way. Liberty refers to a condition, an element of human agency which, while highly esteemed by many, is not valued by all. Nor do all human beings have an opportunity to consistently exercise their liberty. Many people would not accept the claim that those who do not consistently act freely are, in that way alone, fundamentally deprived of what it essentially means to be human. For many, while deplorable, systematic restraints upon the exercise of liberty are not construed as penetrating 'all the way down' into the core of what it means to be human. Likewise, although perhaps less assuredly, one might draw similar conclusions about some forms of inequality and discrimination. Many people are systematically treated unequally: the brute fact of their unequal treatment often does not necessarily yield the conclusion that some essential element of their humanity is thereby denied. The same absolutely does not apply to human dignity. Appeals to dignity characteristically evoke an appeal to some quintessentially human moral essence. To violate a person's dignity is to attack their humanity more fundamentally than to target their liberty and equality. Indeed, those who object to violations of liberty and equality may often, advertently or inadvertently, bolster their claim by appeal to the notion of dignity. That some violations of liberty and equality are so heinous is precisely because their effect is to undermine the dignity of the victims. By invoking the presumed moral essence of humanity, dignity offers a trump card in the denunciation of human rights violations. A final way in which dignity differs from liberty and equality concerns the lack of any sufficiently detailed and comprehensively accepted definition of the ideal. Most refer to a broadly Kantian precept which holds that humanity is fundamentally founded upon individuals' status as ends-in-themselves. We routinely treat non-human animals and the environment as mere means, or instruments, to our ends and goals. As such, non-human material exists as objects, necessarily devoid of intrinsic value or worth. In contrast, human beings are intrinsically valuable. To treat another as a mere object, as many human beings are routinely treated after all, is to violate their dignity.

The widely acknowledged difficulty in seeking to philosophically stipulate the defining features of dignity has largely resulted in an approach which identifies the ideal by its violations. Intuitively, most of us today would consider slavery as a violation of the slave's dignity. Similarly, many would argue that being exposed to crippling destitution and chronic ill-health violates people's dignity. Linking dignity directly to equality, many would agree that systems of apartheid or formally caste-based social systems amount to violations of dignity. However, beyond some intuitively uncontroversial examples, it becomes increasingly difficult to construct a list of acts and beliefs which all, or at least most, people would label as violations of human dignity.[18] Even the Kantian formulation, despite the number of authors who invoke it, could be interpreted as denouncing a vast range of existing practices as essentially a denial of dignity given the extent to which much economic and bureaucratic management involves forms of instrumental rationality which precisely conceives of many human beings as human capital: means to the ends of generating profit or maximising efficiency.

I will proceed cautiously in my deployment of human dignity in the following pages. While I would not expect everyone to agree with this particular approach, I shall equate dignity with part of what it means to endorse the principle of seeking to be loyal to the idea of humanity. Given that I associate that disposition with a commitment to human rights as IHRL, I shall typically assume that violations of IHRL will, all other things being equal, constitute attacks upon human dignity also.

Social context

Any attempt to formulate a human rights-based response to cultural diversity must necessarily acknowledge the social basis and context of human agency. We are all social beings. If society were of little or no importance for our lives and well-being, then there would be no real need to take diversity seriously.

Human rights have been consistently criticised for what is alleged to be their general neglect of the social basis and context of human life. In some respects this criticism is unjustified.[19] The social dimension of human life and human rights is frequently referenced in numerous human rights declarations, treaties and instruments. Our social existence is also fundamentally acknowledged within the category of social and, increasingly, cultural rights which enjoy increasing prominence within human rights. Such rights focus precisely upon the social and cultural conditions which confront many human beings in order to ensure the establishment and protection of social environments which support, rather than obstruct, the protection of human rights. One should also add that the entire edifice of IHRL is dependent upon the construction of a highly complex institutional infrastructure, which itself is only possible as a direct consequence of the existence of an extremely detailed set of social conditions and relationships.

I think that part of the misplaced criticism of human rights' neglect of the social dimension of human existence can be understood as a response to the moral weight attached to a particular type of individualism within some forms of human rights philosophy. In this respect, the criticism has more merit. Historically, human rights thinking has been significantly influenced by liberal philosophy. At the risk of unduly simplifying a very complex relationship, many liberal contributions to human rights have reproduced an account of human agency as ultimately reducible to a distinct, formally conceived-of sovereign individual who radically precedes the social conditions in which he deliberates and acts. Contractarian theories exemplify this approach insofar as they argue that a commitment to some form of human rights can be generated out of the mutually self-interested deliberations of sovereign individuals (Rawls 1971, 1993; Gauthier 1986). Typically, this process of individual deliberation is pictured as taking place within a hypothetical, pre-social domain in which the actual characteristics of embodied human agents are excluded and 'left at the door', so to speak. This way of thinking has attracted a deluge of criticism. For current purposes, one of the most important aspects of that body of criticism concerns the need to recognise human rights as a distinctly social good which, in the words of Appiah, 'cannot be reduced to the satisfaction of a collection of individual desires' (2005: 127). Contractarian theories typically assume an initial moment of political constitution in which the contracting parties exist in a state of equality: no one has disproportionately more bargaining power than anyone else. Needless to say, the world to which human rights responds bears no resemblance to that (admittedly appealing) fiction. Justifications of human rights, particularly those which aim to reconcile human rights with an acknowledgement of diversity, cannot appeal to such fictions and hope to remain relevant to the real world.

In the real world there exist human beings who are fundamentally influenced by their surrounding social conditions. Not just our actual lives but also the concepts we deploy to evaluate those lives are fundamentally affected by the social conditions which support them. The three core ideals of liberty, equality and dignity are all, as I discussed above, utterly immersed in and entwined with social conditions. The exercise of liberty can only be secured within suitably conducive social environments. Discrimination invariably targets human beings' social and cultural identities and commitments. Even human dignity requires the establishment of material conditions which protect people from the de-humanising effects of extreme destitution.

However, to say that the social dimension of human existence is integral to human rights is not to say very much about the specific substance or character of such conditions. I shall begin to address this now in the knowledge that subsequent chapters will develop and refine the account I draw upon.

Our identities and commitments are formed through our relations with others. We become who we are through our interactions with others. No one ever truly lives alone and none of us can ever truly 'drop out' of society. Our agency is fundamentally relational in character. Marilyn Friedman describes relational agency thus:

> according to the relational approach, persons are fundamentally social beings who develop the competency for autonomy through

social interaction with other persons. These developments take place in a context of values, meanings and modes of self-reflection that cannot exist except as constituted by social practices. (Friedman 2000: 40)

Annette Baier (1986) has more succinctly coined the term 'second persons' in her attempt to express the irrefutable empirical observation that we only become persons through our relations with others. The lives of others are integral to our own. If this were not the case, then the hateful prejudices of others would have no fundamental effect upon those they target and we would be justified in requiring the victims of such prejudice to simply look the other way and not be so sensitive.[20]

While our relational nature is empirically irrefutable, what is less clear is precisely what the moral significance of this might be. After all, part of the motivation behind human rights has been (and remains) protecting individuals from the unwarranted and harmful effects of others' behaviour and beliefs. In acknowledging the relational character of human identity do we not we run the risk of a consequent diminution of the continuing need for the establishment of protective barriers between self and other? This is highly complex and will be returned to throughout this book. For the time being, it should suffice to say that it is possible to both acknowledge human interdependency and defend human rights. Indeed, defending human rights can only effectively be realised precisely through recognising human interdependency. I am not alone in pursuing this approach to human rights. One of the leading voices in this approach is that of Seyla Benhabib who similarly seeks to recognise the socially relational character of human agency whilst remaining committed to a normative ideal of self-determination. She writes, 'only when members of a society can engage in free and unrestrained dialogue about their collective identity in free public spaces can they develop narratives of self-identification, which would unfold into fluid and creative re-appropriations of their own traditions' (2011: 76). What human rights are committed to is not the conservative objective of reinforcing existing social relations for their own sake. Nor do they serve to only support an individual's continuing membership of a cultural or political community. Rather, human rights offer the opportunity for individuals to extend upon, revise or even radically transform existing identities. In Carol Gould's (2004: 62) terms, human rights have a quintessentially transformative potential. Acknowledging the relational character of human agency and identity does not entail abandoning individuals to a socially determinist outlook.

Conclusion

This first chapter has covered a wide expanse of complex, philosophical terrain. I have identified a principle, that of loyalty to the idea of humanity, as a possible basis for the origins and continuing motive force for a commitment to human rights. I have enumerated my understanding of the content of existing human rights and outlined separate understandings of the three core ideals which IHRL draws most heavily upon. Finally, I have made a beginning upon the complex task of reconciling the necessary acknowledgement of the social basis and context of human agency with a continuing commitment to human rights.

Suggested reading

- Andrew Fagan, 'Philosophical Foundations of Human Rights', in Thomas Cushman (ed.), *Handbook of Human Rights* (New York: Routledge, 2012), pp. 9–22.
- Jonathan Glover, *Humanity: A Moral History of the Twentieth Century* (London: Pimlico, 2001).
- James Griffin, *On Human Rights* (Oxford: Oxford University Press, 2008), chapter 1.
- James Nickel, 'Human Rights', in Edward N. Zalta (ed.), *The Stanford Encyclopedia of Philosophy* (2014), <http://plato.stanford.edu/entries/rights-human/> (last accessed 27 July 2016).

Notes

1. As Samuel Moyn (2010) has recently argued.
2. Alessandro Ferrara (2003) also views human rights in such terms. He views this argument as originating within Hegel's philosophical vision of humanity and a response to what Hegel referred to as the 'slaughter bench of human history'.
3. One of the most influential political philosophers of the past fifty years, John Rawls (1999) excludes almost all social and economic rights from his account of what should be considered as universally applicable human rights. I consider Rawls's argument in greater detail in Chapter 2.

4. Strictly speaking the UDHR is not a legally binding instrument since it is a declaration and not a convention. However, many domestic jurisdictions now recognise the UDHR as an essential component of customary law and thus legally binding.
5. Chapter 2 will discuss in far greater detail the arguments of those who insist that the justification of human rights amidst cultural diversity requires precisely this kind of roll-back of human rights.
6. Seyla Benhabib (2011) also analyses human rights through this prism of jurisgenerativity.
7. Within this group one may include Cranston (1973), Nozick (1974) and more recently Kukathas (2003), although Kukathas argues in support of only one fundamental right: freedom of association.
8. Charles Taylor (1985: 213) has coined the term 'exercise concept' in his critique of negative liberty. I consider another aspect of Taylor's critique below.
9. Of course, precisely what constitutes a 'Western' ideal or value is a question rife with potential pitfalls. For the moment, I will assume that the reader has some intuitive sense of what Gray and Langlois (or anyone else for that matter) are referring to. In the following chapter I will outline a constructivist understanding of culture which picks out the distinctly politically contingent character of such labels as 'Western' or 'non-Western'.
10. In many such instances, the focus is upon non-interference in the affairs of other cultural communities. Needless to say, this does not necessarily equate with a commitment to individual negative liberty since the political organisation of some such communities may routinely interfere in their members' affairs. This will be explored further at various points.
11. Some readers may be minded to consider Kant's (1970) definition of 'enlightenment' as precisely requiring overcoming such forms of 'self-incurred tutelage', 'immaturity' and promoting the capacity of daring to think for oneself. Clearly, the grounds for *possessing* human rights cannot be so demanding given just how many people would thereby fail to qualify!
12. At this stage I am merely attempting to set out a sufficiently detailed formulation of autonomy as positive liberty. Some of the key implications of this formulation for the application of human rights amidst diversity will be explored in much greater detail in subsequent chapters.
13. This phrase is inspired by the title of Iris Marion Young's book *Justice and the Politics of Difference* (1990). Young's analysis of the social and political sources of discrimination and inequality has exerted a profound influence upon the entire field.
14. A particularly tragic example of this can be found in those policies of forcibly removing indigenous children from their families and rehoming them in white families.

15. Chapter 4 will analyse the right to cultural identity in far greater detail and I will argue that limits to the right are essential if we are to avoid jeopardising some people's human rights.

16. Note the phrase 'ways of being and believing'. This term of art will recur throughout this book and is intended to refer to those systematic elements of established cultural communities which distinguish one community from another. As I shall discuss in greater detail in subsequent chapters, I do not approach ways of being and believing in an essentialist manner. They do change and develop and they are subject to internal and external interpretation and contestation. However, they do pick out an enduring and pervasive sense of phenomenological realities through which individual and collective identities are formed and reproduced.

17. I am, of course, aware of just how underdeveloped this core argument remains at present. It will be developed and refined as we proceed.

18. Schacter (1983) does attempt to list conduct and ideas which he argues can be reasonably considered to violate dignity.

19. As Allen Buchanan writes, 'the authors of the UDHR in particular took considerable pains to make it clear that the individuals to whom this document ascribes rights are social beings, but they underestimated the resilience of false perceptions' (2013: 87).

20. This is a huge issue and will be returned to in later chapters where a far more detailed explanation and defence will be offered.

2

Culture and Transcending Relativism

Key questions

1. Why has culture typically been considered to be incompatible with defending human rights?
2. Why have human rights defenders and theorists been accused of being morally censorious or intolerant?
3. Can one support relativism and human rights simultaneously?
4. What is 'relative universality' and how does it affect the justification of human rights?
5. Why does John Rawls propose a narrower range of human rights than is currently found in IHRL?
6. What does it mean to state that public norms and private practices should not converge?
7. Why might it not be a good idea to allow states and regions to pursue a 'multi-speed' approach to human rights?
8. Which rights are included in the so-called third generation of human rights?
9. What does it mean to say that human rights defenders should 'bear in mind' the significance of religious and cultural factors?
10. How have social scientists conceived of 'culture'? Why is this important for human rights?

Introduction

This chapter confronts a perennial question in human rights theory and practice: to what extent can human rights be reconciled with a recognition of the cultural basis of human agency and the promotion of cultural diversity? I shall argue that the debate has moved beyond the futile intellectual slanging match which some universalists and many relativists have been engaged in for decades. I consider specific critiques of the alleged cultural bias of many human rights norms and values. I challenge claims made within this body of literature by deconstructing 'culture' and challenging the claim that human values and norms can be singly aligned with separate and discrete geo-cultural blocs. The chapter concludes with a claim which will then be defended in far greater detail in Chapter 3. Namely, that a commitment to diversity is not best served by subscribing to the view that the 'West', or 'Africa', or 'Asia', or 'Islam' can be defended as singular, discrete blocs and that the consequence of seeking to do is to stifle and oppress the myriad ways of being and believing found within such spaces.

Speaking past each other: the unhelpful argument between universalism and relativism

Human beings inhabit cultures and the cultures we inhabit are often highly varied and different from each other. Both human rights theorists and IHRL cannot, and increasingly do not, ignore such indisputably important features of human existence. The promotion of cultural diversity is now a well-established component of human rights in the twenty-first century. However, acknowledging and promoting cultural diversity has been, and in some respects remains, a highly complex and controversial area of human rights theory and practice. Indeed, it is reasonable to state that reconciling a commitment to human rights generally with a commitment to recognising the value of cultural diversity remains a key challenge for the justification and application of universal human rights norms. A challenge which has yet to be entirely satisfactorily met. Many human rights theorists and practitioners insist that the continuing normative legitimacy of human rights norms depends upon the doctrine's capacity to accommodate a very broad range of culturally based ways of being and believing. In order to enjoy genuinely universal credibility, human rights are required to affirm the manifest diversity of human life, which, in turn, entails a thorough engagement with the differing existing realities of such life. Reconciling the promotion of human rights with that of cultural diversity is, however, fraught with a number of potentially very serious conceptual and practical pitfalls. As Peter Jones (2001: 27) has written, 'at best . . . diversity can seem inconvenient for, and at worst fatal to, the universality claimed for human rights'. The long-standing dispute between universalism and relativism offers the best vantage point from which to perceive the difficulties which diversity can raise for human rights.

It is undeniable that there have existed and there continue to exist many long-established cultural communities and civilisations which do not fully share or may even fundamentally reject the normative value of liberty, equality or the inherent dignity of human beings as values which should underpin the ways in which all human beings should be governed. Such communities and civilisations will often question or reject the claims that all human rights should be sufficiently respected within or across all cultures. Such claims appear to mark the limits of a human rights-based principle of respecting cultural diversity. If we possess our human rights by virtue of being human, as the conventional mantra states, then where we happen to be at any time should be ultimately irrelevant to our entitlement to the possession of our human rights. On the most rudimentary of universalist approaches, individuals' membership of any given cultural community can have no legitimate bearing upon the moral justification of their entitlement to human rights. Indeed, the tendency within this perspective is to largely ignore any consideration for cultural practices and beliefs except where they appear to entail, condone or seek to justify human rights violations: culture is thereby typically construed in somewhat negative or critical terms. Torture, starvation, the denial of rights to vote, the imposition of stifling restrictions on freedom of expression and the denial of gender equality are thus denounced as morally intolerable irrespective of where such violations occur. As the Preamble to the 1993 Vienna Declaration and Programme of Action (VDPA) proclaims:

> The World Conference on Human Rights reaffirms the solemn commitment of all states to fulfil their obligations to promote universal respect for, and observance and protection of, all human rights and fundamental freedoms for all in accordance with the Charter of the United Nations . . . The universal nature of these rights and freedoms is beyond question.

From a rudimentary universalist perspective, an appeal to established custom or tradition can never condone or justify the violation of human rights. Violations are simply inexcusable irrespective of how deeply rooted they may be within the collective identity of any given cultural community. Thus, human rights and the norms they fundamentally rest upon are universally valid and others' refusal to acknowledge them as such is liable to being construed as acts hostile towards human rights. Non-compliant cultural communities may thereby become targets for reform and intervention by other communities which (legitimately or otherwise) lay claim to the moral title of defenders of the faith of human rights.

In response, many have criticised this approach for being unduly censorious or morally intolerant. The strongest advocates of this form of criticism consist of those who explicitly reject moral universalism in favour of an opposing doctrine which is typically referred to as cultural and moral relativism. Relativism is an established way of thinking about the sources and status of moral reasoning and beliefs. It has been defined in the following terms:

> moral relativism . . . often takes the form of a denial that any single moral code has universal validity, and an assertion that moral truth and justifiability, if there are such things, are in some way relative to factors that are culturally and historically contingent. (Wong 1991: 442)

Moral relativism rejects the claim that there can exist moral principles and forms of moral identity that are not themselves fundamentally shaped by social and cultural conditions: morality is a constituent element of distinct social forms. Moral relativism has sometimes been confused with other doctrines, such as nihilism. Nihilists argue that morality has lost its rational authority and ability to legitimately command our compliance with moral dictates: nihilists view morality (and indeed humanity also) as a myth. In contrast, relativists do not deny either the existence or the potential efficacy of morality. They do deny the legitimacy of purportedly universal moral doctrines but they do not thereby consider morality to be a purely arbitrary or random phenomenon. A relativist will typically argue that morality does exist, or rather that different moralities exist across time and space. The common origin of these moralities is culture, or society. Cultures and societies have differed, and do differ, fundamentally, as is readily apparent in the bewildering range of different moral beliefs and customs to be found 'out there'. Morality is fundamentally shaped by society and there is not (empirically speaking) a common, entirely agreed upon moral code for all existing societies, which is affirmed by all peoples. What is morally permissible in Toronto may be morally taboo in Tehran. Likewise, an act which is morally condemned in London may be widely endorsed on the streets of Lahore or Lusaka. At least, so the relativist must argue.

A recurring feature of the relativist-inspired critique of human rights consists of the specific charge that human rights are burdened by a continuing and unshakeable ethnocentric bias. According to the *Oxford English Dictionary*, ethnocentricity is:

> centred on one's race or ethnic group; based on or characterised by a tendency to evaluate other races or groups by criteria specific to one's own; having assumptions or preconceptions originating in the standards, customs, etc., of one's own race or group.[1]

In keeping with the claim that all substantive moral norms and values necessarily originate in and grow out of some specific cultural soil, some critics of human rights have argued that human rights have decidedly 'Western' historical roots. Based upon an assumption that morality can never transcend such origins but is somehow bound to the cultures which produced them, a number of authors argue that human rights all too often embody and thereby discriminate in favour of norms and values which are, in effect, culturally partial and limited (see Pollis and Schwab 1979; Mutua 2002, 2007). From this position it is sometimes argued (but just as often simply implied or assumed) that the very partiality of the morality which underlies a commitment to IHRL serves to invalidate any attempts to universalise the application of the doctrine, particularly where predominant ways of being and believing are not founded upon a commitment to liberty, equality and dignity. Makau Mutua, who has persistently sought to draw attention to what he considers to be the destructive effects of ethnocentricity in many approaches to justifying and practising human rights, has stated that 'as currently constituted and deployed, the human rights movement will ultimately fail because it is perceived as an alien ideology in non-Western societies' (2002: 14).

Bridging the gap: an appeal to relative universality and the ecumenical approach

There are two distinct versions or manifestations of relativism. The first is typically referred to as descriptive relativism and consists of an empirical claim, which is most frequently found within the writings of social anthropologists and sociologists. On this view, the ever-expanding body of ethnographic evidence continues to demonstrate the sheer extent to which cultures can and do fundamentally differ from each other. In many respects, the accuracy of this empirical claim is secondary to the implications of relativism for human rights. At the heart of the relativist critique lies a normatively *prescriptive* claim which holds that fundamental and incommensurable cultural diversity is, in itself, morally valuable and worthy of everyone's support. Prescriptive relativism builds upon its descriptive counterpart but is, in principle at least, separable from an account of how human life is actually organised. Indeed, many supporters of prescriptive relativism argue that the doctrine becomes more valuable as the homogenising threat of globalisation increases: the less actual cultural diversity there is, the more valid are appeals to protect existing diversity against the threatening tide of 'Mac-World' globalisation.

Prescriptive relativism is ultimately intellectually incoherent and should really be understood as a form of pluralism. On strictly relativist grounds, if the legitimacy of any moral value or norm is inextricably tied to its cultural basis, then the proposed moral value of espousing cultural diversity is similarly conditional upon the distinct cultures in which it is found. Not all cultures value diversity. Many consider the cultural differences of others as posing a threat to their ways of being and believing. On strictly relativist grounds, then, a commitment to espouse diversity can only be demanded within those cultural settings in which diversity is actually widely upheld and esteemed. In appealing to diversity as a principle which *ought* to be lauded by *all* cultures, prescriptive relativists have lapsed into a form of moral universalism and are unavoidably laying claim to a universalist principle, albeit one which is consciously based upon a greater concern for the value of diversity and the need to avoid succumbing to cultural intolerance and censoriousness. In this way, we may collectively begin to transcend the somewhat protracted slanging match between universalists and relativists and embrace the objective of establishing a more constructive universalist understanding of the value of cultural diversity for human rights. In so doing, attention may be redirected towards cultural ways of being and believing which may be consistent with an admittedly redefined understanding of the universalism of human rights.

Over the past two decades or so, the debate surrounding the relationship between human rights and cultural diversity has evolved significantly. Acknowledging the importance of culture for human beings and of the value of cultural diversity for human rights is no longer conventionally considered as fundamentally incompatible with justifying human rights. An alternative intellectual ground has been cleared, which attempts to reconcile human rights with culture and cultural diversity. The eminent US human rights scholar, Jack Donnelly refers to this new approach as a form of 'relative universality', which he defines as 'a form of universalism that also allows for substantial space for important (second order) claims of relativism' (2007: 282). Prior to Donnelly, other human rights scholars such as the previously quoted Makau Mutua, referred to this new approach to human rights as a form of ecumenicalism. Mutua argues that the ecumenical approach requires that 'the cultures and traditions of the world must, in effect, compare notes, negotiate positions, and come to agreement over what constitutes human rights. Even after agreement, the doors must remain open for further inquiry, reformulation and revision' (2002: 74).

The relative universality/ecumenical approach derives a great deal of its philosophical impetus from a position which differs significantly from those views which hold that substantive moral truths are ultimately *discovered* (not created) by human beings through the exercise of reason which is itself constitutively independent of the social and cultural conditions which human beings inhabit. The natural law tradition of thinking about human rights, for example, holds that fundamental moral truths in some sense pre-exist actual human communities. This is quintessentially expressed in John Locke's appeal to life, liberty and property as natural rights existing within the state of nature. The legitimacy of any form of legal or political authority is fundamentally conditional upon the extent to which law- and policy-makers respect these natural rights. A great deal of human rights thinking remains deeply influenced by this set of assumptions and claims. On this view, the appropriate role of human deliberation over human rights is restricted to identifying the best means for applying the moral ends enshrined within the doctrine of human rights: deliberation is restricted to an instrumental role. In contrast, many contributors to the relative universality/ecumenical approach place much greater stress on the potentially constitutive role of human deliberation over what may be considered to be morally authoritative rights for any given community. Mutua's arguments drive this way of thinking firmly towards a position which, in a very real sense, would leave it up to separate communities of human beings to ultimately determine what is to count as a genuine human right for them. The political motivation for this kind of approach appears to be largely driven by a desire to overcome a recurring situation which is represented as (often hypo-critical) geo-political elites deploying the language of universal human rights as a means for imposing their continuing hegemony over other less powerful cultures and civilisations. Human rights thereby provide a new means for seeking to punish non-compliant partners and rivals within deeply unequal geo-political institutions and fora.

The relative universality/ecumenical approach is internally varied and raises some very important questions for any attempt to justify human rights in ways which do not simply condemn or ignore the sheer diversity of human cultures. Different theorists within this emerging tradition defend different accounts of the specifically universal basis of human rights norms. However, most contributors agree that what is to count as distinctly universal human rights cannot be intellectually imposed from above, but ought to flow out of a continuous dialogue with the full range of diverse ways of being and believing which are still to be found across the globe. Of course, any attempt to establish some form of universal morality from an actual or hypothetical global forum of actually existing practices and beliefs is a potential hostage to fortune. As I wrote in the previous chapter, human rights exist as a response to inhumanity and the sheer extent of inhumanity threatens to undermine any attempt to establish universal moral values on purely empirical grounds. Various authors recognise this problem and have attempted to fashion a universally legitimate account of human rights in a way which recognises cultural diversity whilst simultaneously ring-fencing some account of moral agency or the reasonable agent from the vagaries of how human life is actually led in many places. John Rawls's book *The Law of Peoples* (1999) exemplifies this attempt to square human rights with diversity and warrants a closer analysis.

Since the publication of a series of articles during the 1980s which culminated in his book *Political Liberalism* (1993), Rawls has sought to frame regulative principles for the legitimate governance of diverse societies. The focus of his work was primarily restricted to reconfigur-ing the public sphere of a single, constitutionally democratic political community. *The Law of Peoples* extended Rawls's vision to relations between states, as well as within states. In so doing, it focuses more heavily upon human rights. Three elements are particularly important to understanding Rawls's approach to human rights as expounded in *The Law of Peoples.*

First, he distinguishes between comprehensive liberalism as comprising a collection of substantive and reasonably contestable moral commitments and political liberalism which comprises what he defends as regulative principles which all sufficiently free and reasonable peoples can accept. He considers comprehensive liberalism to be merely one of a number of very different moral conceptions of the good present in the world today.[2]

Second, he argues that a commitment to reciprocity is essential to developing a legitimate account of global justice within a complex and culturally diverse world. His focus upon the ideal of reciprocity seeks explicitly to forestall the effects of the unequal distribution of power and influence. He writes:

> when terms are proposed as the most reasonable terms of fair cooperation, those proposing them must think it at least reasonable for others to accept them as free and equal citizens, and not as dominated or manipulated or under pressure caused by an inferior political or social position. (Rawls 1999: 14)

Finally, while he insists that a commitment to the universal validity of human rights can be shown to be reasonable and legitimate, the enumeration of human rights he offers falls far short of that existing body of IHRL, which I refer to in Chapter 1 and which my account of human rights is based upon. In effect, he excludes all of those human rights contained within Articles 19–30 of the UDHR, which would exclude a human right to democracy and a range of human rights to economic, social and cultural goods. For Rawls, the purpose of human rights within a globally just order is as follows: 'they restrict the justifying reasons for war and its conduct, and they specify limits to a regime's internal autonomy' (1999: 79). Gaining a sufficiently detailed understanding of Rawls's proposals in this regard requires an analysis of each of these elements.

Rawls's analysis of liberalism and his distinction between political and comprehensive liberalism has its origins in his *Political Liberalism* (1993). Simplifying a complex series of arguments, Rawls argues that modern complex societies do not yield a reasonable consensus in support of comprehensive liberalism as a distinct account of the morally good life.[3] Because not all who are subject to the jurisdiction of the 'liberal' state share the values and ideals of comprehensive liberalism and because this state of affairs is 'reasonable', the moral legitimacy of the liberal state must be secured upon a more procedural and less normatively substantive basis. In effect, this requires that the state refrain from discriminating against those individuals and communities who, for example, do not consider personal autonomy to be the principal ingredient for leading a good life. Similarly, it will require the liberal state refraining from prioritising forms of education which emphasise a primarily secular or religious world view. Comprehensive liberalism is characterised as no longer enjoying (if it ever did) a justified and reasonably privileged place in determining the basis and scope of political authority. Political liberalism, in contrast, seeks to secure conditions of mutually reciprocal respect amongst diverse communities and individuals who adhere to potentially incommensurate comprehensive moral doctrines. Achieving this will require the state adopting a certain distance from any substantive moral doctrine, including comprehensive liberalism. The philosophical basis for Rawls's argument lies in ethical pluralism.[4] Pluralism holds, in effect, that there are many different ways to lead a morally good life. Many of these ways may even be incommensurate with one another. Thus, pluralism rejects the claim that moral value can be evaluated or measured by reference to a single scale (such as utility) or a single, purportedly ultimately valuable ideal (such as personal autonomy). Rawls's commitment to and formulation of ethical pluralism extends beyond the more conventional liberal understanding which seeks to restrict moral legitimacy to those ideals and practices which comply with the central liberal ideals of equality and individual liberty.

It would, I believe, be a mistake to view this development in Rawls's thought as an abandonment of Kant in favour of Hobbes, as some critics have characterised the development in his thinking about justice. Rawls was clearly concerned to forestall the potential of the state to induce strife and conflict through a too close association with one constituency amongst the many who are subject to its jurisdiction. However, he did not thereby commit himself to the principle of *whatever* prevents strife and conflict is necessarily, on these grounds alone, legitimate. The apparently pragmatist turn in his thought is tempered by his continuing commitment to the principle of reciprocity which has always been fundamental to his account of justice. Rawls's concern to establish a just global order upon the principle of reciprocity can be understood, if only implicitly, as an attempt to avoid the charges levelled at those human rights proselytisers accused of, inadvertently perhaps, seeking to impose the partial values of the globally power-ful upon the globally weak. It also, more explicitly, accords the kind of 'voice' to 'non-Western' peoples which an overly ethnocentric approach to human rights has been accused of suppressing. In accord-ing such prominence to the ideal of reciprocity, Rawls effectively seeks to dramatically broaden the constituency of legitimate participants in the debate concerning what the basis of a just global order ought to be. The terms of this debate are also thereby altered so that it is no longer to be understood as a process of 'us' enlightening 'them' in our values and ideals but rather, as with Mutua's proposal, opening up the terms of the debate in a manner which no longer privileges the discourse of one constituency over all others.

Adopting a less substantively prescriptive approach to the basis and scope of a globally just order does not entail an abandonment of human rights. However, in Rawls's view, it does require a distinct paring down of the doctrine. Rawls argues that a just global order cannot simply extend respect to all existing cultures and societies. However, he also insists that such an order may comprise societies other than simply liberal ones. He addresses his account to what he refers to as liberal peoples and decent hierarchical societies. While liberal peoples are characterised by their espousal of a comprehensive panoply of human rights, decent hierarchical societies are based upon a commitment to a more limited range of rights. Thus, the global order may require that such societies share a commitment to life, liberty, property and to formal equality, which Rawls describes as the core of human rights. However, they do not necessarily need to thereby commit to the more comprehensive range of human rights enshrined within IHRL and found within most liberal constitutions. Also, and arguably most importantly, whilst political power must not be the sole preserve of a single constituency, decent hierarchical societies need not be commit-ted to the principle of universal suffrage. Nor need it be necessary for every member of such societies to possess substantively equal oppor-tunities to access and influence the principal decision-making fora. Finally, decent hierarchical societies are characterised as such by the absence of any necessary commitment to individualism (in its various forms) as essential for their normative legitimacy. The fundamental political unit is thereby more likely to be an association or community, rather than the individual citizen. Rawls insists that the comprehensive doctrines of such societies are not fully unreasonable. He writes, 'these doctrines must admit a sufficient measure of liberty of conscience and freedom of religion and thought, even if these freedoms are not extensive nor as equal for all members of the decent society as they are in liberal societies' (1999: 74).

For Rawls the law of peoples applies to both liberal and non-liberal societies alike. While war-like societies are excluded, he argues that casting membership in these terms serves to overcome the cultural partiality and limitations of an account of human rights as necessarily requiring a conversion to comprehensive liberal values and ideals. He clearly states that 'it is crucial that the Law of Peoples does not require decent societies to abandon or modify their religious institutions and adopt liberal ones' (1999: 121). For him, a globally just order does require the establishment and protection of a limited range of human rights as fundamental freedoms, but this does not amount to an insistence that the entire globe comply with 'Western' (idealised) standards. For Rawls, the law of peoples asks people to adopt a standpoint of 'fair equality with all other societies' (1999: 122). A commitment to this particular principle, he insists, is not a commitment to an exclusively 'Western' idea since the concept of fair equality is not the sole preserve of 'Western' civilisation but is a principle which all societies committed to a stable peace and lack of hostility and conflict can reasonably endorse and apply.

The significance of Rawls's political philosophy extends far beyond the specific concerns of human rights theorists. However, his vision of the relationship between human rights and cultural diversity provides a highly sophisticated illustration of what a commitment to relative universality/ecumenicalism could mean for the global application of human rights. His approach is clearly deeply sympathetic to the concerns of theorists such as Mutua, who seek to protect the universal validity of human rights by allowing for a far more localised reformulation of human rights. As others have argued more recently, many supporters of human rights have been accused of simply 'hoping for too much' (Cohen 2004) through their continuing commitment to basing human rights upon ideals and values which can be reasonably objected to by some. The principles enshrined within the law of peoples aim to extend the constituency of the reasonable authors of what human rights are by including some non-liberal peoples. Mutua, in particular, has consistently argued that the global legitimacy of human rights has suffered from its too close association with liberal democracy. Liberal democracy might thereby be understood as merely one of a number of substantive political ideologies which human rights allow for. Liberal democracy is merely one of a number of players in a game which it has too often sought to referee.

A final important element of Rawls's contribution to reformulating the relationship between human rights and cultural diversity concerns the relationship between the public norms of any given sovereign authority and the private practices which citizens subject to that authority actually pursue. At the risk of simplifying a very complex series of arguments and debates within legal and political philosophy, the Rawlsian approach (which many theorists explicitly identify with) argues that public norms and private practices should not converge. Sovereign authorities that exercise jurisdiction over diverse societies will necessarily be confronted by a broad range of differing private practices.[5] Securing sufficient legitimacy within such diverse societies necessitates, or so it is typically argued, the formulation of a political morality that no one of the constituent ways of being and believing can claim as its own. Public norms must, therefore, take a primarily procedural form, which enables the sovereign authority to adopt a largely impartial standpoint vis-à-vis the beliefs and practices of those over whom it exercises its authority. As such, this Rawlsian approach to formulating the requirements for legitimate legal and political authority appears to add an important element to the relative universality/ ecumenical approach and its desire to reformulate human rights in ways which can better speak to a far broader population of cultural communities.

The relative universality/ecumenical approach to human rights clearly accords significant weight and value to what are envisaged as distinct peoples or cultural communities: culture is central to this approach. In addition, the approach also seeks to promote cultural communities' capacity to both contribute to the global determination of which human rights should be binding for all and, beyond this, which rights may be recognised as valid for those separate peoples and communities themselves.[6] Rawls provides a distinct enumeration of precisely which human rights, on his view, are genuinely universal. Others, such as Mutua, anticipate different collections of human rights for different communities. Many defenders of human rights would (and do) take great issue with any proposal that different communities might pursue different versions of human rights. In seeking to respond effectively to cultural diversity, theorists such as Rawls and Mutua appear to be potentially opening the door to a multi-speed approach to human rights, much as some theorists discuss multi-speed approaches to regional unions, such as the European Union. Clearly, these are important concerns which require a closer analysis, which will be provided shortly. However, before turning to this task, I shall consider one obvious objection to the kinds of anxieties which the relative universality/ecumenical approach raises for many defenders of human rights. Thus, one might attempt to dispel worries by simply stating that this is all mere philosophising and, as such, the likelihood of any of it actually impacting upon IHRL is highly remote. An appeal to positive law might appear to assuage the concerns of many. Is this the case? Is IHRL genuinely sufficiently immunised against the likelihood that recognising culture and cultural diversity in ways proposed by Rawls and Mutua may result in a global and localised retraction of IHRL?

Institutionalising culture and cultural diversity

There is an extensive body of IHRL and related declarations, instruments and institutional bodies which together are explicitly concerned with recognising the importance of cultural community for individuals and the need to positively espouse the value of cultural diversity. As the so-called third generation of human rights, cultural rights may be relative newcomers but are an established category of IHRL. The principal components of the category of cultural rights are the following: Article 27 of the UDHR; Article 15 of the ICESCR; Articles 13 and 14 of the ICESCR in respect of education; similarly in respect of education, Articles 28 and 29 of the Convention on the Rights of the Child (CRC); Article 27 of the ICCPR in respect of minority rights; International Labour Organization's (ILO) Convention 169 in respect of indigenous peoples' rights; the UN Declaration on the Rights of Indigenous Peoples (UNDRIP); the UN Declaration on the Rights of Persons Belonging to National or Ethnic, Religious and Linguistic Minorities; and Article 2 of the UNESCO Convention on the Protection and Promotion of Diversity of Cultural Expressions. In addition to the treaty monitoring bodies which oversee the respective conventions, the UN has also recently established a special procedures mandate in the form of the Special Rapporteur in the field of cultural rights, who is charged with monitoring states' commitments to cultural rights across IHRL.

Underlying this established body of IHRL is an explicit recognition of the importance of culture for individuals' enjoyment of all human rights and, just as significantly, an acknowledgement of the importance of the cultural context for human rights generally. In respect of the latter, repeated acknowledgements of the cultural context of human rights can be found in numerous UN declarations and resolutions. Foremost of these include Article 5 of the VDPA, Article 1 of the UNESCO Universal Declaration on Cultural Diversity and several UN General Assembly Resolutions, including GA Resolution 64/174. The general position these instruments support is the need to recognise that the promotion of human rights is entirely consistent with the promotion of cultural diversity: the object of human rights is not to enforce cultural hegemony or homogenisation. This commitment to cultural diversity is thereby seen as entailing the need to recognise the significance of the differences in existing cultural perspectives upon human rights principles. A stock wording has emerged to express this position, exemplified by Article 5 of the VDPA and the Preamble to GA Resolution 64/174 which state that 'the significance of national and regional particularities and various historical, cultural and religious backgrounds must be borne in mind'. Collectively, these developments can be understood as an explicit response to the allegation both that human rights can be insensitive to the cultural basis of human life and that specific human rights campaigns can be unduly ethnocentric in simply assuming that others should follow the same instrumental paths to the shared ends of any specific human right. As such, IHRL's recognition of culture and cultural diversity represents a qualified endorsement of some of the arguments found within the relative universality/ecumenical approach. However, the requirement that 'cultural and religious backgrounds must be borne in mind' most certainly does not equate to the kind of roll-back of IHRL which authors such as Rawls and Mutua propose. Perhaps this qualified acknowledgement of culture and cultural diversity prompted the most recent development within IHRL which sought to accord even greater significance to the effects of culture upon human rights.

In 2011 the UN Human Rights Council (HRC) passed Resolution 16/3, entitled *Promoting human rights and fundamental freedoms through a better understanding of traditional values of humankind.* Having been established to promote and protect universal respect for all human rights and fundamental freedoms, the chief mandate of the international community's foremost human rights body is to make recommendations on situations of violations of human rights. While the founding resolution of the HRC lacks any reference to 'culture' in relation to the responsibilities of the mechanism, its Preamble reaffirms the language of the VDPA which states 'that all human rights are universal, indivisible, interrelated, interdependent and mutually reinforcing, and that all human rights must be treated in a fair and equal manner, on the same footing and with the same emphasis'. It also noted that all states regardless of their cultural system have an obligation to promote and protect human rights. However, despite the absence of any grounds for taking action on value-laden matters of morality, it is within this setting that the inter-governmental Council has approached the debate on the impact of cultural practices and beliefs on the universal element of human rights.[7]

In 2009, during the 12th session of the HRC, Belarus, China, Russia, Singapore and Sri Lanka tabled the resolution *Follow-up and Implementation of the Vienna Declaration and Programme of Action: Promoting human rights and fundamental freedoms through a better understanding of traditional values of human kind.* By launching the discourse of an undefined set of 'traditional values of human kind', this resolution introduced unprecedented language within the scope of the Council. The resolution recognised that all cultures share common values belonging to humankind which contribute to the advancement of human rights and requested that the High Commissioner for Human Rights convened a workshop on how 'a better understanding of traditional values of human kind underpinning international human rights norms and standards can contribute to the promotion and protection of human rights and fundamental freedoms'. The resolution was adopted, although the voting process (twenty-six votes in favour, fifteen against and six abstentions) demonstrated a clear geographical divide. A majority of votes against the adoption of the resolution emanated from European and 'Western' states whereas the majority of votes in favour were those of African and Asian states. In the two years between initiating the focus upon traditional values and the final passing of Resolution 16/3 various working parties deliberated and argued over several significant issues, including the need for any acknowledgement of traditional values within IHRL, how traditional values might be understood and defined, and even to what extent traditional values might justify a restriction of some human rights within some cultures. The outcome of this process is exemplified by Articles 3–5 of the resolution, which state:

3. *Affirms* that dignity, freedom and responsibility are traditional values, shared by all humanity and embodied in universal rights instruments;
4. *Recognizes* that the better understanding and appreciation of these values contribute to promoting and protecting human rights and fundamental freedoms;
5. *Notes* the important role of family, community, society and educational institutions in upholding and transmitting these values, which contributes to promoting respect for human rights and increasing their acceptance at the grass roots, and calls upon all States to strengthen this role through appropriate positive measures[.]

The language of Resolution 16/3 clearly resonates with the general spirit which permeates the relative universality/ecumenical approach. It also complies with the broader UN requirement that religious and cultural factors must be *borne in mind*. However, one of the most revealing features of the HRC's engagement with the notion of traditional values was the clear and significant differences of opinion expressed within the working parties and more formal HRC proceedings, which led to the final resolution. Put simply, what may be referred to as established liberal-democratic states parties persistently opposed the whole concept of traditional values. The composition of the HRC ensured that their cause was bound to fail, although many of those states parties which supported the entire initiative suggested that they would have preferred even greater significance being accorded to traditional values than that which appears in the final resolution. It can be said then that Resolution 16/3 embodies and exemplifies precisely the kinds of divisions and concerns which defenders of the relative universality/ecumenical approach appeal to: the existence of a clear division amongst geo-cultural and regional blocs over precisely what the relationship between human rights and cultural diversity should be. However, it remains constrained by the body of established UN IHRL which serves to limit how far concessions may be on the grounds of culture. Similar constraints do not apply to regional bodies.

While the UN has clearly sought a realignment with the importance of culture and cultural diversity, various regional human rights bodies have gone further in seeking to enunciate a more ostensibly culturally sensitive formulation of human rights. The most important of these clearly testifies to the influence of the ethos of the concept of relative universality and is found in the spirit and letter of several regional human rights declarations. Thus, the Preamble and Articles 17(3) and 18(2) of the African Charter on Human and Peoples' Rights explicitly evokes an appeal to so-called traditional values as underpinning and directing the content of the African version of human rights, which the Charter expounds. The Preamble states, 'taking into consideration the virtues of their historical tradition and the values of African civilization which should inspire and characterize their reflection on the concept of human and peoples' rights'. The Cairo Declaration on Human Rights in Islam subordinates all of the Declaration's provisions to the authority of Shari'a. Article I(a) states, for example, that 'all human beings form one family whose members are united by submission to God and descent from Adam'. Finally, Article 6 of the recent ASEAN Human Rights Declaration includes a provision which requires the balancing of individual freedoms with what are referred to as 'responsibilities to all other individuals, the community and the society where one lives'. These declarations represent a formal diffusion of the spirit of human rights across the globe. However, as significant elements of each of them illustrate, the precise letter of which human rights exist where and to what extent clearly departs from the UN's position on what bearing cultural differences in mind should entail. Clear and substantial disagreements exist between the drafters of these regional accounts of human rights and the UN's version outlined above.

The final institutional embodiment of the relative universality/ ecumenical approach within established IHRL can be seen in the mechanism which enables states parties to UN covenants to enter reservations against specific aspects of those covenants. Reservations enable states to exercise their sovereignty over matters which are culturally or religiously controversial for them and, it is claimed, the populations they exercise jurisdiction over. As will be analysed in a later chapter, the covenant with the largest number of reservations entered against it is the CEDAW. Reservations against specific articles of the covenant emanate predominantly from amongst Islamic states and notionally secular states with large majority Muslim populations. Rarely do such states argue against the principle of gender equality, and they tend to assert instead that some provisions are dispensable to achieve that end in their respective societies.

It should be abundantly clear then that the acknowledgement of culture and cultural diversity is not restricted to philosophers and human rights theorists. Culture and cultural diversity are firmly established components of IHRL. While largely restricted to debates over what might constitute the most appropriate means to achieve universal human rights norms, the institutionalisation of culture and cultural diversity are clearly straining towards a more fundamental reassessment of precisely which human rights norms may be genuinely universal with regional declarations providing the strongest manifestations of this impulse. Having discussed the basis for the arguments which support some form of renegotiation and having summarised the key institutional developments in this area, I now turn to evaluate the assumptions and implications of this entire phenomenon.

Analysing what's at stake

Human rights clearly have to embrace cultural diversity and the importance of culture for human well-being. It would be politically and conceptually disastrous for a doctrine which must claim universal validity to be capable of being accepted by only some communities of peoples and individuals. The promotion of cultural diversity and the value of culture are essential to human rights: period. As I demonstrated above, the debate is no longer aligned along starkly opposing lines, in which both camps only agree upon one thing: that acknowledging diversity and culture is incompatible with justifying human rights. However, a demarcation line is and must still be drawn between human rights and some ways of being and believing. The principled position is clearly stated in paragraph 18 of General Comment 21 of the Economic, Social and Cultural Rights Committee which states that 'no one may invoke cultural diversity to infringe upon human rights guaranteed by international law, nor to limit their scope'. The same language is also expressed in Article 2(1) of the UNESCO Convention on the Protection and Promotion of Diversity of Cultural Expressions and Article 4 of the UNESCO Universal Declaration on Cultural Diversity. Many will intuitively consider some practices to be incompatible with respect for fundamental human rights, irrespective of how formally established those practices are within specific cultural communities. In this respect, an albeit rather tentative attempt to identify which practices may be included in this category has been initiated by the UN in the specific context of women's rights. Thus, in 2009 an Expert Group were tasked to identify and examine so-called harmful cultural practices (HCPs) against women. Amongst a number of important insights, the report provides a definition of HCPs, as including 'FGM [female genital mutilation], dowry-related violence, acid attacks, so-called 'honour' crimes, and maltreatment of widows' (UN Division for the Advancement of Women 2009: 4). I shall return to discuss this issue in far greater depth in a subsequent chapter.[8] Given how little further substantive progress has been made in formulating a comprehensive list of HCPs, we are better placed, at this time, to pursue a different approach in analysing what is at stake and focusing instead upon a series of conceptual and methodological moves and stratagems which this whole area of debate draws heavily upon. The greater part of my discussion will specifically focus upon explicit and tacit understandings of culture which authors appeal to since underneath it all lies 'culture'.

A commitment to human rights cannot include the principle of according an unconditional equality of respect for all ways of being and believing. Demarcation lines must be drawn. After all, human sacrifice was once an established cultural practice within some communities and today many cultures and religions continue to formally discriminate against people on the basis of their identity. However, the simultaneous acknowledgement of this principle and of the need to protect and promote diversity and culture must be ever mindful of the charge of simply narrowly defining what constitutes valid ways of being and believing in accordance with an unduly narrow set of ethnocentric criteria. In his critique of recurring attempts to define such criteria, Mutua writes, 'it says that diversity is good so long as it is exercised within the liberal paradigm' (2002: 3–4). In other words, others' ways of being and believing are acceptable only so long as they comply with the ways of being and believing which allegedly characterise the 'Western' (comprehensive) liberal belief systems which, on

Mutua's terms, have exercised and largely continue to exercise hegemonic control over human rights ideals and institutions. At this juncture, other authors might head down what I consider to be a largely futile avenue which focuses upon the surface-level credibility of such claims, such as whether ostensibly 'Western' prejudices are really so widespread within the theory and practice of human rights. However, far more valuable insights can be achieved by digging deeper into the conceptual soil out of which this debate ultimately grows, the most important of which is the very notion of culture.

Generations of social anthropologists and sociologists have debated and disagreed over precisely what we are referring to when we describe patterns of human behaviour as manifestations of 'culture'. The *Oxford English Dictionary* defines culture very succinctly as comprising 'the ideas, customs, and social behaviour of a particular people or society'.[9] Most of us, I am sure, have some intuitive sense of ways of being and believing which are more distinctly influenced by culture than others. Most of us can recognise the influence of culture upon universal features of human behaviour, such as how and what we wear and what we eat. The perceived culturally based differences between different patterns of human behaviour entail some sense of the boundedness of distinct human cultures. Any attempt to identify and laud (or condemn) cultural differences entails referencing specific cultural communities, such as *the* African-American community, *the* community of ethnic Russians residing in eastern Ukraine or *the* community of Sunni Muslims residing in Iraq. The distinctiveness of different cultural communities necessarily entails some acceptance of the tangible boundedness of such communities. To many who identify with them, or are identified by others as belonging to such communities, the basis and content of membership is anything but artificial and constructed. Hence, the *Blut und Boden* (or blood and soil) markers of many insiders' claims to embodying distinct forms of culturally based identity. Up until the late 1960s and early 1970s many academic accounts of culture tended to reinforce members' perceptions of the essential and immutable basis of the distinct constitutive elements of their respective communities. Academic accounts of culture would frequently reference the causal properties of various structural conditions which, unperceived by the members of the communities themselves, nevertheless sought to explain why they practised and believed in the particular ways they did. What was not questioned was the extent to which such communities might be far less stable, distinct and integral than many of their members imagined them to be.

Clearly, all of those theorists who insist that human rights are unduly influenced by 'Western' ideals and practices, or those who appeal to some alternative forms of 'Asian' or 'African' ways of being and believing are necessarily appealing to the notion that such distinct and separable cultural configurations actually exist. Everyone who asserts that gender equality is a *'Western'* ideal is necessarily trading upon a very well-established set of assumptions, which include *the* 'West' exists and can be reasonably separately identified from other geo-cultural configurations; that gender equality is a distinctive component of the normative identity which references to the 'West' entail; that 'non-Western' attitudes towards gender equality must either reject or deviate from the 'Western' conceptualisation of the ideal and so forth. African, Asian, European and Islamic formulations of human rights must all assume the existence of some geo-cultural referents which enable one to define and distinguish between different understandings of human rights. All of this is fundamentally and conceptually objectionable, as I shall now argue.

Over the past forty years or so, an alternative account of culture has gained ascendency within the social sciences. Summarising a complex set of debates and analyses, it is now widely acknowledged that all forms of cultural identity are constructions. No culture has an essence or an immutable set of characteristics which serve to constitute the authentic manifestations of identity. While many members of cultural communities continue to seek to protect what they imagine to be their essential ways of being and believing, these ways are, ultimately, 'imagined', as Benedict Anderson (1991) has written of national identity. This does not mean, of course, that appeals to such identities are thereby any less urgent, passionate or in some cases, deadly. Indeed, some people's experience of their identity as fragile and endangered can lead to campaigns of hatred and ethnic cleansing. However, the implications of correctly understanding the ultimately contingent and constructed basis and shape of any given form of cultural identity are profound for understanding how we might respond to appeals to protecting established identities.

Conceiving of cultural communities as tangible but constructed entities enables one to discern the role of politics and power in the construction of any specific community's identity. To understand a community as imagined does not entail viewing that identity as based upon a collection of random or arbitrary components. Thus, what are presented as the essential signifiers of any particular community are the products of and are subject to political contestation, which is itself situated within highly influential contexts of time and place. For example, what it means to be 'German' has clearly changed over the past 150 years in ways which have had devastating effects upon many human beings during the 1930s and 1940s in particular. The weight which Christians attach to the authority of Scripture has changed (and divided) that global community even during the past two decades. In recent months during 2015 and now 2016 the status of 'refugee' or 'asylum seeker' has been subject to radically different representations, which are largely influenced by others' politically motivated attitudes towards them.

As with any political process, it is also crucial to scrutinise precisely who has the means to effect and influence the construction of identity. This extends to include *intra-* and *inter-*cultural forms of identity. Various authors have made invaluable contributions to expanding our appreciation of these dynamics but arguably one of the most important contributions was made by Edward Said in his seminal work *Orientalism* (1985). Said argued that identity was fundamentally relational in character, so that no collective form of identity is ever entirely self-constituting and constructed from purely and authentically immanent components. Drawing upon a tradition of thinking which includes Giambattista Vico, Hegel and Antonio Gramsci, Said sought to demonstrate how the hegemonic constructions of both Occidental and Oriental identity was the consequence of an unequally dialectical relationship between the two civilisations, which emerged as part of the empirical expansion of European powers in the seventeenth, eighteenth and nineteenth centuries. Both the very delineation of a geo-cultural space referred to as *the* Orient and the constituent elements of what were presented as essentially defining *the* Oriental were largely, if not entirely, Occidental constructions. However, the dialectical twist consisted in the fact that the collective form of the constituting identity (the Occident) was also a construction whose shape was inherently entwined with the pejorative representation of the Occident's significant and constituted other: the Orient. The West was represented as being rational and scientific because the East was irrational and prone to myth. The West was represented as heading towards rational, bureaucratised and largely democratic government because the East was still mired in forms of despotic and charismatic authoritarian governance.

At worst, such constructions sought to legitimise the imperial raping and pillaging of others' lives and environments. At 'best', they served as attempted justifications of 'our' duty to civilise 'them', which is epitomised by the so-called white man's burden. Said alerts us to the need to scrutinise the precise nature of the relational dynamics which prevail between any two or more parties to the construction of collective identities. While the constituting party is most strongly placed to attribute an identity to its significant other, both parties' identities are, in a very real sense, interdependently constructed. The implications of Said's (and others') insights extend well beyond genealogical studies into the formation of West and East. Understanding identity as a relational construction, which always occurs within a political context, provides for forms of analysis which destabilise all appeals to distinct collective identities and recast how we ought to think of the relationship between human rights and culture.

I wrote above that the anti-essentialist conception of culture as a constructed phenomenon is firmly in the ascendency. Indeed, many who argue for the need to protect particular ways of being and believing simultaneously reference and endorse this conception of culture. Very few academics writing in this area will argue that any particular form of collective identity is based upon some essential, natural basis. However, it is difficult to fully understand appeals to preserving and protecting such identities without making an appeal to some purported essence of the culture, whether it consist of language, land, religious practice or other sets of established customs. The persistence of such phenomena is not, in itself, a justification for their preservation. If all forms of collective identity are ultimately contingent, as the anti-essentialist position insists, then change is not loss, but merely change. Kwame Appiah (2005) has argued in these terms in his critique of what he calls the 'preservationist ethic'. As I will discuss in greater detail in the following chapter and given the largely paradigmatic status of the anti-essentialist perspective within the literature, it is surprising just how many legal decisions and public policies are based upon a conception of cultural community as something which warrants protection in its own right. From UN instruments to US Supreme Court rulings, the insistence that specific communities' ways of being and believing should be protected has received consistent and concerted support. Typically, such rulings and policies appeal directly to the claim that some loss or diminution to the cultural community ought to be prevented and avoided.

One can understand and sympathise with the apparently empathetic motivations for such a position but it amounts to a failure to fully appreciate the implications of correctly understanding the construction of culture. All too often, as Madhavi Sunder (2001) has written, a policy of cultural survival simply ignores (and can thereby serve to support) existing intra-cultural inequalities and discrimination. Or, following on from Edward Said's (2000) critique of Samuel Huntington's so-called *Clash of Civilizations* thesis, it can have far wider and catastrophic consequences in which attempts to protect the West from the East and vice versa completely overlook how each necessarily constructs the other, albeit in politically unequal ways. Seeking to preserve identities can, at times, serve only to affirm conditions of inequality and, at worst, outright inhumanity.

The passage above may alarm some readers. I could be construed as simply denouncing and rejecting all attempts to support diversity through a wholesale denial of the authenticity of any form of collective identity. On this view, a rejection of the preservationist ethic or policies of cultural survival will serve only to provide succour to the forces of cultural homogenisation and the replacement of long-established ways of being and believing with the necessarily rootless and bland commodities of global consumer capitalism; that an acknowledgement of the contingency of all cultural constructions inadvertently reinforces an entirely profane impulse towards perpetual destruction and reconstruction. This is certainly not my intention and I believe a commitment to human rights is essential to leading us away from such dystopian scenarios.

A return to universality

To this point I have argued that human rights are an essentially human construction which, more specifically, draws its substance and motivation from a commitment to the ideal of humanity. Humanity, in all of its rich diversity, must therefore be fully represented in the form which the doctrine of human rights takes in the process of the doctrine's continual development. Humanity cannot be the sole preserve of a select few, nor can the norms and institutions which support it be coercively imposed from above. As many have argued before me, commitments to human rights require human deliberation. This, in effect, is precisely what the likes of Mutua and Rawls are arguing for when they insist that the identification of genuinely universal human rights should be the outcome of a deliberative process, which does not unduly load the dice in favour of narrowly liberal norms and values. However, the basis and shape of any such deliberative process must itself presuppose the legitimacy of core human rights norms if it is to avoid the risk of simply reinforcing existing inequalities and cultural practices which are fundamentally oppressive. Many of those who agonise over the potentially oppressive character of simply presupposing the legitimacy of human rights norms are themselves drawing upon precisely those ideals on which human rights are fundamentally based – liberty, equality and human dignity – in their denunciations of what they see as forms of moral intolerance or censoriousness exercised in the name of human rights. There can be no denying the fact that the name of human rights has been too often invoked to lend justification to acts and policies which cause large-scale human rights violations. Similarly, there can be no denying that human rights campaigns have all too often suffered from a lack of cultural awareness and sensitivity. As I will discuss in greater detail throughout this book, the ends of human rights may be achieved in various ways. However, the challenge which foregrounding cultural belonging and diversity raises for human rights is precisely one which also acknowledges the extent to which some cultural communities' predominant practices and beliefs can be harmful for the human rights of some members and non-members alike. This is precisely the alternative vision of a deliberative process espoused by the likes of Seyla Benhabib (2011). The deliberative process cannot exclude or systematically jeopardise the very ideals upon which it rests in the first place. This is not intended as a means for loading the dice in favour of merely one parochial normative doctrine, but is simply entailed by the requirements of humanity. The ultimate value of culture and cultural diversity must always be measured in respect of their effects upon human beings and their fundamental human rights. To reassert a claim which will be far more satisfactorily defended in the following chapter, cultures which systematically prevent and deny some members' fundamental rights to effectively participate in the construction and reconstruction of the communities' collective identities cannot be uncritically affirmed from a human rights perspective.

Setting aside the inherent problems with referring to any collection of human phenomena as 'Western' (or 'African', 'Asian' or 'Islamic'), human rights is not a doctrine which privileges 'Western' sensibilities. There have been and continue to be countless campaigns across the globe which explicitly reference human rights as the driving force behind their struggles to overcome systematic denials of liberty, equality and human dignity. Some of these campaigns were waged against 'Western' imperial powers during the anti-colonial movements of the 1950s and 1960s. The moral authority of human rights for many independence movements clearly transcended the alleged geographical origins of human rights and provided an essential tool by which to combat and ultimately overcome imperial domination. Similarly, many grass-roots campaigns for social, economic and political justice across the globe appeal directly to human rights in their struggles with internal oppression, whether this be within nation-states or more narrowly distinct cultural communities. This vernacularisation of human rights provides a powerful objection to anyone who seeks to categorise a commitment to gender equality, for example, as an exclusively 'Western' ideal. It should also be clear that human rights should not be considered as essentially incompatible with some ways of being and believing, as such, but rather that they take principal aim at those instances of the exercise of power which perpetuate continuing inhumanity. No society or culture is immune from outbreaks of inhumanity, nor is any society or culture *essentially* inhumane since no society or culture can legitimately claim to possess an essential character. Some who claim that there exists a fundamental incompatibility between respect for human rights and respect for existing cultural traditions and beliefs are undoubtedly seeking only to reinforce their continuing power and control. From the perspective of a commitment to liberty, equality and human dignity there are no good moral reasons why we should connive in such attempts by the few to dominate the many.

One must also question the presumption that cultural diversity is best promoted by protecting the boundaries of existing communities. Many authors have written of the existence of so-called internal minorities within minority cultures (Green 1995; Sunder 2001). One of the very real dangers of granting a degree of self-governance rights to established minority communities is that these may then be used to stifle or suppress internal dissidents and those who, recognising the constructed character of culture, seek to change the community from within. In recent years, even some communities which many considered to be positively emblematic of possessing a single and shared identity or nomos have been shown to contain reformist constituencies.[10] The principle of diversity is not well served by simply displacing the problem of the denial of members' voices within cultural communities. Conceiving of cultures as possessing some essential identity is not only, as we have seen, conceptually incoherent, but, more importantly perhaps, incompatible with a genuine commitment to protecting and promoting cultural diversity. Conservation and preservation can, sometimes, stifle and frustrate innovation and change. Reconciling a commitment to human rights and to the promotion of cultural diversity is not best served by subsuming the myriad of different ways of being and believing within singular geo-cultural parameters, such as 'Asia', 'Africa', 'Europe' or Islam, in the same way that, as will be discussed in Chapter 4, the rights of women cannot best be secured by imagining that 'women' represent a single, shared constituency. Promoting diversity from within a human rights-based perspective is poorly served by attributing singular characteristics and traits to what are imagined to be discrete constituencies of human beings.

Conclusion

This chapter has traversed a complex intellectual and legal terrain. I have considered various long-standing ways of looking at and evaluating the challenge of diversity for human rights. I have enthusiastically endorsed the now established claim that human rights not only cannot ignore culture and cultural diversity, but that the cause of human rights requires a qualified endorsement of the importance of culture and cultural diversity. I have raised concerns over the persistence of essentialist understandings of culture within some attempts to fashion a human rights-based assimilation of culture. Many ways of being and believing can be shown to be consistent with, or at least not a violation of, IHRL. However, not all can be so considered. This last claim has been mostly suggested in what I have written above and it requires a detailed explication and defence, which Chapter 3 will now provide.

Suggested reading

- James Griffin, *On Human Rights* (Oxford: Oxford University Press, 2008), chapter 7.
- Steven Lukes, *Liberals and Cannibals: The Implications of Diversity* (London: Verso, 2003), chapters 1–4.
- Alison Dundes Renteln, 'The Significance of Cultural Differences for Human Rights', in Cindy Holder and David Reidy (eds), *Human Rights: The Hard Questions* (Cambridge: Cambridge University Press, 2013), pp. 79–99.

Notes

1. <http://www.oxforddictionaries.com/definition/english/ethnocentric?q=ethnocentricity#ethnocentric__7> (last accessed 27 August 2016).
2. Recall that I summarised the principal themes of political liberalism in the previous chapter.
3. See Kukathas and Pettit (1990) for a detailed analysis of Rawls's distinction between comprehensive and political liberalism.
4. For discussions of pluralism and its relevance for international ethics see Paul et al. (2003); Walzer (1994).
5. For the moment, I understand 'private practices' as referring to all those ways of being and believing which individual citizens commit to. I will subsequently question the extent to which such practices can rightfully be referred to as 'private'.
6. The separateness and distinctness of peoples and cultural communities is a highly important issue within this broader focus upon human rights and culture. As such, I will consider it in greater detail later in this chapter.
7. See Fagan and Fridlund (2016) for a critical analysis of this issue.
8. I also consider this in greater detail in Fagan (forthcoming, 2017b).
9. <http://www.oxforddictionaries.com/definition/english/culture> (last accessed 27 August 2016).
10. I am thinking specifically here of the Amish and the Jehovah's Witnesses communities in the United States.

3

A Right to Cultural Identity

Key questions

1. Why did human rights theorists and practitioners largely ignore cultural identity in the past?
2. Why do some argue that identity should be included in legislating for diverse societies?
3. Why is so-called ascribed identity important to human rights?
4. How does the 'politics of recognition' differ from a 'colour-blind' approach to combatting discrimination?
5. What are some of the key justifications for a right to cultural identity?
6. What do cultural rights include?
7. Must IHRL include collective rights as a legitimate category of human rights?
8. Does a right to cultural identity justify cultures accusing some of their members of being disloyal towards the culture?
9. How should human rights defenders respond to culturally oppressive communities?
10. In what ways can human rights influence the construction of the collective identity of any given cultural community?

Introduction

This chapter focuses upon the complex relationship between identity and human rights. I argue that the conventional approach to human rights that has largely sought to ignore individuals' cultural identity is unsustainable. I consider the arguments in support of the claim that we are all deeply influenced by our (variable) cultural surroundings. I proceed to analyse the arguments which specifically seek to defend the existence and legitimacy of collectivist rights to cultural identity. I consider how such rights have been established and upheld in various legal decisions and instruments. I then consider more critical engagements with collectivist rights to cultural identity. I argue that a human rights-based approach cannot endorse an account of cultural community as inherently valuable. Some cultures include oppressive hierarchies which cannot be easily avoided by those whom they target. I conclude that a right to cultural identity can be justified only on the basis of recognising and defending the essentially constructed character of all cultural communities. The purpose of human rights in this context is to create the opportunity for people to make and remake their cultural communities in ways which are not dominated by oppressive tradition and custom.

Acknowledging the undeniable reality of cultural identity

Some readers may remain sceptical of the importance I and others attach to the cultural context of human agency. It is undeniably the case that successive generations of human rights theorists and practitioners largely, if not entirely, ignored individual human beings' actual identities when formulating and applying human rights norms. Indeed, prior to the wider attention which so-called identity politics began to attract from the 1980s onwards, human rights theorists largely endorsed liberalism's principled exclusion of any sustained consideration of individuals' specific and differing identities from the determination of core constitutional and legislative reasoning. Why?

Historically, liberalism emerged as a response to centuries of oppression and discrimination enacted through political and legal systems which formally distinguished between different collective categories of human beings. Human beings' largely, if not entirely, ascribed characteristics had provided the grounds upon which centuries of oppression and discrimination were practised and ostensibly justified. The combination of moral individualism and a succession of political and social revolutions sought to remove any consideration for individuals' ascribed identities from the political moralities which liberal states drew upon in their attempts to establish just political and legal systems. Most theorists held to the firm conviction that genuine equality could only be achieved through an adherence to what became widely known as a 'colour-blind' approach to any and all forms of identity-based discrimination, including those which continued to attract widespread prejudice and outright hatred from others within formally liberal societies.

The principle of formal equality was based upon and entailed a corresponding commitment to an abstract and asocial account of individually sovereign moral agents from which any distinguishing characteristics or attributes were necessarily stripped away. Successive generations of liberals and then human rights theorists attempted to restrict any consideration of identity to the so-called private sphere in which individuals were understood as being sufficiently free to experiment with various ways of being and believing. Within the somewhat fantastical world of ideal liberal political thought, many argued that the state and the broader public sphere should adopt a position of neutrality or impartiality towards any and all forms of individuals' professed identities and culturally informed commitments. Laws and policies should thus take no position on the importance of cultural belonging which some individuals attest to, nor should any specific ways of being and believing enjoy any form of preferential treatment through state action. Advocates of this approach would occasionally point to those states which expressly discriminated in favour of some culturally based religious, racial and ethnic communities as continuing evidence of the kind of state-sanctioned discrimination liberalism was justified in seeking to avoid in the part it played in the evolving narrative of modernity. For their part, many human rights theorists typically supported the liberal diagnosis of the inherently damaging character of any forms of preferential treatment in their focus upon the effects felt by minorities within such societies. Liberals and human rights defenders were largely united in their evaluation of the threat which any attempt to legislate for identity generally posed to the pursuit of a politically and legally just order of things. However, beginning in the 1980s, the identity-excluding paradigm attracted increasing and concerted criticism through the emergence of the phenomenon of so-called identity politics.

The full range of the intellectual, political and cultural components of identity politics cannot be satisfactorily summarised here (see Kenny 2004). However, some of the most salient elements are directly relevant to an analysis of human rights and its relationship with cultural diversity. Thus, a core motivation for the politicisation of identity consists of the claim that colour-blind attempts to overcome identity-based oppression and discrimination have largely failed: overcoming inequalities of opportunity cannot be achieved by ignoring the identities which racists, homophobes and bigots pay so much attention to in their vilification of others. The critique of the colour-blind approach does not stop at a concern for the technicalities of public policy, but goes much deeper into the body of beliefs and assumptions from which the colour-blind approach derives. A significant part of what distinguishes those who seek to politicise identity from those who insist the state should remain neutral towards cultural differences is a radically different understanding of the bases and public significance of individuals' culturally based ways of being and believing.

Critics of the colour-blind approach typically reject both the empirical validity and the moral value of the asocial account of individually sovereign agency, which generations of liberals have adhered to. Whatever the motivations may have been for conceiving of individuals in such asocial terms, we are not well served by relegating constituent components of our personal identities to the status of utterly private and discretional objects of choice or preference. Many of the ways of being and believing which many individuals adhere to exert profound effects upon a vast range of highly significant aspects of human life. Some of these extend to include commitments and assumptions which many liberals and human rights theorists simply assumed were capable of transcending the inherent partiality of the private sphere, such as an account of individual agency as necessarily always retaining the capacity for culturally undetermined forms of deliberation, the value of individual choice and discretion, and even the very separation of the public from the private sphere. The essence of this alternative perspective can be simply stated: many of us are who we are as a consequence of the culturally based ways of being and believing we adhere to and identify with. If such commitments were entirely on a par with other individual preferences, such as a taste for expensive wine, women and song, then the state would be entitled to insist that individuals must bear the costs of any adverse consequences of their expensive tastes. However, the adverse effects some experience from their identity-based commitments cannot be so easily avoided by simply renouncing those commitments. For example, even if it were possible for African-Americans in the United States to avoid the effects of racism by becoming less culturally African-American and more culturally Caucasian and middle class, one is entitled to question why they should be expected to do so. Even assuming that such radical exercises of choice over largely ascribed forms of identity were feasible, why should victims of discrimination be expected to comply with others' norms, values and practices as a condition of avoiding such discrimination? A defender of the colour-blind approach might counter that no cultural community is prioritised within systems committed to remaining neutral on the value of cultural belonging. On this view, no member of any community should feel that they have to become more like the members of some other community in order to enjoy similar opportunities and treatment. Regardless of how well intentioned such appeals may be, the depth and extent of racism within many societies, including the United States, testifies to the naïvety of such approaches.

As I argued in Chapter 1, human identity is not constructed through a succession of radically existential individual choices. Manifestly, the construction of anyone's personal identity draws heavily upon pre-existing cultural resources and forms, whether they be highly formal-ised systems of religious and cosmological beliefs or the often far more banal and mundane practices of the more overtly profane domain of life. We also become who we are as a consequence of our continuing interactions with others. These interactions are themselves largely con-stituted by forms of collective cultural discourses, which pre-exist those individuals who develop the means to communicate through them. As Charles Taylor writes:

> people do not acquire the languages needed for self-definition on their own. Rather, we are introduced to them through interaction with others who matter to us – what George Herbert Mead called 'significant others'. The genesis of the human mind is in this sense not monological, not something each person accomplishes on his or her own, but dialogical. (Taylor 1992: 32)

Like the feminist advocates of relational agency I discussed in Chapter 1, Taylor's insight is heavily indebted to a broadly Hegelian tradition of thinking about agency which fundamentally rejects visions of rational agents as capable of constituting themselves *de novo* and in isolation from others. Taylor also develops upon a Hegelian insight when he argues that the mutual effects which agents can have upon each other's sense of themselves can be either beneficial or deeply damaging. The extent to which anyone becomes who they are as a result of interact-ing with others creates the possibility of others' prejudices and hatred effectively penetrating the 'inner citadel' of the individual self and causing untold damage to one's sense of self-worth. As Taylor states:

> the thesis is that our identity is partly shaped by recognition or its absence, often by the misrecognition of others, and so a person or group of people can suffer real damage, real distortion, if the people or society around them mirror back to them a confining or demeaning or contemptible picture of themselves. Non-recognition or misrecognition can inflict harm, can be a form of oppression, imprisoning someone in a false, distorted, and reduced mode of being. (Taylor 1992: 25)

The effects of pronounced and prolonged forms of prejudice do not magically stop at some purportedly impermeable inner boundary of the pure self. Nor can the harmful effects of the vilification of one's community be mitigated or avoided by simply looking the other way, or turning the other cheek. The ease with which some can hold to such assumptions is itself evidence of continuing discrimination and oppression despite the legal recognition of formal equality. We are all of us deeply influenced by our cultural surroundings. Some of us are more aware of and sensitive to this fact as a consequence of being the victims of long-standing prejudice and discrimination.

Taylor's diagnosis of the cultural basis of inequality is accompanied by a far more constructive approach to combatting discrimination, which is typically referred to as the 'politics of recognition'. In stark contrast to the colour-blind approach, advocates of the politics of recognition approach insist that public policies should not only acknowledge the existence of differing cultural communities, but should generally affirm and espouse the inherent value of such communities. Discrimination can be countered not by encouraging its victims to manifest fewer of the characteristics which racists, for example, see as being somehow essential to being black, but rather by positively extolling, through state policies and legislation, the value and virtues of the identities which members of such communities adhere to. Culture affects us all and thus a concern to laud and espouse culture is not merely a partial or contingent good but an essential value. Taylor states, 'due recognition is not just a courtesy we owe people. It is a vital human need' (1992: 26). Or, as another Canadian philosopher argues, cultural belonging should be thought of as an essential and primary good, which all sufficiently rational individuals are capable of recognising and espousing (Kymlicka 1989). Where once cultural identity was deliberately excluded from any consideration within law- and policy-making, the politicisation of identity seeks to establish a new principle which calls for a general presumption in favour of recognising the value of cultural belonging and identity. Given the persistence of discrimination, the extent to which our identities are formed through our relationships with others and the extent to which others' prejudices can harm us, such a principle has a great deal to commend it.

A right to cultural identity

I can see no absolutely compelling reason why the 'vital human need' for others' recognition of one's cultural community *must* entail a com- mitment to a rights-based approach. Indeed, the later part of this chapter will analyse a range of highly problematic issues which such an approach raises for defenders of the integrity and value of cultural belonging. However, it is undoubtedly the case, as with attempts to protect many other human goods, that a significant number of theorists consider rights to be the most normatively defensible and institution- ally effective instrument for the promotion and protection of existing cultural communities. This is a highly complex and nuanced field of study. In order to focus upon the core issues in respect of rights claims the remainder of this section will address two crucial questions. First, how is a right to cultural identity typically argued for? Second, pre- cisely which elements of any given cultural community are afforded protection by existing and proposed rights to cultural identity?

The basis of a right to cultural identity

While they remain a relatively small constituency within political and social philosophy, those theorists who argue for a right to cultural identity do so in a variety of ways and draw upon a variety of different traditions of thought. It is possible, however, to identify some key and recurring elements within their arguments.

To begin with, most argue that the right to cultural identity is ultimately grounded upon the contribution cultural belonging makes to individual well-being. Feeling 'at home' in one's culture can be essential for many individuals' broader sense of self-worth and self-respect. This claim presupposes a commitment to the kind of arguments I considered above which insist that our identities are fundamentally fashioned through culturally based forms of human interaction. Culture plays an indispensable role in fashioning who we are as individuals and what we consider to be of value for ourselves and for others. What follows from this is the claim that the value of cultural membership cannot be ultimately reduced to individuals' exercise of radical choice or discretion. Cultural communities are, in a very important sense, not at all like private associations, such as bird appreciation societies, student societies or sporting clubs. To conceive of cultural communities as akin to associations that are instrumentally formed through voluntary agreement and for a single and specific purpose is to misunderstand entirely the importance of culture and the deep and wide-ranging effects which cultural communities can have upon their members. If cultural communities did not possess this kind of power and significance, then there would be little justification for attaching so much importance to preserving and protecting them. As Bhiku Parekh correctly claims:

> cultural communities are not voluntary associations like clubs, political parties and pressure groups . . . they are not deliberate human creations but historical communities with long collective memories of struggles and achievements and well-established traditions of behaviour. We do not join but are born into them, and are not so much their members as part of them. (Parekh 2006: 161–2)

Other advocates of a right to cultural identity have provided more specific accounts of precisely which collective characteristics of a given cultural community justify according rights to them. Thus, Avaishai Margalit and Joseph Raz (1990) outline a moral, as opposed to a legally positivist, justification for national self-determination, which they base upon a generalised account of cultural community. They identify six characteristics which any community must satisfy in order to legitimately claim a right to self-determination:

1. The community must possess a common character and distinct identity.
2. Members of the community will be significantly influenced by it such that individuals' well-being will be affected by what happens to the community as a collective entity.

3. That individual membership of the community is based upon mutual recognition: no one can unilaterally declare themselves to belong to a group which does not recognise their claim as bona fide. This presupposes the existence of some distinct, specific and relatively settled criteria for membership.
4. That membership of the community is the primary constituent of someone's identity. This allows for inter-sectional axes of identity (being both a woman and a Muslim, for example) but recognises the extent to which many individuals will identify themselves as primarily influenced and affected by one axis of community membership.
5. That membership of such communities is primarily based upon ascribed characteristics and is fundamentally secured through a sense of belonging, rather than the outcome of sustained effort. As Margalit and Raz state, 'one cannot choose to belong. One belongs because of who one is' (1990: 447).
6. Finally, such communities must be of a sufficient size and scope, which must extend beyond mere face-to-face communities.

Margalit and Raz refer to communities which possess these six characteristics as *'encompassing groups'* in which 'Individuals find . . . a culture which shapes to a large degree their tastes and opportunities, and which provides an anchor for their self-identification and the safety of effortless secure belonging' (1990: 448; original emphasis).

Writing with a different collaborator, Margalit developed upon this defence of the basis of a right to cultural identity in his work with Moishe Halbertal. Together they argue that a right to cultural identity is fundamentally founded upon and entailed by an individual right to identity. They argue that an individual's right to identity is not itself an instrument for the pursuit of some purportedly more fundamental good or capacity but should be understood as being 'basic and primary' (2004: 543). The capacity to develop and express an identity is an essential moral good from which other goods and values derive. They include within their argument a vital and highly significant distinction between two different statuses of personhood. Thus, they distinguish between the status of the person, which constitutes the irreducible substrate of human identity and may be compared with the Kantian conception of the faculty for pure reason as a stable and fixed form. In addition, however, they also argue that each of us possesses and is constituted by our personality identity which is directly affected by the cultural communities we adhere to. They argue that:

> the individual right to culture stems from the fact that every person has an overriding interest in his personality identity – that is, in preserving his way of life and the traits that are central identity components for him and the other members of his cultural group. (Margalit and Halbertal 2004: 542)

Our personality identity is distinctly not immune or radically detached from the cultural communities in which we develop our sense of self. According to Margalit and Halbertal, our agency may not be entirely shaped by our cultural surroundings, but the greater part of the content of our selves most certainly is. Our identities are of fundamental importance and value to all of us. Our identities are necessarily derived from diverse cultural environments. The indispensable importance of developing and expressing our identities entails, so it is argued, a right to identity and thus a right to culture given the claim that all identities are shaped and fashioned within a cultural context.

What is protected by cultural rights?

The prevailing convention amongst those who write upon cultural rights from a more overtly legal perspective restricts the application of such rights to a limited collection of communities (Capotorti 1991; Thornberry 1991). On this view, the enjoyment of distinct rights to cultural identity is restricted to religious, ethnic, indigenous and linguistic communities. Such groups may be understood as consisting of largely ascribed forms of identity and embodying what Thornberry refers to as a 'shared consciousness' (1991: 57) which is borne by the individual members of the communities. It is not at all clear, however, that the principled justifications of the basis for a right to cultural identity should be restricted to only those included within the legal convention. So-called encompassing groups may very well be found amongst other established communities. I shall return to this important point in greater detail later in this chapter. Accepting, for the time being, that rights to cultural identity may be legitimately claimed by at least those members of those communities recognised by international human rights lawyers, what precisely do such rights afford?

The task of classifying cultural rights has been made easier by Jacob Levy (1997). He identifies eight different forms of cultural rights within both established IHRL and normative justifications of cultural rights:

1. *Exemptions.* Typically, these consist of exemptions from laws and regulations which are considered to be significantly incompatible with core customs and beliefs within a particular community. For example, in the United Kingdom, Sikh males have been exempted from the requirement of wearing a crash helmet whilst riding a motorcycle as doing so would require them to remove their turbans.
2. *Assistance.* The state may provide specific assistance to some cultural communities which is not afforded to other citizens. For example, state funding may be provided to support the learning of some native language.
3. *Self-government.* Some communities enjoy varying degrees of self-government over either general areas of governance or specific areas considered to be essential for protecting the identity of the community.
4. *External rules.* The protection of highly symbolic goods and resources has been established in many domestic jurisdictions in order to prevent the potentially damaging consequences of outsiders' interventions within the affairs of a community. An example of this is provided by the legal protection of tribal or indigenous peoples' land through property laws which forbid non-members of the community acquiring title to land.
5. *Internal rules.* This provides one of the most controversial areas for debate amongst supporters and opponents of cultural rights. Internal rules comprise a very broad range of potential constraints upon members' behaviour. Typically, it is argued that the distinct identity of any given community entails a degree of compliance with the core customs and beliefs which that identity is largely based upon. The legal enforcement of such constraints often raises the highly complex question of the degree to which communities are entitled to claim the loyalty of their members to established ways of being and believing. Supporters of such internal rules generally argue that internal dissidents can simply exit the community if they cannot be reconciled to its ways. While internal rules are merely one amongst eight forms of cultural rights, they are arguably the most important for any formulation of the basis and scope of a right to

cultural identity and will be analysed in far greater detail later in this chapter.

6. *Recognition/enforcement of traditional legal codes.* This is an area which has attracted significant interest in recent years. Some have argued that culturally diverse societies are best served by forms of legal pluralism in which members of given communities should have the opportunity of legally regulating their own internal affairs in accordance with their own established legal traditions and practices. For example, heated debate regularly flares up over proposals that Muslim communities within liberal democratic societies should be subject to the law of Shari'a. The use of the so-called *Gacaca* courts for pursuing restorative justice for victims of the Rwandan genocide provides a much-discussed example of this cultural right.

7. *Representation of minorities in government.* There are numerous examples of the executive and legislative bodies of nation-states granting specific representation to minority communities through blocs in national parliaments or ministerial offices in government.

8. *Symbolic acknowledgement.* Finally, and arguably the least costly and least controversial cultural right, is the wider acknowledgement of the importance of some communities' most important festivals, holidays and days of the Sabbath. By their very nature, these rights tend to be applied to distinctly religious communities but this can raise interesting issues over which communities are recognised by legislative authorities as being 'religious' in the first place.[1]

In various ways these different forms of cultural rights typically serve to delineate the boundaries of the community which they provide protection for. Regardless of how one ultimately understands the construction of the identity of any given cultural community, one is bound to accept that the identification of boundaries is an essential feature of identifying any particular cultural community. Following on from this, individuals' enjoyment of the specific rights afforded by membership of a protected community, such as a Sikh's exemption from wearing a crash helmet, necessarily entails the establishment of some entitlement criteria. Put simply, only sufficiently and authoritatively recognised members of the given community can be entitled to benefit from the right in question. This raises a number of very interesting and challenging issues which will be addressed in due course.

The (apparent) necessity of collective rights

The recurring and central justification offered for a right to cultural identity appeals to the well-being of any given community's individual members. In this way, the value of a right to cultural identity appears to be essentially instrumental in character. The focus upon individual members of cultural communities is in keeping with the conventional ethos of a human rights-based approach which accords intrinsic moral value only to individual human beings. An instrumentalist understanding of a right to cultural identity also establishes a clear moral criterion for evaluating between any specific claims to the possession of a right to cultural identity. On this approach, only individual members of any given cultural community can be said to possess the right. The right is then held against public authorities who have a duty to provide for the enjoyment of the right in exactly the same way public authorities have duties to provide for rights against torture or rights to health care. It is conceivable that such duties may be extended to include cultural communities in ways which are similar to the increasing claims made in respect of extending human rights obligations to transnational corporations. However, this morally individualist approach to human rights is deeply at odds with approaches which consider the cultural community to be the necessary bearer of the *collective* right to cultural identity. The right to cultural identity has been consistently argued for in value collectivist terms. Indeed, many defenders of the right insist that many actual instances of rights to cultural identity are fundamentally incompatible with morally individualist approaches. In effect, others' a priori adherence to moral individualism is criticised as incompatible with identifying and providing for those conditions which justify the need for some forms of cultural rights in the first place.

The value collectivist alternative to the morally individualist approach to a right to cultural identity is based upon a number of highly significant claims. Arguably the most fundamental is the claim that distinctly social human goods do exist and that many cultural communities must be understood as such. On this view, cultures can and do exist as non-individuated goods 'whose value cannot be reduced to the satisfaction of a collection of individual desires' (Appiah 2005: 127). Many supporters of specifically indigenous peoples' rights claims to exclusive and collective protection of ancestral lands argue that such land can only be properly understood in these terms. It is thereby argued that a failure to understand this has proven to be disastrous for many communities who have lost access to and use of their ancestral lands as a consequence of others' securing freehold title to tracts of land through legal systems which fail to adequately recognise the value of collective goods. As I shall explore in greater detail in Chapter 6, a coherent case can be made in support of indigenous peoples' collective rights claim to land as an essential means for securing the identity of the community. Others, such as Jovanović (2005) have argued that the existence of collective human rights is already unequivocally recognised in such core human rights treaties as the Genocide Convention (Convention on the Prevention and Punishment of the Crime of Genocide 1948). Genocidal acts are perpetrated against individual human beings only by targeting their shared, collective identity. On this view, acknowledging the possibility of genocide as a particularly heinous human rights violation (as opposed to the 'mere' crime of murder) entails an acceptance of non-individuated social human goods. After all, any given individual's claim to be a victim of genocide is entirely dependent upon their being recognised as a member of the group under attack. As David Ingram (2012) has argued, some human rights are only possessed by some individuals as a consequence of their belonging to a particular community of people.

After establishing the existence of social goods, the value collectivist argument in support of the necessity of collective rights to cultural identity proceeds by developing upon a claim which many other contributors to this area of theory and practice broadly acknowledge, namely a right to cultural identity entails distinguishing between voluntary and ascribed forms of belonging and membership. Even those who argue against a collective right to cultural identity acknowledge that many forms of cultural belonging and membership are not best understood in entirely voluntarist terms. Value collectivist supporters of a collective right to cultural identity differ fundamentally from their more morally individualist counterparts in their insistence that recognising that some forms of cultural belonging and membership are based upon ascribed characteristics of individual identity formation excludes conceiving of cultures in individualist terms. As I discussed above, writers such as Parekh (2006) are adamant that the kind of cultural communities deserving of rights protection should not be understood as mere associations of entirely freely consenting and contracting individuals. Many cultural communities are widely considered to be valuable precisely because of many of their members' presumed reliance, if not dependency, upon them. If they were not so considered then it would seem reasonable to argue that the members of threatened cultural communities should simply renounce their damaging attachments and align with less vulnerable, more prosperous, communities. In much the same way that some of us wonder why many individuals continue to support persistently failing football teams one might, on this approach, suggest that people should switch allegiance when the pain becomes too great to bear.

Acknowledging the ascribed character of some forms of cultural belonging entails a re-evaluation of many assumptions surrounding the continuing capacity of many individuals both to be members of their communities and to retain the effective capacity for autonomous deliberation and action. Beginning with Michael Sandel's (1982) critique of Rawls's contractarian model of justice, an entire constituency of theorists have come to argue that all cultural communities cannot be fundamentally judged on the basis of their compatibility with the autonomy ideal. Thus, Parekh (2006) has argued that opportunities for leading autonomous lives are often not prerequisite for many individuals' well-being. In many cases members' ability to benefit from membership of communities based upon largely ascribed characteristics is essentially incompatible with any sustained autonomous reflection upon the basis of cultural membership. He argues:

> if a cultural community respects human worth and dignity, safeguards basic human interests within the limits of its resources, poses no threat to outsiders and enjoys the allegiance of most of its members, and thus provides the basic conditions of the good life, it deserves to be respected and left alone. (Parekh 2006: 177)

Value collectivist defenders of a collective right to cultural identity insist that the right is not conditional upon the culture affording generalised opportunities for the persistent exercise of individual autonomy.

Another highly important component of the value collectivist case for collective rights appeals to the sheer importance of cultural belonging for many. Put simply, theorists such as Parekh argue that many cultures are entitled to their members' general compliance with those customs and beliefs through which the recurring identity of the culture is expressed. Respecting any given cultural community requires, Parekh argues, members' identification with and endorsement of those specific and distinctive traits which, to a certain extent, serve to differentiate cultural communities from each other. A certain degree of loyalty can therefore be demanded of members as a condition of their continuing membership. Parekh (2006: 158) extends this argument further in his discussion of members whose persistent failure or refusal to comply with core cultural tenets may be described as perpetrating a form of cultural treason. He discerns evidence of this idea in various forms of abuse which some cultures have developed to describe members who defy core cultural traits, such as describing some people of African descent as 'Coconuts' (brown on the outside and white on the inside), or describing some Asians as 'bananas' (yellow on the outside, white on the inside).

At one, value collectivist, level it seems reasonable to argue that members of communities are required to comply with core and distinguishing features of their respective communities. This ostensive duty to culture will be strengthened if members derive specific benefits only as a consequence of their membership of a cultural community which, for example, may enjoy exemptions from laws or access to specific benefits designed to protect and promote the community. Individual members' loyalty to their culture might also appear to be reasonable if one accepts the claims made for the sheer importance of cultural belonging for many people's well-being and sense of worth. However, the notion of loyalty to culture significantly affects the conventional ways in which the relationship between rights and duties is understood within the human rights doctrine. IHRL is largely predicated upon the view that individual human beings are owed rights by the state and, in some instances, the broader international community. Individual nation-states are free to determine the varying extents to which citizens may be required to declare their allegiance to the flag, so to speak. Individual loyalty to a specific collective is not, however, typically understood as a precondition for anyone's claims to human rights. The principal duty-bearer within IHRL is, of course, the state. The claim that, under some circumstances, individual members of specific cultural communities are required to remain loyal towards those communities in order to enjoy access to the collective human rights invested in those communities fundamentally challenges and confuses the conventional understanding of what individuals must do in order to possess their human rights. Granting collective rights to cultural communities raises the prospect of establishing a new collective actor within IHRL, which already has the power to significantly affect people's lives and their enjoyment of their human rights.

For many, recognising collective rights to cultural identity necessitates acknowledging the legitimacy of cultural communities enjoying specific protections against external actors and, when necessary, demanding compliance from members as a condition of their membership. The collective right to exist is clearly established within IHRL and affords protection to those forms of community discussed above: ethnic, linguistic, indigenous and religious communities. Some contributors to this debate have effectively challenged this convention and have argued that the proper basis of any community's claim to rights protection should be founded upon the strength of the so-called expressive purpose of the community, which is not, necessarily, restricted to those communities recognised by IHRL (Gutmann 1998). As a criterion for an entitlement to the possession of collective rights the concept of the expressive purpose of the community suffers from a degree of indeterminacy. Generally, the concept is typically used in ways which closely resemble Margalit and Raz's (1990) concept of encompassing groups, which I considered earlier. Thus, expressive purpose can be understood as a largely analytical, rather than substantive, concept. It is not intended to specifically exclude communities which may have a strong, distinct but largely disliked identity. It does not provide a means by which the state may legitimately seek to liberalise communities as a condition of granting them legal recognition and standing. Rather, it is concerned with the significance of the community's core identity in the lives of its members. A society dedicated to exhibiting the films of Ingmar Bergman will, all other things being equal, have a relatively weak expressive purpose, whereas the Catholic Church will have a particularly strong expressive purpose, given the broad influence of its teachings upon the lives of Catholics. Theorists such as Amy Gutmann argue that the stronger the expressive purpose of a community, the greater are its claims to being afforded protection by the state even in cases where the expressive identity in question may be discriminatory towards members and non-members. Citing the example of discriminatory religious communities in the United States, Gutmann argues that 'respecting the freedom of churches to discriminate in this way may be necessary to respect the . . . moral convictions of its members as expressed through their church, whose primary purpose is spiritual' (1998: 17–18). The enjoyment of collective rights to cultural identity is not, therefore and on this reading, conditional upon those communities' full compliance with core liberal ideals.

As various value collectivist defenders of a collective right to cultural identity argue, such a right has been broadly recognised within numerous legal jurisdictions: collective rights to cultural identity exist as positive forms of law. They have also been legally upheld in precisely those terms considered immediately above. Many cultural communities have successfully secured the legal protection of customs and practices which are demonstrably discriminatory. Typically, courts in many jurisdictions have argued that communities with a sufficiently compelling and established expressive purpose have a right to survive as collective entities and not merely aggregations of separate individual members. Thus, what Madhavi Sunder refers to as the 'principle of cultural survival' (2001: 499) has been routinely upheld by the US Supreme Court. A similar principle has also been referred to in the justification of prioritising the collective right of a community to survive by preserving its core traditions and beliefs over the separate rights claims of dissatisfied or dissident members. Many such rulings simply assume that the expressive purpose of a given community can be identified and justified as such. Once the expressive purpose of the community has been established, it is then deployed as the criterion by which to evaluate the claims of those who do not necessarily seek to leave the community but aim to change those aspects they consider to be unduly traditional or morally intolerable. The principle of cultural survival offers little support to those who appeal to external norms in their attempts to undermine core aspects of their cultural community. In such instances, the collective right of the community to exist in its established form typically trumps the individual rights claims of disaffected members. Such individuals have no right to demand that their community should change by, for example, abolishing the offending tradition or practice. As the old adage proclaims, 'when in Rome, do as the Romans do'.

Critical perspectives

Cultural communities exist to the extent that their distinguishing traditions, practices and beliefs exert tangible and significant effects upon the identities and well-being of many of their members. The value collectivist argument for collective rights to cultural identity appears particularly well suited for those types of community, such as geographically isolated indigenous peoples, who generally comply with the ways in which cultural community is conceived of by many value collectivists. Value collectivism also speaks to other cultural communities in which members' identity is significantly influenced by a single, ascribed commitment. However, many of us are not like this. Many of us far more closely resemble the vision of the cosmopolitan self, which theorists such as Jeremy Waldron espouse. He writes, 'the cosmopolitan may live all his life in one city and maintain the same citizenship throughout. But he refuses to think of himself as defined by his location or his ancestry or his citizenship or his language' (1995: 95). Not everyone seeks a right to a single cultural identity nor identifies with a single community. Cosmopolitans proffer an alternative vision of identity formation to that espoused by value collectivist defenders of a right to *a* cultural identity.

In the spirit of diversity and pluralism one may be tempted to argue that there is sufficient room for both approaches to co-exist within a broad human rights tent. Generally, I think this is a reasonable and principled position to adopt. People whose sense of identity is primarily derived from a single cultural community should not be required to actively embrace cosmopolitan norms in order to claim their human rights. Nor should individuals who take their cultural bearings from multiple sources be required to commit to only one of these as a means for enjoying access to various cultural rights. I will develop this claim further in my subsequent chapter upon the rights of indigenous peoples. The world does not need to be entirely populated by cosmopolitan selves in order to be said to be just. However, other concerns can be raised over granting collective rights to even some of those communities which do broadly comply with the value collectivist account of cultural community.

From within a rights framework no one can seriously argue that all cultural communities have a right to recognition and respect. Some communities have been and remain utterly intolerable or, to use Margalit and Raz's (1990: 449) term, 'pernicious'. The difficulty, however, consists in defining precisely what it is that makes some communities' ways of being and believing thoroughly pernicious and thus undeserving of rights protection.

Some would argue that practices and beliefs which are, for example, systematically and unashamedly racist should not enjoy rights protection. One of the most recent examples of this can be found in the debate over the flying of the Confederate flag outside public buildings in some southern states of the United States. I have already shown that the US Supreme Court has granted rights protection to discriminatory groups and the Dixie flag is undeniably construed by many of its defenders and opponents alike as purposely discriminatory insofar as it symbolises a cultural heritage that was partially constructed through the celebration of slavery and a deeply racist ideology. The banning of the Confederate flag does not aim to destroy the culture of 'Dixie' but it does intend to remove from that culture overtly racist symbols. This specific entitlement is denied on the grounds that many peoples do have an interest in taking pride in their ways of being and believing, but this sense of pride cannot include taking pride in being a racist or a bigot. While slavery was an undeniably significant element of the South's culture and economy, not everyone who identifies with the culture of the South today would agree that the Confederate flag and the culture it represents are inherently racist or bigoted. One may accept the principle that cultural rights should not be extended to racist communities but disagree fundamentally over whether a particular community in question is racist. In such instances, legislators run the risk of failing to uphold a principle of protecting and defending cultural diversity through imposing an empirically partial collection of values and norms upon others simply because they are in a position to do so.

Many theorists who are concerned by the danger of ethnocentrically imposing partial norms and values upon others find a solution to the problem in the so-called right of exit remedy. Thus, the challenge is how can legislators within culturally diverse jurisdictions simultaneously avoid discriminating against some communities' ways of being and believing whilst also avoiding simply condemning individual members of those communities to having the predominant customs and practices imposed upon them? Theorists spanning a range of philosophical perspectives, including liberalism and communitarianism, argue that the individual right of exit must be a prominent component of any political morality capable of meeting the challenge of cultural diversity.

Defenders of the right of exit conceive of it in differing ways. One may distinguish between those who think of the right in largely negative terms and those who interpret the right in more positive terms. The negative–positive spectrum owes much to the differing ways in which many theorists conceive of individual liberty and those differences are clearly discernible in various formulations of the right of exit. Thus, the negative end of the spectrum is exemplified by Chandran Kukathas (2003). He argues that the right of exit should be the sole basis for securing individual freedom within diverse societies. Indeed, he goes so far as to state that all rights are derived from the sole, fundamental right of freedom of association and its necessary correlate: freedom of dissociation (exit). States are not required to provide any other goods beyond upholding an individual's right to dissociate from a community. At some level, states are required to assume that all forms of individual association are, in essence, voluntary, or at least, that individuals always retain the capacity to renounce their commitments. He conceives of the right of exit in thoroughly formal terms, which entails that states are not required to provide what some others might consider to be pre-requisite to any individual's effective exercise of exit. Kukathas insists that a state committed to upholding only this fundamental right is best positioned for regulating culturally diverse societies in a way which is mutually tolerant and respectful of individuals' (negative) liberty.

Other formulations of the right of exit also accord a great deal of importance to its capacity to regulate diversity but formulate the right in distinctly more positive terms. Thus, Joseph Raz (1986, 1994) argues that the right of exit enables states to avoid unduly intervening in the internal business of differing communities. However, he argues that the effective capacity of exercising the right requires states' commitment to promoting and protecting a broader public political culture based upon the ideal of personal autonomy. Raz considers the exercise of the right of exit to be heavily dependent upon individuals' capacity for auton-omy. Further, in accordance with more positive conceptions of liberty, Raz argues that individuals generally cannot achieve autonomy simply by being left alone by outsiders and the state. Autonomy can only be achieved in suitably supportive social environments and the state has a moral duty to promote and protect such environments. Once this duty is discharged, however, state regulation of cultural communities should be largely restricted to upholding the right of exit.

Raz's formulation of the right has been criticised by a number of theorists who look to the right of exit as the means for prevent-ing liberal political moralities being, in some sense, imposed upon non-liberal communities, or communities which do not esteem the autonomy ideal. Thus, Parekh (2006) argues that the autonomy ideal cannot provide a normative foundation for regulating culturally diverse societies since autonomy is, he insists, a culturally partial ideal which only some communities espouse. Interestingly, Raz's specific formulation of the autonomy ideal lends some inadvertent weight to Parekh's claim insofar as Raz depicts autonomy as a cultural value which is only valid within what might somewhat imprecisely be described as liberal, 'Western' societies. Like Kukathas, Parekh argues that the right of exit should be understood in terms which leave the decision to stay or go entirely for individuals themselves to determine. If individuals do not leave communities which are not manifestly oppressive, then the state has no grounds for seeking to regulate the internal affairs of the community. The more overtly negative formulation of the right of exit appears to its supporters to perform a vitally important task of restricting state regulation of cultural communities and placing the onus of evaluating the worth of any community upon individual members of the community.

There is an extensive body of literature which challenges specifically the assumption that the right of exit requires only a concern for individuals' formal opportunity to leave. Many have argued that individuals' ostensive choice not to leave a community can be construed as evidence of their endorsement of the community's ways of being and believing. Much of this literature has been motivated by specific concerns over the plight of women in many formally patriarchal societies. Thus, I will reserve a far more detailed engagement with this approach for the next chapter which addresses diversity and the rights of women. Setting to one side for the moment an analysis of the assumptions which many supporters of the right of exit harbour about individual agency, I wish to focus on another area of critical concern which a heavy reliance upon the right of exit raises.

The right of exit focuses upon disaffected individuals. It affords those individuals the formal opportunity to avoid those aspects of their cultural communities which they have become deeply dissatisfied with. It offers an ostensive remedy to what might be thought of as the victims of some cultures. The right of exit is so appealing to so many precisely because it does not directly concern itself with the cultural practices and beliefs which are the cause of concern for some members. It does not require public authorities taking an independently evaluative position on the practices and beliefs in question. However, as others such as Sunder (2001) argue, a primary reliance upon the right of exit can serve to frustrate and prevent efforts at internally reforming cultures' ways of being and believing. The right effectively presents disaffected individuals with a 'like it or leave it' scenario. Setting to one side the questions I address in the next chapter concerning the viability of some individuals being able to exit their communities, the right of exit appears to leave some with little real alternative to a form of exile from communities which they actually seek to change and do not wish to abandon. This is more than a merely technical concern over which legal mechanisms may work to prevent forms of cultural oppression. Indeed, as Sunder argues, it goes to the heart of how culture is conceived of by legal systems and how such conceptions may serve to reinforce forms of purportedly essentialised cultural identities.

Sunder argues that the right of exit typically serves to reinforce a policy of cultural survival, which is itself based upon an assumption that cultural communities ought to be able to survive. Rights to cultural identity offer additional and more substantive support for this policy. One problem with this approach is that it often assumes that the identity of the community is relatively settled. Indeed, many legal rulings in favour of a community's right to survive seek to protect what the conventionally authorised leaders of the community claim is the expressive purpose of the group against internal dissenters' challenge to that interpretation. What is sometimes in question is precisely the process by which the constitutive identities of cultural communities are constructed and manufactured. Supporting one side within such disputes rests upon an assumption that there exists a genuine interpretation of practices and beliefs which must be accepted as a core condition of membership of the community. In some instances, the very fact of the dissenting voices will serve to refute that assumption. A policy which seeks to remedy this problem only by granting a right of exit to the dissident individuals may serve to subvert the processes by which constructed cultural identities change and develop. Even if those individuals are effectively able to leave, they are surely entitled to question why they should do so. The grounds of their opposition to aspects of their community cannot be determined by appealing to the presumed essence of the community's identity without thereby utterly contradicting what most authors in this area conventionally recognise: all cultural identities are constructions. The question of what form any cultural community should take cannot be legitimately settled by what the current power-holders in such a community assert to be the 'truth' of its ways of being and believing. The right of exit can be accused of effectively undermining and subverting the process of internal contestation and reform.

Of course, attaching significance to the possibility of dissident individuals being able to contest dominant cultural practices and beliefs implies that the capacity to do so is normatively valuable. Arguing that the capacity for internal dissent is valuable often assumes an appeal to the fundamental human rights of such members and a claim that maintaining a right of exit is not sufficient to protect these rights. Value collectivist supporters of a collective right to cultural identity are often explicit about the potential implications of this for some individual members' human rights. The value collectivist David Ingram states that 'a collectivist group right . . . preserves and protects the cultural identity of a group by permitting the group to limit the basic human, constitutional, or statutory rights of its own members to believe and behave as they individually think fit' (2012: 280). This unequivocal statement appears to point to a particularly troubling impasse. I have argued that many individuals' enjoyment of a right to cultural identity is best served by their access to collective rights to cultural identity and that such collective rights are typically best understood in the terms outlined by various value collectivists. However, some value collectivists explicitly recognise the potential for deep conflict between the collective rights of the community and the separate rights of individual members. How can this conflict be resolved in ways which comply with the understanding of human rights I defended in Chapter 1 but which do not ultimately dismiss the importance of cultural belonging for many?

The current UN Special Rapporteur on cultural rights has written that 'negotiating culture with human rights concerns inherently questions, delegitimizes, destabilizes, ruptures and, in the long run, destroys oppressive hierarchies' (UN General Assembly 2012: 18). This raises a core question: from a human rights-based perspective, which conditions serve to confirm culturally based hierarchies as 'oppressive'? At the core of any credible human rights-based understanding of culturally oppressive hierarchies is an account of why cultures matter morally. Peter Jones expresses the general human rights answer to this question when he writes, 'if cultures matter morally, it is because they matter to and for people and, if that is so, the issue of how people are to count morally must precede rather than follow our encounter with cultures' (2001: 45). Thus, rights to cultural identity can be held collectively insofar as a collective right to indigenous land, for example, cannot

be disaggregated into individual title claims but the value of any such
right is ultimately to be justified by the benefit it intends to uphold:
indigenous peoples' retention of their ancestral lands. Individual lives
can sometimes benefit from the protection and promotion of collective
goods. What is impermissible from a human rights-based perspective is to enable communities to exercise such rights in ways which
are detrimental to the human rights of their members. Communities
can and do make claims upon their members. In many instances such
claims will not be significant enough to warrant the concerns of human
rights defenders. When they do pose such a threat, however, it is perfectly appropriate to engage in forms of critical analysis of the specific
issues as part of the process of determining whether such claims are
consistent with the principles of human rights.

   What is required for this process of critical analysis and engagement to proceed in a normatively legitimate manner is a regulatory
framework, based upon a series of crucial elements. Arguably the most
important of these elements is how cultural community is conceived of
in the first place. I have argued that a narrowly individualist approach
to cultural identity has consistently failed to acknowledge and provide
for the significance of cultural belonging for many. Indeed, one could
argue that the narrowly individualist approach is based upon a false (or
naïve) account of all forms of human agency and identity formation to
the extent that it neglects the essentially relational nature of identity.
However, in responding to these shortcomings, some value collectivists have unduly essentialised the phenomenon of cultural community. Different cultures take a bewildering range of differing forms. The
nature of members' relationships with one or more cultural communities is also profoundly diverse and complex. Conceptual formulations
of rights to cultural identity too often unduly simplify an inherently
complex and diverse set of human realities. Some of us derive much of
our core ways of being and believing from a single normative source,
others are constructed out of a myriad of cultural elements. What all of
these cultural communities have in common is their essentially constructed and historical character. Many of those members of largely
closed, apparently static communities may well view their culture in
essentialist terms. Their perceptions are deeply influential and will
affect their communities' relations with anyone who is perceived as a
threat to perpetuating allegedly timeless and primordial practices and
beliefs. However, the mere perception of a custom or belief as being

somehow essential to the continuing identity of a community does not serve to justify them as such. A regulatory framework for determining rights to cultural identity must, therefore, be based upon epistemological considerations and not merely political concerns. Regardless of how strongly many may hold to it, the myth that cultural communities are not ultimately human constructions can play no role in considering the basis and scope of rights to cultural identity.

The alternative to thinking of cultures in such essentialist terms is to conceive of them as constructed phenomena whose identity is, to varying degrees, contingent and inherently contestable. Conceiving of cultures in these terms does not result in trivialising the importance of culturally based forms of identity for human beings. But it does point towards a rather different understanding of the relationship between rights and cultural identity. Most importantly, this approach indicates the need to assess the specific claims of collective rights to cultural identity in accordance with the process by which those claims emerge and are expressed. Put simply, cultural ways of being and believing cannot be coercively imposed upon members by, for example, denying the opportunity or fundamental legitimacy of members of the community deliberating upon the precise way in which those ways of being and believing have been constructed. Questioning the elders' view of a given custom or belief should not be construed as heresy or a form of intolerable cultural dissent. Nor should outsiders be forbidden from raising questions over the claims made by some insiders within communities concerning what they consider to be entirely beyond critical scrutiny.

In turn, this approach calls for a different way of understanding *who* comprises the community. Recognising the constructed character of collective identities allows for a normatively far more desirable understanding of who is authorised to represent the constituent components of the community's identity. In some instances, such as debates over national identity for example, this approach may serve to fundamentally disrupt the very notion of some shared and distinguishing traits and characteristics. In others, it may still allow for some forms of centralised decision-making within the community but will require evidence of extensive consultation and deliberation within and sometimes outside of the conventionally designated boundaries of membership. Ultimately, a human rights-based approach to rights to cultural identity must embrace what Seyla Benhabib refers to as the movement from ascription to association. She writes, 'only when members of a society can engage in free and unrestrained dialogue about their collective identity in free public spaces can they develop narratives of self-identification, which unfold into fluid and creative re-appropriations of their own traditions' (2011: 76). A commitment to human rights does not necessarily entail that all individuals must be constantly reflecting upon the contingent and constructed nature of all human identity. It does, however, require the establishment of institutional settings within which this collective process is genuinely possible.

A human rights-based approach to rights to cultural identity must also refrain from endorsing arguments which posit an unconditional right to recognition as such. Defenders of human rights are not required to necessarily affirm existing cultural identities. Some of these identities are, after all, formed through the actions of oppressive hierarchies, as is the case with many patriarchal cultures and their effects upon many women. Affirming these identities would amount to a clear violation of the normative basis and purpose of human rights. Indeed, not all forms of collective identity politics aim at preserving the identity which mobilises political action in the first place. Many women's organisations are precisely concerned with challenging and overcoming traditional conceptions of femininity. Other campaigns, such as those pursued by the so-called *Dalit* (or untouchable) communities in India, are similarly concerned with overcoming and transforming the identities which others have largely attributed to them. As Kwame Appiah writes, 'a movement for poor people does not seek to affirm their identity *as* poor people' (2005: 141; original emphasis).

Finally, and by way of concluding this chapter, any human rights-based approach to cultural identity must ultimately focus upon what is fundamentally capable of uniting us and identifying what we have in common. No one can live outside of a cultural context and we are each of us partly as we are as a direct consequence of our culturally based relations with others. Human rights have generally begun to better acknowledge these essential truths of the human condition. To this extent, it is entirely correct that the relational character of our identities is sufficiently recognised by IHRL. However, cultural differences also have an awesome power to divide us and, at worst, to promote impulses towards hatred and fear, which are entirely incompatible with our potential for acting in accordance with the tenets of humanity. One way of subverting and seeking to prevent identity-based conflict is through institutionalising the insistence that all forms of cultural identity are constructed and that we are all of us who we are because of our relations with others and not in spite of them. Rights to cultural identity must, therefore, be handled with extreme caution since they can all too easily serve to propagate the conditions for inhumanity and thus the very, ever-present, threat from which human rights aim to protect us.

Suggested reading

- Peter Jones, 'Groups and Human Rights', in Cindy Holder and David Reidy (eds), *Human Rights: The Hard Questions* (Cambridge: Cambridge University Press, 2013), pp. 100–14.
- David Ingram, 'Group Rights: A Defense', in Thomas Cushman (ed.), *Handbook of Human Rights* (New York: Routledge, 2012), pp. 277–90.
- Paddy McQueen, 'Social and Political Recognition', *The Internet Encyclopedia of Philosophy* (n.d.), <http://www.iep.utm.edu/recog_sp/#H7> (last accessed 27 July 2016).
- Charles Taylor, 'The Politics of Recognition', in Amy Gutmann (ed.), *Multiculturalism: Examining the Politics of Recognition* (Princeton: Princeton University Press, 1994), pp. 25–73.

Note

1. I consider the question of how law has typically sought to define 'religion' in Chapter 7.

4

The Rights of Women – Patriarchy, Harm and Empowerment

Key questions

1. Generally, how has feminism contributed to the development of IHRL?
2. Is 'multiculturalism bad for women'? If so, must human rights abandon support for cultural diversity?
3. Why do some women not protest against the oppressive conditions they are exposed to?
4. In recent years, how has the UN engaged with harmful cultural practices?
5. Why has the CEDAW proved to be so controversial for many?
6. Why do some theorists argue that gender equality asks too much of human rights?
7. Is it fair to accuse many human rights defenders of suffering from a 'saviour mentality'?
8. What are some of the strengths and weaknesses of the right of exit?
9. Must one be committed to defending liberal values and norms in order to comply with the requirements of human rights?
10. How does acknowledging the fact of so-called adaptive preferences influence the application of women's human rights?

Rejecting culture

Simultaneously promoting the principles of respect for human rights and respect for cultural diversity is a conceptually and practically challenging task. As I have argued to this point, it is entirely correct and necessary that advocates of human rights engage with the myriad forms of culturally based identities which individuals adhere to and experiment with. Human rights cannot effectively speak to and for many people's most important interests and concerns while remaining wedded to a so-called colour-blind approach to human identity. The need to assimilate and acknowledge the importance of cultural identity has become an established feature of international human rights law (IHRL). Cultural rights have become integral to the theory and practice of human rights. However, recognising the need to engage with culturally based forms of human identities exposes human rights advocates to a challenge which threatens to strike at the very normative foundations of the doctrine. There exist long-established forms of culturally based ways of being and believing which are, in various ways and to varying degrees, deeply incompatible with core human rights norms and values, such as individual liberty, equality and dignity. The existence of such ways of being and believing constitute a potentially profound challenge to the continuing appeal of human rights norms within communities which adhere to differing and opposing norms and values. Nowhere is this more so than in respect of those ways of being and believing which deny gender equality and the rights of women.

An extensive body of academic literature and research has demonstrated the extent to which women and girls across the world suffer as a consequence, in large part, of being exposed to the customs, practices and beliefs that are often considered by the communities' leaders as essential to maintaining many cultural communities' collective identities. As one researcher has stated, 'no social group has suffered greater violation of its human rights in the name of culture than women' (Rao 1995: 169). Many theorists and activists have argued that the one objective of recognising the collective rights of many cultures' rights to enjoy continuing access to what are argued to be core and distinguishing ways of being and believing and the other objective of recognising women's and girls' rights to liberty and equality are entirely incompatible. Many consider the appeal to cultural rights as providing a very poor alibi for patriarchy, misogyny and the wholesale disempowerment of over half of the human population in many parts of the world. If we are to consider women and girls as constituting a category of identity (a controversial claim which I shall discuss in greater detail below), then we appear to be confronted by a potentially intractable conflict within the broader domain of identity politics and human rights.

Many who consider cultural rights as harmful for women and girls base their position upon a series of feminist-inspired insights. Foremost amongst these is the claim that many forms of social, cultural, political and economic power are themselves manifestations of patriarchy. Patriarchy is typically taken to refer to an extremely broad and diverse set of ways of being and believing which are nevertheless united by their consequences or effects: establishing and reinforcing the unequal power of men within the institutions that exert a significant influence over the lives of all. On this general view, even ostensibly incompatible and opposing ideologies, religions, political systems and cultural practices are united in their disproportionate promotion of the ostensive interests of men within each constituency. When seen through the lens of patriarchy as a critical construct, the world is far less diverse than many (men) assume it to be. Patriarchy is a core feminist concept and has been deployed by many theorists and activists. One of the most prominent of such theorists is Susan Moller Okin who famously declared that 'multiculturalism is bad for women'. For Moller Okin, 'most cultures are patriarchal, then, and many (though not all) of the cultural minorities that claim group rights are more patriarchal than the surrounding cultures' (1999: 17). She extended her general analysis to include consideration of group rights for minorities and argued that many such rights are in effect, if not intention, anti-feminist to the extent that they uphold patriarchal ways of being and believing. She stated that group rights 'substantially limit the capacities of women and girls of that culture to live with human dignity equal to that of men and boys, and to live as freely chosen lives as they can' (1999: 12).

Other feminist-inspired theorists have refined Moller Okin's original perspective and presented a more nuanced account of the basis and effects of patriarchy. One such theorist is Ayelet Shachar (2001) who has specifically focused upon the wider concern for gauging the effects of cultural rights upon many women. Shachar has developed an important concept which she refers to as the 'paradox of multicultural vulnerability . . . which refers to . . . the ironic fact that individuals inside the group can be injured by the very reforms that are designed to promote their status as group members in the accommodating, multicultural state' (2001: 3). She argues that the policies which aim to protect and promote cultural diversity in the name of defending minority communities against majority prejudice or discrimination raise the prospect of enhancing power hierarchies within such communities at the expense of the weaker members of those communities, who, in many cases, are women and girls. A well-intentioned ethical objective may prove harmful for many women and girls as a consequence of strengthening the capacity of patriarchal communities to maintain their internal identity. Shachar, and others such as Anthias and Yuval-Davis (1989), have argued that many women are so vulnerable within so many communities precisely because they are accorded the role of embodying and upholding the key symbols and rites through which the identity of the community is expressed. The irony of the paradox of multicultural vulnerability is compounded by the well-documented ethnographic fact that many cultural communities esteem many of their female members as the necessary bearers of the group's continuing identity. This is particularly apparent in customs and rites surrounding marriage and reproduction, which are typically highly formalised and rigid. Many such customs and rites are effectively defined by men, as is the allocation and distribution of the roles the customs and rites entail. The insistence that women comply with such roles is thereby based upon unequal power relations and serves to severely restrict women's opportunities to pursue other potential life choices, such as marrying outside of the community, remaining single or choosing not to have children. Women's status as key bearers of the group's identity further serves to expose them to the charge that any desire to deviate from their allotted roles constitutes a form of cultural disloyalty. Women are thereby required to prioritise what others claim are the interests of the community over their own wishes, or even to comply with a view which holds that women can have no legitimate interests of their own that are independent of those of the community. Shachar argues that this harm is particularly apparent within cultural communities that are committed to what she refers to as a form of 'reactive culturalism'. For her, reactive culturalism 'entails a strict adherence to group's traditional laws, norms, and practices as part of an identity group's active resistance to external forces of change, such as secularism or modernity' (2001: 35). Thus, reactive culturalism is often most apparent within communities who consider their 'true' identities to be threatened or endangered. In many such instances, she argues, 'images of women and of the family frequently become symbols of a nomoi group's "authentic identity"' (2001: 36). The rights of women and girls are, one may surmise, often most at risk within communities which consider themselves to be most in need of some forms of collective rights protection.

One does not have to self-consciously identify with feminism in order to discern the extent to which cultural ways of being and believing can have devastating consequences for many women and girls. Arguably one of the most significant examples of the threat culture can pose begins with the influence cultural values exert upon many parents' decision to abort girl foetuses on the grounds that, particularly first-born, infants should be boys. UN demographers have estimated that there are some 117 million 'missing girls', who would have been born but for selective abortion. Campaigners refer to this practice as 'gendercide'.[1] With every year which passes, a further 2 million girls are estimated to have been selectively aborted. Gendercide is most widely practised in China and India, which together account for almost 100 million missing girls. The practice appears to have been strengthened by advances in medical technology and the ability to identify the sex of a foetus at a progressively earlier stage in vitro.

Those girls and women who are born then routinely experience discrimination and oppression as a direct consequence of a multitude of culturally based expectations. It is estimated that some 135 million girls and women have undergone female genital mutilation (FGM) specifically within twenty-nine countries in the Middle East and Africa where the custom is most common.[2] According to World Bank indicators and as of 2014 only 70 out of 173 countries have introduced specific criminal legislation which identifies marital rape as a crime. In many countries it remains perfectly legal for a man to rape his wife in accordance with a belief that rape is consistent with a man's conjugal rights. Despite being illegal in many countries, forced marriage is widely practised in accordance with cultural norms and customs. In Afghanistan some 40 per cent of all marriages are forced and over half of these brides are under the age of sixteen. One in four women are estimated to be the victims of domestic violence during their lifetimes. Cultural attitudes reinforce domestic violence and even extend to influence the victims' perceptions of their suffering. Thus, in Egypt some 94 per cent of women think it is acceptable for a man to beat his wife on grounds such as burning his food, arguing with him, going out without telling him and refusing sex. Seventy per cent of women in India similarly consider domestic violence to be justified on such grounds (Fagan 2010). Finally, many women and girls are the victims of inappropriately named 'honour killings' in which a father or other male relative murders a woman or girl judged to have severely dishonoured the family's reputation. The UN estimates that there are some 5,000 'honour killings' each year, although many consider this figure to be a gross underestimate. Very large numbers of women and girls are being aborted, are suffering and are dying as a direct consequence of their own and others' adherence to ways of being and believing which, in many cases, are considered to be essential to the survival of the group's collective identity. For many women and girls, culture is a matter of life or death.

Human rights and cultural harm

At one level, IHRL can be understood as embodying a comprehensive account of 'harm'. Torture, slavery, the denial of freedom of conscience and religion are, along with the many other human rights provisions, legally and morally proscribed because they have a profoundly harmful impact upon those whose human rights are violated. As a moral criterion, 'harm' is essential to human rights. However, a human rights-based response to cultural diversity requires a narrower focus upon practices which are significantly harmful but which nevertheless are prescribed by long-standing culturally based ways of being and believing. So-called cultural harms can differ from harms which result from the exercise of brute force, or the pursuit of utterly partial interest, or mere wanton and arbitrary acts of violence in several, highly significant, ways. For example, the intentions behind the actions which cause harm to others will often be very different. The male elders of the community may seek to deny young girls' access to formal schooling on the grounds that, in so doing, they are protecting the widely accepted and gendered division of labour which, they claim, is essential to sustaining the identity of the community. This motivation is different, I believe, from one based upon purely misogynistic hatred of educated women. Similarly, many victims' perception of the harms they experience will be affected by the extent to which the community with which they identify ostensibly legitimises the harm, as is the case in many instances of FGM. Indeed, recognising that culture affects many victims' experience of the harm raises profound questions (which will be addressed below) concerning the extent to which outsiders may legitimately claim that intolerable harms have occurred. In recognising the extent to which culture can affect the perceptions and experiences of many human beings, one must simultaneously acknowledge the extent to which the formal acknowledgement of cultural rights complicates any subsequent reliance upon notions of harm in determining the limits of such rights in various instances.

While the concept of cultural harm remains underdeveloped within human rights theorising, it has featured in several recent UN forays into the field of cultural rights and cultural diversity. Thus, in 2011 the HRC conducted a specific study into the role of traditional values in the implementation of human rights, concluding that some such values are harmful to the more vulnerable and marginalised members of some communities, and reasserting that traditional values can never be legitimately elevated above human rights commitments. The study resulted in Resolution 16/3 of the HRC which proclaimed the need to recognise the constructive role which so-called traditional values can play in the implementation of universal human rights norms. Other international initiatives recognise the harmful potential of many cultural practices, as evidenced by the Document of the Copenhagen Meeting of the Conference on the Human Dimension of the CSCE (Copenhagen Convention 1990), the Vienna Declaration and Programme of Action (1993) and the Beijing Platform for Action on Women's Rights (1995). However, the key instrument for identifying the harmfulness of some culturally based ways of being and believing in respect of women is the 1981 UN Convention on the Elimination of All Forms of Discrimination against Women (CEDAW).

The CEDAW is highly significant in many respects. First, it recognises that identifying and addressing the violations of human rights which many women suffer from requires a specific focus upon women as a distinct category. Thus, alongside the protections afforded by the other instruments of IHRL, the CEDAW aims to address the distinct violations women suffer from *as* women. As such, women are exposed to an additional range of potential harms than those which men may be exposed to. The CEDAW thereby offers a response to a frequent feminist criticism of IHRL, namely that far too many instruments of IHRL ignore the specific vulnerability of many women by prescribing a gender-neutral body of laws and provisions (Charlesworth 1995; McColgan 2000). The CEDAW recognises that many women suffer human rights violations because they are women and, further, that correctly identifying human rights violations requires delineating a field of violations which are unique to women.

Just as importantly, the CEDAW explicitly extends the writ of IHRL beyond its conventional restriction to the public sphere. Feminists have consistently argued that the distinction between the public and private spheres which is endemic to liberal-democratic legal and political systems is both artificial and harmful (Pateman 1988). A core objective of the public/private distinction is to limit the law's capacity to regulate relations within the private sphere. Thus, for example, family law has been deeply influenced by the perceived need to adhere to an assumption that relations within families should not be subjected to legal regulation. Many feminists have argued that one consequence of this has been to expose many women to systematic abuse and discrimination perpetrated by men within many families. By seeking to largely exclude the state's capacity to intervene within the private sphere, law effectively ignores one of the principal sites of women's oppression. As Donna Sullivan has written:

> within this conceptualisation of the law as a constraint on the power of the state, many abuses against women have not been acknowledged as human rights violations because they are committed by private persons rather than by agents of the state. (Sullivan 1995: 126)

Article 1 of the CEDAW recognises that threats to women's human rights often emanate from beyond the so-called public sphere and extends the focus of the CEDAW to include the social and cultural domains also.

The CEDAW proceeds to focus extensively on the wrongfulness of many established cultural practices. The CEDAW's response to the place of culture in human rights makes a fundamentally important contribution to the understanding of the sources of human rights violations, by extending its focus beyond state institutions and actions by state bodies. Thus, Article 2(f) specifically identifies states parties' obligations to combat discrimination found within various cultural customs and practices. In this way, the CEDAW legally recognises the iconic feminist insight, that the 'personal is political', and thereby draws culture into the human rights regulatory domain. Article 4(1) licenses the adoption of policies of affirmative action (or positive discrimination) as temporary measures designed to overcome systematic discrimination against women. Article 5(a) commits states parties to take appropriate measures to:

> modify the social and cultural patterns of conduct of men and women, with a view to achieving the elimination of prejudices

and customary and all other practices which are based on the idea of the inferiority or the superiority of either of the sexes or on stereotyped roles for men and women.

In writing upon the implications of Article 5 for gender relations within the Middle East, Ann Elizabeth Mayer writes that compliance with Article 5 entails:

> where cultural constructs of gender were an obstacle to the achievement of women's equality, it was the culture that had to give way – not that women's rights should be sacrificed in situations where their realization would require modifying local social and cultural patterns. (Mayer 1995: 179)

Article 10 recognises the role education can play in combatting culturally based forms of discrimination against women and calls for:

> the elimination of any stereotyped concept of the roles of men and women at all levels and in all forms of education by encouraging coeducation and other types of education which will help to achieve this aim and, in particular, by the revision of textbooks and school programmes and the adaptation of teaching methods.

Finally, in respect of those provisions that are most relevant for combatting culturally based forms of discrimination, Article 16 recognises the role which culturally based forms of marriage and family life can play in the denial of women's human rights across a broader range of life activities and opportunities. The article requires that marriage and family relations be conducted in accordance with the principle of equality between men and women. Article 16 thus extends the writ of IHRL into what many have considered to be the veritably sacred and untouchable domain of marriage and family. This is particularly important for many reasons, not the least of which is because marriage and family are often the cultural sites in which women's obligation to uphold the collective identity of the community is most powerfully asserted. As Julie Mertus has written, 'women's obligations in societies are often defined in terms of their obligations in the family' (Mertus 1995: 135).

Through its various provisions and subsequent General Recommendations issued by the treaty monitoring body which oversees it, the CEDAW can be credited with establishing a legal instrument which specifically addresses the distinct status and vulnerability of women, extends the explicit focus of IHRL beyond the public sphere, recognises that human rights violations can also occur within cultural communities, and finally provides the most comprehensive and legally authoritative source for identifying the culturally based harms to which women are typically vulnerable. Systematic violations of women's rights continue to occur across the globe, but the CEDAW provides an essential instrument in recognising many long-established culturally based ways of being and believing as morally intolerable violations of human rights. So I contend, at least. Not everyone shares this view, however.

Hoping for too much?

The specific content of the CEDAW underlines the extent to which the requirement of respecting women's human rights can often conflict with the requirement of ostensibly respecting distinct culturally based ways of being and believing. Unfortunately, the CEDAW's attempt to resolve this conflict through the prioritisation of women's human rights has met many challenges.

The first of these challenges emanates from within the system of IHRL and consists of the multitude of states parties' reservations which have been entered against specific provisions of the CEDAW. States which have ratified UN human rights treaties may nevertheless declare that their compliance with the terms of the treaty does not extend to include those articles which they have entered reservations against. The CEDAW has attracted more states parties' reservations than any other of the core human rights treaties. Specifically, Articles 2, 5, 7, 9, 15 and 16 have received the largest number of reservations. The 1969 Vienna Convention on the Law of Treaties has established that some articles of a human rights treaty are central to the 'object and the purpose' of the treaty and that it should therefore not be legally permissible to enter reservations against them. In respect of the CEDAW, Articles 2 and 16 have been deemed to be core provisions. Despite this, many states have entered reservations against these provisions which, recall, respectively require states to address cultural and social forms of discrimination against women and to establish marriage and family relations on a basis of equality between men and women. The majority of those states which have entered reservations against Article 2 are sub-Saharan African states and have typically argued that prevailing religious and ethnic customs are incompatible with gender equality. The majority of those states which have entered reservations against Article 16 have insisted that the provisions of the article are in conflict with the requirements of Islamic Shari'a law (Freeman 2009). Notwithstanding the 1969 Vienna Declaration, such states show few signs of bending to the will of IHRL, and the specific forms of women's human rights violations covered by respective articles of the CEDAW are legally unprotected. Many women are suffering as a consequence of the apparently intractable conflict between universal human rights norms and some forms of culturally based ways of being and believing. How might this conflict be resolved?

In a previous chapter I discussed one general response to the conflict between human rights norms and culture. Thus, those who have endorsed an ecumenical or relative universality approach to implementing human rights have cautioned against 'hoping for too much' from normatively substantive norms and values (Cohen 2004). On this view, supporters of human rights should not seek to cajole or coerce others into accepting the norms and values which many liberals take to be integral to the human rights doctrine, but which are not, in fact, universally endorsed. Rather, it is argued that human rights defenders should aspire towards securing a shared moral consensus via a process based upon a mutually respectful understanding of one another's normative differences. Respecting the cultures of others thereby provides an argumentative bridgehead for accepting that highly significant moral differences are inevitable and the associated claim that others should not be required to change or fundamentally adapt to what are all too often presented as 'Western' norms and values. For some, such as Charles Beitz (2009), a continuing commitment to substantive gender equality as a key human rights norm places human rights at odds with very many established cultural ways of being and believing, and thereby threatens to undermine the moral appeal of human rights within such communities. On this reading, a commitment to gender equality is typically conceived of as being unduly ethnocentric in character. Advocates of women's rights, such as Moller Okin (1999), are criticised for failing to distinguish between the highly significant differences of experience and interests which different communities of women across the world possess. On this view, there is no single, essential condition of femininity, and so-called Western visions of the empowered woman cannot and should not seek to legislate for all women everywhere. It is thereby argued that, by insisting upon gender equality as a non-negotiable human rights norm, some within the human rights community run the risk of setting normative aspirations too high; of hoping for too much from human rights. For its defenders, this alternative vision and analysis of the scope of human rights certainly appears to better fit the reality of states' relationship with the CEDAW and the broader aspiration of women's rights across the globe.

The cultural basis and context of human agency and identity cannot be ignored by the human rights community. However, of those who argue that the acknowledgement of culture requires a re-evaluation and limitation of human rights norms and values, none, to my knowledge, argue that this should extend to include what we might conceive of as unequivocally intolerable harms, such as torture, slavery, denial of the basic means for subsistence and other distinctly 'measurable' harms. Thus, no one would argue that we should tolerate a contemporary culture's insistence that human sacrifice is an essential feature of their collective identity. Nor would the ecumenical or relative universality approach condone systematic infanticide as an established cultural practice. Some account of cultural harm remains integral to any determination of the scope and limitations of the implementation of human rights norms and values. However, not all harms are as overtly measurable and identifiable as human sacrifice or the murder of infants.

Whose harm is it, anyway?

The identification of what constitutes harm is a deeply complex and highly politicised domain. The attribution of harm to others necessarily involves the appeal to some account of human agency and the minimal requirements for human well-being. For the sake of argument, we might assume that the identification of some harms is relatively uncontroversial, regardless of the wider context in which the harm occurs. The identification of a great many other harms is, however, far more problematic. Some principal defenders of the ecumenical or relative universality approach to human rights explicitly argue that far too many 'Western' accounts of human rights are based upon a disrespectful and patronising account of the need to save others from their purportedly oppressive cultural surroundings. Thus, Mutua (2002) condemns many more normatively substantive understandings of human rights as afflicted by what he describes as a 'saviour mentality', which he compares to the 'white man's burden', which defenders of colonialism once appealed to in an attempt to justify their domination of others. Mutua argues that the construction of the identity of a saviour requires that of a victim, who is in need of being saved, even if the ostensive victim is not aware that they are in need of saving. Human rights defenders, some of them at least, are thereby condemned for recreating a hierarchical relationship which, while ostensibly very differently motivated than those who appealed to a 'white man's burden', nevertheless serves to maintain neo-colonial relationships.

A similar analysis is presented by Bhiku Parekh (2006) who also seeks to challenge what he characterises as a prevailing set of assumptions among many so-called liberals, which are exemplified by their characterisation of non-liberal ways of being and believing as inherently oppressive or discriminatory. Like Mutua, Parekh argues that the urge to characterise others as being necessarily victims of their specific cultural communities is, irrespective of its motivations, deeply disrespectful to those individuals and to their communities. Parekh argues that the analysis such a characterisation is based upon is also typically false. He argues that, rather than claiming to know others' interests better than they themselves do, human rights defenders should generally take people at their own word. Parekh considers the practices of arranged marriages and even some forms of FGM which may confront young adult Asian women in the United Kingdom. He writes:

> in the Asian view individuals are an integral part of their family, and their lives belong not just to them but also to their families . . . If young Asians are happy for their parents to choose or help them choose their spouses, they have chosen to be chosen or co-chosen for, and their choices should be respected. (Parekh 2006: 275)

While he recognises the need to remain attentive to the potential pressures and coercion some young women may be subjected to, Parekh effectively grounds his account of cultural harm upon the overt consciousness of individuals. The legitimate identification of specific harms therefore requires that the victims of these harms experience and evaluate them as such. Despite Parekh's awareness of just how deeply influential culture can be in forming individuals' perceptions and interests, he proposes that what would be a core legislative principle for regulating cultural diversity should be based upon the ideal of a freely deliberating sovereign agent, that is, an individual whose capacity for deliberation, in some areas at least, remains sufficiently independent of the ways of being and believing which have shaped them.

The right of exit: a possible solution to the problem?

As I have already argued above, any defensible account of human rights requires some developed notion of what constitutes intolerable harm. In many cases, identifying harm is a relatively unproblematic task. However, there remain many other areas in which describing others' cultural practices as causing harm to those exposed to them raises significant problems for any attempt to reconcile respect for human rights with respect for cultural diversity. Some argue that the task of identifying HCPs should be largely accorded to individuals themselves. On the face of it, this position has much to commend it. For example, it complies with a principle which has been integral to the development of the liberal political morality which human rights emerged out of and which esteems the moral sovereignty of the individual as the basis upon which legitimate systems of legal and political governance should be based. It also appears to offer a way by which we might avoid scenarios in which cultural outsiders claim to know what is best for insiders. Human rights should not revert to forms of neo-colonialism, no matter what the intentions may be for seeking to intervene in the internal affairs of others.

Within the domestic sphere of many separate national jurisdictions, the so-called individual right of exit has offered an ostensibly effective instrument for enabling states to regulate culturally diverse societies in ways which prevent the state from imposing a single, partially espoused political morality upon all of those diverse ways of being and believing which are subject to the state's jurisdiction. As Robert Nozick has written, 'individual communities may have *any* character compatible with the operation of the framework. If any person finds the character of a particular community uncongenial, he needn't choose to live in it' (1974: 323–4; original emphasis). The right of exit should be understood as integral to an individual's human right of freedom of association. The right of exit offers a means by which the basis and constitution of community relations can be regulated in a manner which does not demand the eradication of cultural differences. Arguably the most detailed philosophical defence of the right of exit has been presented by Chandran Kukathas (2003) whom I briefly considered in the previous chapter.

Kukathas argues that the legitimate regulation of culturally diverse societies should be based upon the twin ideals of negative liberty and mutual toleration. Legitimately governed culturally diverse societies do not require the state to discriminate in favour of distinctly, that is to say, substantively liberal norms and ideals. A normatively legitimate response to the fact of cultural diversity requires recognising that we are most certainly not all liberals now. Many entirely legitimate communities practise their own ways of being and believing. No single community within what he depicts as an 'archipelago of separate jurisdictions' (2003: 4) should be able to demand compliance from others to their partial norms and values. Thus, the key criterion for the legitimacy of any community is not the proximity of its norms and ideals to a 'Western', liberal vision of the good life, but the extent to which individual members have a formal right of exit from any community. For Kukathas, the evidence of the legitimacy of any single individual's exercise of the right is simply whether he or she actively chooses to dissociate from other groups of individuals they previously associated with.[3]

For those seeking to vernacularise human rights principles in order to better respond constructively to cultural diversity, the right of exit appears to provide a powerful resource and a potential ground for identifying the criteria for determining the value of any given cultural community: leave the task of judging cultures to their individual members and trust in their ability to know their own minds. The right of exit appears to offer a powerful instrument for the purpose of reshaping human rights amidst diversity. A core motivation would be to extend the ethical appeal of human rights in such a way as to counter the claims that human rights principles unduly reflect 'Western', liberal values and ideals. In seeking to re-establish human rights on grounds which do not ultimately depend upon support from partial ideals, the right of exit approach obviously entails an acknowledgement

of the right of many non-liberal cultures to exist. The very designa-
tion of some of these cultures as 'non-liberal' raises the possibility
that the protection of some of their defining traditions, practices and
beliefs may require the suspension of some of their members' human
rights, especially, for example, some of the rights enshrined within the
CEDAW. On the face of it, this implication might cause some human
rights defenders significant anxiety. Against this, maintaining the individual's right to exit any community they have come to disapprove of
offers apparent reassurance against the prospect of cultural communities being afforded a *carte blanche* to oppress some of their members.
The right thereby seeks to uphold what is widely acknowledged as
a fundamental value, which has profoundly influenced the development of human rights: individuals' capacity for normatively deliberating upon their own commitments and core preferences. From this,
one can derive the following maxim: if individuals do not seek to leave
their cultural communities there can be no legitimate basis for external
interference or intervention within such communities. The individual
right of exit might thereby become recognised as a core human right
within a complex and diverse global order. Is the right of exit capable
of bearing such a heavy moral load?

On being unable to leave

Individuals may be prevented from exiting their communities in a multitude of recognisable ways. They may be physically prevented from
leaving by other members of the community. They may be effectively
prevented from leaving by being exposed to extreme threats against
their life or person. Their community may be geographically isolated
from any other community and in such a way which makes it practically impossible for them to escape to the 'nearest town'. Very few, if
any commentators to this debate would seriously suggest that states do
not have some role to play in combatting such effective forms of constraint and severe restrictions on freedom of movement. However, a
far more problematic category consists of people who, on the face of it,
are not physically imprisoned within their communities and do appear
to possess sufficient opportunities and means to seek to exit from culturally based conditions which it seems reasonable to conclude are
harmful and should be avoided. Those who argue that the right of exit
provides a powerful, if not sufficient, instrument for combatting forms

of cultural oppression would generally conclude that no further action should be taken in such cases. I disagree.

Maintaining the individual right of exit from communities which some of their members come to feel estranged from appears to offer a means by which cultural communities may be afforded collective cultural rights to their core ways of being and believing whilst simultaneously providing a legal instrument by which individuals (and not public authorities) may directly overcome any community's attempts to coercively impose its values and norms upon its members. However, combining a right to cultural identity and a right of individual exit, under a single normative perspective, raises an interesting and highly important issue. Recall that the strongest arguments supporting rights to cultural identity focus upon ascribed forms of identity: ways of being and believing which many individuals themselves consider to be central to who they are as members of specific communities. However, the effective possibility of exercising the right of exit necessarily entails that individuals are capable of viewing themselves as, in some ways, fundamentally distinct from, or independent of, their communities. In many cases, the capacity to step back from one's culturally derived commitments and beliefs will be retained. Under such circumstances it seems reasonable to conclude that the commitments of those who choose not to leave should be respected. Individual sovereignty takes precedence. However, this approach rests upon an assumption that all of the individuals who have not sought to exit their communities may thereby be understood as having affirmed the community's ways of being and believing. That *not* saying 'no' amounts to consent. While the principle of respecting individuals' normative deliberations is central to the philosophy underlying both human rights norms and the appeal to a right of exit as a basis for regulating cultural diversity, it should not be universally upheld – or so I argue. Setting the limits to a right to cultural identity upon the right of exit will, inadvertently perhaps, contribute to the persistence of ways of being and believing which are significantly harmful for some individual members. Moreover, in some instances, the right of exit will not suffice to prevent the harm, because what is harmed is precisely individuals' capacity to effectively initiate any such course of action: they are largely unable to say 'no'. Some individuals' lack of overt opposition to their cultural fate is a consequence of the harm they are exposed to. A principle of respecting this lack of opposition is to respect cultural conditions which expose some individuals to intolerable wrongs and mistreatment. This claim raises many complex questions which I engage with later in this chapter. What is required now is a concrete illustration of the predicament I have raised. In keeping with the focus of this chapter upon women's rights, the example I shall now focus upon is domestic violence.

Domestic violence is a universal phenomenon and affects women and girls across a vast range of social and cultural communities and spaces. There appear to be no cultures in which women do not suffer domestic violence. It has been estimated that one in four women will be the victims of domestic violence during their lifetimes. In the United States at least 20 per cent of women have been estimated to have been physically and psychologically abused by their partners or ex-partners. In Bangladesh at least 50 per cent of all adult women have been the victims of domestic violence (Fagan 2010). The UN Secretary-General Ban Ki-moon stated in 2007:

> violence against women and girls continues unabated in every continent, country and culture. It takes a devastating toll on women's lives, on their families, and on society as a whole. Most societies prohibit such violence – yet the reality is that too often, it is covered up or tacitly condoned. (Fagan 2010: 76)

In 1993, the UN recognised violence against women as a human rights violation through the Declaration on the Elimination of Violence against Women (DEVAW). Articles 1 and 2 of DEVAW define violence as including physical, sexual and psychological acts.

Despite its global prevalence and the UN's recognition of violence against women as a human rights violation, domestic violence is still not specifically recognised as a crime within many national jurisdictions. There is also little evidence to suggest that classifying domestic violence as a human rights violation has had any significant effect upon reducing its prevalence. Many perpetrators and far too many victims appear not to share others' views on the morally intolerable nature of domestic violence. Thus, one of the most shocking aspects of domestic violence consists of how many women in some parts of the world appear to endorse being physically, sexually and psychologically abused by their male partners. Ninety-one per cent of women surveyed in Zambia consider it reasonable for their husbands to abuse them under circumstances such as burning food and refusing sex. In Haiti the figure is 48 per cent and in Cambodia it is 46 per cent. In Swaziland some 60 per cent of men surveyed believe that a man has a right to beat his wife (Fagan 2010).

To reiterate, domestic violence is a universal phenomenon and is not restricted to 'non-Western' cultures. 'Westerners' cannot claim the moral high ground on this issue. Many 'Western' perpetrators of domestic violence reference cultural factors when asked to account for their behaviour, such as the sexual objectification of women and girls (Gadd 2012). However, it appears that the formalisation of attempts to justify domestic violence is more established and powerful in some cultural communities than in others. The consciousness-raising effects of the feminist and women's rights movements are more apparent in some cultures than in others. In some cultures, it is clear that established ways of being and believing serve to prevent the consolidation of a view of domestic violence as a human rights violation. The effects extend to perpetrators and victims alike.

Many victims of domestic violence manage to escape from their abusive partners. Any woman's ability to do so will be affected by a range of external factors, such as the existence of sufficient numbers of women's refuges, support from public officials and authorities, the opportunity to be financially independent from their partners and the like. Many other victims of domestic violence do not leave their abusive partners. The absence of the kind of facilities outlined above will obviously greatly diminish women's effective ability to leave. In many parts of the world the lack of public provision for victims reflects the wider cultural acceptance and tolerance of men abusing their partners. In these instances, women are effectively denied any real opportunity to establish a new life. More disturbing, however, are instances where domestic violence is recognised by public authorities as both a crime and a human rights violation, where there does exist some public provision and yet where victims refuse to leave their partners. Research has focused upon the role of culture in preventing such women from seeking to exit the wider communities within which the abuse occurs.

The role which women and girls' compliance with formally established cultural expectations of wives, mothers and dutiful daughters plays in preventing victims seeking to leave abusive relationships has been demonstrated by two recent studies into the experiences of some women of South Asian descent, living within the United Kingdom (Muslim Women's Network 2013). Both reports studied a number of avowedly Hindu, Muslim and Sikh women and other community members residing within the UK. The studies examined the multitude of attitudes and responses to domestic violence within these communities. Both studies identified a widespread reluctance amongst victims to discuss, protest against or seek to avoid the abuse they suffer. Both studies identified a range of cultural and religious factors which explain victims' apparent acceptance of their suffering. Five different cultural factors which explain women's responses to domestic violence were identified by these studies:

1. There exist cultural and religious barriers to women even initiating discussions about sexuality and thus, what may or may not be appropriate behaviours within a sexual relationship.
2. There exist cultural obstacles to victims' seeking help from within and outside the community, including well-founded fears of being excluded from the family and community if they reveal themselves to have been the victims of abuse.
3. The vocabularies of many South Asian languages do not include terms for designating forms of specifically sexual abuse, severely restricting some women from even referring to their experiences as 'abuse'.
4. There exists a widespread cultural expectation of female obedience to their menfolk, and victims of domestic violence are liable to be dismissed or blamed for causing their own abuse by not being sufficiently obedient.
5. The recurring cultural and religious mechanism underlying many of these barriers is the extremely powerful aversion to shame and dishonour prevalent within many of these communities.

As one of the reports states:

there is a tendency to prioritise protecting the 'honour' of the community over the safeguarding of vulnerable girls . . . it does appear that silence in the name of avoiding shame and preserving honour, is allowing men to continue operating with impunity, therefore fuelling sexual violence against girls and women further. (Muslim Women's Network 2013: 28)

Over 80 per cent of the women studied in one of the reports explicitly referred to the fear of being disowned by their family and community if they reported the abuse they suffered. One victim stated:

> my own family didn't let me disclose [the] sexual violence [received] from my husband and I was emotionally blackmailed by them saying that I have a big mouth and don't think about their reputation in the community. (They) also said that by religion you have to satisfy your husband's needs. (Rehal and Macguire 2014: 10)

Another victim testified to the influence exerted by religious and cultural beliefs upon her own mother. She stated, 'I was experiencing sexual and domestic abuse from my husband, and disclosed to my mum in the hope that she loves me and will protect me. Instead I was shown the main door and was told that the door is closed to me forever' (Rehal and Maguire 2014: 11).

Finally, a Hindu victim of domestic violence, from another report, described her conditions in the following terms:

> my culture is like my blood – coursing through every vein in my body. It is the culture into which I was born and where I grew up, which sees the woman as the honour of the house. In order to uphold this false 'honour' and 'glory' she is taught to endure many kinds of oppression and pain in silence. In addition, religion also teaches that her husband is her god. Fulfilling his every desire is her religious duty. A woman who does not follow this path in our society has no respect or place in it. She suffers from all kinds of slanders against her character; she has to face much hurt entirely alone. She is responsible not only for her husband but also for his entire family's happiness. (Saghal 1992: 188)

Many women from within these communities are not seeking the kind of redress which is potentially available to them. They are not availing themselves of the formal right of exit afforded them by the law. They are not seeking the support of existing public and charitable resources. Nor are they initiating criminal proceedings against the perpetrators. Despite having formal opportunities of redress, many victims of domestic violence within such communities fail to seek to end their suffering. Must we therefore conclude that such women are, in some meaningful sense, tacitly or explicitly consenting to their plight?

Suffering injustice

The focus of this chapter necessarily includes a concern with the criteria for legitimately identifying human rights violations. There exists an established body of conventional legal procedures for correctly identifying state and non-state acts (and omissions) which violate the human rights-based duties and obligations of nation-states. These will depend upon many factors, beginning with the state's ratification of the relevant treaty or instrument. However, the conventions for identifying human rights violations are rendered problematic by the argument that respecting others' ways of being and believing requires affording them the ultimate say in whether or not a practice is genuinely harmful in respect of human rights. I have discussed above how understandings of what constitutes cultural harm challenge the assumption made by many human rights defenders that harm is identifiable even where the victims have adapted themselves to others' attempts to justify the harm. Human rights defenders have been accused of being too keen to identify victims of human rights violations in practices and customs which have prevailed for centuries in many communities. The right of exit offers an apparent instrument in which the sovereignty of individuals can be respected and the role of identifying intolerable practices can be accorded to those closest to the action, so to speak. On this alternative approach, identifying human rights violations in some areas requires that the purported victims perceive themselves as such. Such a position draws heavily upon the well-established principle of equality of respect for the opinions and commitments of all individuals. Many a legal and political theorist has cautioned against embarking upon the slippery slope of the state presuming to know how citizens should authentically act and think. Is the challenge of domestic violence any different in this respect?

I understand the domestic violence endured by the women in the studies above to be a specific manifestation of a cultural harm with deeper roots. Empirical studies into domestic violence have consistently identified what Leonore Walker (2009) refers to as the 'battered woman syndrome'. Some domestically abused women manifest forms of learned helplessness which serve to severely undermine their capacity to emotionally detach from their abusive partners. The battered woman syndrome may co-exist alongside other, more overtly material forms of dependency, but it is an identifiably separate factor in some victims' psychological adaptation to the abuse they are exposed to. What the studies discussed above serve to show is a dimension of psychological adaptation which is even more powerful than that found within the battered woman syndrome. Victims' adaptation to their abuse is undeniably affected by deeply established discriminatory cultural values and norms. Women are able to endure their suffering precisely because, to a certain extent, their formal status within the broader cultural framework of meaning validates such treatment. Domestic violence is one manifestation (of potentially many) of this deeper form of cultural harm which precisely consists of values and norms which systematically and severely discriminate against women and girls. But, how is it possible that women can so effectively adapt to such harmful ways of being and believing?

Empirical studies have demonstrated the remarkable capacity human beings have for inflicting suffering upon innocent others in the name of some purportedly 'higher purposes' (Haney et al. 1973; Milgram 1974). Of interest here, however, is our capacity to adapt to and even identify with forms of injustice and suffering of which we are the victims: our capacity to accept others' mistreatment of us. Thus, a body of psychological studies have identified what initially might appear to be an irrational response by members of communities which are unequivocally oppressed or disadvantaged, such as racial minorities, outcast communities or the destitute across a range of industrialised societies (Lerner 1980; Major and Schmader 2001). Many victims of overt discrimination and severe disadvantage systematically develop dispositional attitudes and beliefs which directly endorse the narratives and theories which aim to support the status quo by blaming the victims. Victims blame themselves for their own plight. Major and Schmader have referred to the kind of cognitive construal processes by which victims come to identify with their own diminished status as 'chronic belief systems' (2001: 177). These studies evoke the question once posed by Wilhelm Reich when he stated:

> what has to be explained is not the fact that the man who is hungry steals or the fact that the man who is exploited strikes, but

why the majority of those who are hungry *don't* steal and why the majority of those who are exploited *don't* strike. (Reich 1971: 53)

Reich's question and the body of empirical research above also bears a close affinity to another body of research, which is specifically concerned with explaining how deprived individuals come to downwardly adapt their stated preferences in accordance with the highly diminished opportunities afforded them within their communities. Jon Elster (1983) first drew concerted attention to what initially appeared as a mere failure in economic rationality amongst members of economically impoverished communities. The poor generally aspire to want far less than others. Gary Becker (1996) was awarded a Nobel Prize for his studies into the adaptive preferences of the poor and this phenomenon's implications for theories of economic behaviour. Others such as Onora O'Neill, Martha Nussbaum and Amartya Sen (1993) have studied the effects of adaptive preferences upon development and gender. Finally, for present purposes, Cass Sunstein (1991) has applied the concept of adaptive preferences to challenge the prevailing view of welfare satisfaction in many accounts of legal and political legitimacy.

Sunstein argues that the principle of equality of respect for individuals' expressed preferences must concern itself with the background conditions under which such preferences are formed. Political and legal principles which ignore the effects of systematic discrimination upon some individuals conflict with the requirements of genuinely democratic legal and political systems. He states that 'respect for preferences that have resulted from unjust background conditions and that will lead to human deprivation or misery hardly appears the proper course for a liberal democracy' (1991: 12). Sunstein challenges the claim that such citizens' preferences can be generally considered to be 'private' and self-determined. Rather, he identifies a range of background conditions which render such preferences as exogenous or external to individuals. Within the category of exogenous preferences Sunstein includes 'a decision of a woman to adopt a traditional gender role because of the social stigma attached to refusing to do so' (1991: 12). Sunstein and the other authors writing upon the phenomenon of adaptive preferences assert the need to respond critically to expressed preferences and desires, in circumstances where there is a reasonable suspicion that the individuals' preferences may be understood as adaptive towards unjust conditions. In such circumstances, respecting such individuals is precisely not best served by endorsing the forms of injustice and oppression they are systematically exposed to. The test of the legitimacy of such systems is thus not the extent to which individuals' preferences are satisfied, since some preferences only exist as a consequence of systematic injustice and oppression.

Counter-arguments

I have argued that many defenders of a right of exit consider it to be an instrument which is capable of simultaneously recognising collective rights to cultural identity whilst avoiding exposing individual members to internal forms of oppression. An appeal to the right of exit would appear to have much to commend it for those seeking to reconcile cultural diversity with human rights norms. However, I have sought to show how it is possible that individuals' effective capacity to even formulate the desire to leave can be severely undermined by established culturally based ways of being and believing. With a specific focus upon domestic violence, I have sought to show how victims can become reconciled to their plight through various cognitive and cultural mechanisms. Domestic violence is a demonstrable harm and no one should be required to tolerate it. It is also, however, a global phenomenon which, in many cases, is underpinned by culturally based attitudes about the status of women. This claim appears to raise the prospect of human rights defenders having to confront the cultural practices and attitudes which support domestic violence. A core element of any such project would necessarily involve advocating strongly for gender equality since long-standing perceptions of the unequal status of men and women clearly exert a profound influence on domestic violence. Any such project, however, would appear to drive a divisive wedge between defenders of human rights and those who argue that greater respect must be accorded to many established ways of being and believing. Those who may be inclined to prevent human rights defenders pursuing this course might take issue with various aspects of my argument. These counter-arguments need to be considered before I finally conclude this chapter.

To begin with, it could be argued that the account of cultural harm which I defend ultimately rests upon an empirically false conception of cultural community. To be trapped inside something presumes the existence of some closed, static and homogenous construction, which has rigid and impermeable boundaries. On this view, I could be accused of perpetuating an all too common but false conception of cultural community as akin to what Steven Lukes (2003: 18) refers to as culture as a 'window-less box' from which it is difficult for anyone, let alone vulnerable women, to exit. As I discussed in a previous chapter, the prevailing view within academia is that cultures are fluid, malleable constructions, the boundaries of which typically overlap in ways which make it very difficult, if not impossible, to identify where one community begins and another ends (Geertz 1973). This is obviously true of many cultures when viewed from a dispassionate external perspective. However, as we saw in Chapter 3, many advocates of collective rights to cultural identity do not conceive of their own cultures in this way. After all, claims to protect distinct practices and customs are typically made precisely on the grounds that such customs and practices are, in some sense, essential to preserving the distinct identity of the community. The cosmopolitan's conception of the field of culture as a huge kaleidoscopic melange of differing and contingent elements is seen by many defenders of distinct cultures as posing a significant threat to protecting their collective identities. The conception of some cultures as distinct and separable has also been endorsed by various constitutional courts in their deliberations over the extent to which the preservation of the identity of some communities justifies placing significant restrictions upon would-be internal dissidents. In some instances, these decisions have directly violated the rights of some women.

One of the most analysed examples of such is the US Supreme Court ruling in the case of *Santa Clara Pueblo v Martinez (1978)*. Julia Martinez was a full-blooded member of the Santa Clara Pueblo tribe. She married outside of the tribe and the couple had two children. One of the daughters was raised on the tribe's reservations and socialised into the customs and practices of the tribe. However, the tribe denied this daughter the right of belonging to the tribe on the grounds that legitimate members of the tribe must have been the offspring of a male member of the tribe. The daughter, Audrey, thus would have been granted membership if her mother had been a non-member, but not her father. The rule is clearly discriminatory and was legally challenged. The US Supreme Court finally upheld the tribe's right to determine their own rules of membership, a decision which resulted in the Martinez

children being denied access to federal services and denied a right to
continue living on the reservation after their mother died. The Court
justified its decision on the 'non-intervention' principle, which in the
words of Ayelet Shachar 'lends precedence to the tribe's own criteria
for satisfying membership rules as a means for ensuring the tribe's
cultural preservation' (2001: 19). As Madavi Sunder (2001) has written,
the US Supreme Court has persistently decided such cases on the basis
of seeking to ensure the survival of various, discriminatory cultural and
religious communities. The *Martinez* ruling exemplifies how legislators
often conceive of collective rights to cultural identity. It seems reasonable to conclude that such ways of thinking have yet to satisfactorily
embrace the view of culture as inherently malleable and fluid, lacking
any essential, core elements of identity.

One might also object to my general argument on the grounds that
victims of domestic violence are not entirely defined by their plight, nor
are many victims entirely trapped within the institutions which serve to
reinforce abusive behaviours. Victims of domestic abuse will invariably
pursue activities and relationships outside the realm of their immediate family and even the broader cultural community which is prepared
to tolerate the abuse. They need not be entirely restricted to the single
role of obedient wife to an abusive husband. All of which is, generally
speaking, most likely true. However, the objection overlooks the extent
to which some relationships and roles can be fundamentally constitutive of an individual's sense of self-worth within some communities
and thereby strike at the core of their capacities for agency. For women
in particular, within some cultural communities, being married is core
to their standing and status within the community. Marriage for many
women can be a double-edged status. On the one hand, it serves to
secure many women's access to various community resources, such
as nationality or legal standing in respect of inheritance and custody
over children in the event of their husband's death. On the other hand,
being married serves to confer a formally subordinate status and standing upon many women. Where the status of being married grounds
and, for some at least, ostensibly 'validates' the treatment meted out by
some husbands to their wives, it should not be difficult to see how this
one relationship can be the source of so much harm for some women.
This does not necessarily entail that they are physically entrapped
within some purportedly, utterly closed community, but rather that
their freedom of deliberation and of movement are, none the less,

severely restricted as a consequence of who their cultures expect and require them to be. Identity-forming and maintaining relations may not, necessarily, exhaust all of an abused woman's activities and commitments, but may still have a significant impact upon core aspects of her identity and opportunities.

Another potential objection to my argument takes its bearings from the type of concern expressed by Mutua (2002) and refers to human rights defenders' alleged predilection towards attributing the status of victimhood to groups of people who simply do not share the same normative commitments as those typically espoused within the human rights community. Thus, it might be argued that my characterisation of women exposed to forms of systematic discrimination and inequality is too quick to depict them as passive victims of ways of being and believing which largely act upon them. In characterising them as passive victims I unduly deny their agency. This concern runs across many debates regarding the status and standing of women in so-called traditional cultures. For example, many opponents of women donning religious clothing argue that women are necessarily coerced into doing so and that the very form of the clothing is often inherently oppressive by insisting upon covering part or all of a woman's body. Thus, many Muslim women's wearing of the niqab or burqa is characterised as unworthy of respect and, as is well known, has even been legally banned in countries such as France.[4] This is, of course, a deeply politicised area of contestation and has come to form a veritable front line on the continuing conflict between defenders of Islam and religious freedom and defenders of a particular understanding of secularism. For present purposes, what is both interesting about this particular issue and challenging for my more general argument is the extent to which many Muslim women do not share many of their would-be saviours' evaluation of the allegedly disempowering effects of their dress rules. Similarly, even if it were possible to conclude definitively that items of clothing are inherently oppressive or discriminatory, human rights defenders will still be confronted by many women apparently opting to comply with such rules. As Shachar wisely comments, 'what makes this situation a truly complex problem is the fact that although they may be subject to such injurious burdens within their communities, women may still find value and meaning in their cultural traditions and in continued group membership' (2001: 61).

The objection that human rights defenders are too quick to reject those commitments which do not satisfactorily comply with conventional liberal values and norms is clearly highly significant and will be returned to in various parts of this book. I shall also consider the objection's specific concern with agency below. For the moment, it is important to distinguish between the wearing of specific clothes and the endurance of domestic violence and all this latter entails. They are clearly not morally equivalent in respect of the nature and gravity of the harms each serves to inflict upon their victims (assuming that the wearing of specific clothes can be considered to necessarily inflict harm upon those expected to do so). Domestic violence, by its very nature, violates women's physical and psychological integrity and often serves to pacify its victims, resulting in severe and lasting restrictions in women's capacity to lead different lives. No one should seriously doubt, therefore, that the morally intolerable effects of domestic violence necessitate perceiving its victims as, in some significant ways, wronged and offended-against parties who are in need of external support and assistance, particularly where the abuse is not generally condemned from within the cultural community. Having said that, I argued above that domestic violence should be understood both as inherently harmful and as a manifestation of a deeper culturally harmful condition, which consists precisely in the denial of equal moral standing and status to men and women. Seen from this perspective, is it not therefore the case that there is a connection between religious dress codes which are discriminately applied to women and domestic violence since both appear to be expressions of gender inequality? This is a very important issue which requires a careful response. My response focuses upon the conditions for the kind of agency which human rights norms and values are committed to establishing and protecting.

I argued in an earlier chapter that we are who we are as a consequence of our relations with others. No human being entirely and endogenously creates their own identity. The interpersonal character of identity formation serves to expose each of us to one another in radical ways. I have argued that human rights norms and values are committed to promoting and protecting a certain type of mutually reciprocal agency. The salience of liberty, equality and dignity to the doctrine of human rights and IHRL calls for the advocacy of human faculties which enable human beings to lead lives which are sufficiently free and dignified, on the basis of equality. Formally established ways of being and believing which systematically deny or seek to obstruct each individual's opportunities to benefit from such ideals are incompatible with the normative prerequisites for IHRL. This can be demonstrated by an analysis of how domestic violence can fundamentally impact upon its victims' agency.

I have argued that domestic violence is a manifestation of a deeper form of cultural harm. This deeper form of cultural harm consists of established forms of relations that are fundamentally incompatible with treating people humanely. What do I mean by this?

As others have argued (Baier 1991; Benson 1994; Mackenzie 2000), our capacity for agency entails a capacity for being capable of initiating an alternative course of action to the one we opt for. The opportunity for the exercise of choice is essential for free agency. An agent's capacity for choice (rather than any specific instance of choosing) can be severely undermined by the attitudes and opinions they have about themselves and their worth. As the literature on adaptive preferences demonstrates, what we ostensibly accept and 'endorse' will be deeply affected by how we esteem ourselves. Our self-conceptions are not a purely private matter of internal mental states. Rather, our own sense of self-worth and value will be directly shaped by the attitudes others exhibit towards us. It is more difficult, all other things being equal, for individuals who develop their identities within cultural conditions which routinely deny their sense of equal self-worth to combat discriminatory and oppressive ways of being and believing.

One reason why many victims of domestic violence do not seek to exit abusive relationships is, as we have seen, that they internalise a diminished role allocated to them. Some women come to evaluate their sense of self-worth and dignity through their experience of being abused. The greater the tangible obstacles are to leaving the relationship and the culture, the increased likelihood of this belief, although, of course, this diminished sense of self-worth and dignity can occur even where few such obstacles exist. Exercising the right of exit entails the capacity for an individual to conceive of herself as an agent capable of initiating a course of action that is inherently critical of the community she seeks to exit. In many cases, this condition will entail an individual conceiving of herself as possessing a worth and dignity independently of her cultural community and the fate accorded to her within it. In

many cases this is no doubt possible, but the extent to which many
victims of domestic violence do not seek exit serves to remind us of
the need to allow for the possibility that not all individuals will retain
this sense of worth and dignity. It is ironic perhaps but in order to confront the intolerable, one must generally have a sufficiently intact sense
of oneself as being someone who deserves to be treated better. As
Mackenzie writes, 'without a sense of her own worthiness as an agent
and of the worthiness of her capacities, her desires, and her beliefs,
an agent will not be able to conceive of herself as capable of effective
action' (2000: 140).

This way of thinking of agency runs counter to the more conventional and prevailing approaches to conceiving of individual agency in
much theoretical literature. The prevailing view concerning the political
and legal regulation of intra-cultural relations remains founded upon
the conventional vision of a sovereign individual agent whose *capacity*
for normative deliberation, as opposed to what is tangibly deliberated upon, cannot be determined or significantly undermined by the
cultural environments they inhabit. On this view, to respect another
agent is precisely to understand them as constitutive ends and not the
mere marionettes of some or other cultural forces. Of course, there is
a vast body of literature on this subject, and however well-honed and
practised are the arguments supporting this conception of sovereign
agency, one of the most interesting challenges entailed by affirmatively
responding to cultural diversity precisely consists of the alternative
understanding of agency this approach rests upon.

To this extent, the account of cultural harm outlined here trades upon
what defenders of a right to cultural identity do and must acknowledge:
an appreciation of just how deep and significant are the effects of cultural
community upon those who develop their identities within them. After
all, a broader policy of respecting cultural communities is defended on
grounds which range from the necessity of this policy for individuals'
exercise of personal autonomy and enjoyment of equality, through to
being essential for upholding the self-respect and purportedly inherent
dignity of those who draw so heavily upon their cultural communities
for orienting their way in the world. None of these arguments holds
that the effects of culture upon individuals can only ever be skin-deep.
Cultural attributes such as race, religion, gender and ethnicity are thus
integral to the construction of many people's identities. In acknowledging this claim, one must at least countenance the possibility that some

such attributes can constitute forms of harm as I have formulated that notion above. This is precisely what I have argued occurs in the case of domestic violence and its effects upon some women's capacity to initiate exit from their harmful plight. Culture can have significantly harmful consequences for some individuals' sense of self-worth and self-respect. Arguments for cultural rights which simply ignore what Shachar refers to as the 'paradox of multicultural vulnerability' (2001: 3) cannot provide a ground for determining the regulative basis of culturally diverse political and legal systems because of their partiality and unfounded wishful thinking.

Towards a more constructive approach

As I stated towards the beginning of this chapter, seeking to simultaneously protect the rights of women and girls and to uphold a principle of respecting cultural diversity is very problematic. Some advocates of women's rights have concluded that rights to cultural identity are necessarily deeply incompatible with protecting the more vulnerable members of such communities, and this is especially the case in respect of women and girls. This conclusion seems ostensibly justified if we continue to conceive of culture in a particular way. As I demonstrated above, despite the widespread academic convention that all cultural communities are contingent, malleable and inherently fluid constructions, far too many advocates of collective rights to cultural identity conceive of distinct cultures in more essentialised terms. Collective rights are argued for precisely on the grounds of the necessity of perpetuating specific practices and customs which are considered by some within the community to be essential to maintaining the community's identity. As Appiah (2005) has written, the prospect of cultures changing their ways of being and believing is typically thought of as amounting to a diminution or loss of identity. The notion of loss implies the existence of common, stable and fixed cultural traits that are essential to the community's collective identity. Policies of cultural survival and much of the wider advocacy of collective rights to cultural identity are thus heavily indebted to a conception of culture which few are willing to explicitly argue for. This entire field of study and advocacy has not yet satisfactorily addressed the full implications of accepting the contingent and constructed character of even the most long-standing and established ways of being and believing.

As Arati Rao writes in respect of women's rights and the essentialist conception of culture:

> the notion of culture favoured by international actors must be unmasked for what it is: a falsely rigid, ahistorical, selectively chosen set of self-justificatory texts and practices whose patent partiality raises the question of exactly whose interests are being served and who comes out on top. (Rao 1995: 174)

The false conception of cultural community is also apparent in the weight many attach to the right of exit as a potential remedy to the possibility of internal oppression. As several authors have argued, the right of exit confronts individuals who are critical of some aspects of their community with a stark 'take it or leave it' option (Green 1995; Shachar 2001; Sunder 2001). By according so much remedial weight to the right of exit, theorists and practitioners contribute to a broader process which thwarts the establishment of any concerted internal deliberation and reflection upon the community's identity. Being critical is effectively dismissed as necessarily setting oneself against one's own community. The right of exit is often little more than a right to exile. As Shachar writes:

> the right of exit solution offers no comprehensive policy approach at all, and instead offers a case-by-case approach, imposing the burden of resolving conflict upon the individual – and relieving the state of any responsibility for the situation, even though, as the accommodating entity it still has a fiduciary duty toward all citizens. Specifically, the right of exit argument suggests that an injured insider should be the one to abandon the very center of her life, family, and community. (Shachar 2001: 41)

Addressing these issues in a way which seeks to avoid a blanket conclusion that women's rights and rights to cultural identity can never be reconciled requires re-engaging with our understanding of the potential role of agency, particularly women and girls' agency, in forming and reforming collective identities. No one should naïvely underestimate how difficult a task this will prove to be. Many cultural communities seem to be in the grip of what Shachar refers to as 'reactive culturalism' and an appeal to mythically pure and uncontaminated cultural norms and values. In some cases, this response may itself be fuelled by a reaction to the attempts of international agencies to establish respect for human rights norms, such as gender equality, upon communities who, for a whole range of complex reasons, perceive human rights as foreign and hostile. However, the only effective long-term approach human rights defenders should pursue in confronting such challenges is to insist upon defending a fundamental concern for enabling the effective empowerment of the disenfranchised and disempowered. It is not so much cultural identity which is inherently intolerable, but the manner in which such collective identities are formed and reformed. Ways of being and believing which seek to deny women and girls' opportunities to effectively participate in the construction of collective identities are fundamentally incompatible with human rights norms. This does not mean that all women and girls must be 'Westernised' in order to be said to genuinely enjoy their human rights. Nor does it mean, necessarily, that religious dress codes must be abolished in order to comply with the principle of gender equality. As many feminists have consistently argued, many women and girls are harmed by some 'Western' attitudes towards femininity also. No effective defence of women and girls' rights can be based upon a 'clash of civilisations' platform since no civilisation is entirely innocent or guilty of violating gender equality. There clearly is no singly true account of empowered femininity for all women and girls everywhere to emulate. However, it is undeniably the case that otherwise very different communities of women and girls across the world experience very similar violations of their human rights, as is evidenced by, amongst others, domestic violence, which I have taken as a key illustration of the challenges confronting the attempt to reconcile human rights with respect for cultural diversity. A concern for empowering women and girls entails an appeal to human rights norms and the development of spaces in which collective identities can be deliberated upon, free from the spectre of criticism and innovation being dismissed as forms of cultural disloyalty or betrayal.

Suggested reading

- Andrew Fagan, 'Cultural Harm and Determining the Limits of a Right to Cultural Identity', *Human Rights Quarterly* (forthcoming, May 2017).
- Susan Moller Okin, *Is Multiculturalism Bad for Women?* (Princeton: Princeton University Press, 1999).

- Cynthia Willett, Ellie Anderson and Diana Meyers, 'Feminist Perspectives on the Self', in Edward N. Zalta (ed.), *The Stanford Encyclopedia of Philosophy* (2015), <http://plato.stanford.edu/archives/fall2015/entries/feminism-self/> (last accessed 27 July 2016).

Notes

1. See <http://invisiblegirlproject.org/the-issue/> (last accessed 27 July 2016).
2. <http://www.unwomen.org/en/what-we-do/ending-violence-against-women/facts-and-figures> (last accessed 27 August 2016).
3. I critically analyse Kukathas's approach in Fagan (forthcoming, 2017a).
4. I discuss this example in greater detail in Chapter 7.

5

The Rights of National and Ethnic Minorities

Key questions

1. Is nationalism entirely incompatible with the purpose of human rights?
2. What are some of the key factors underlying minority rights claims?
3. Why do so many individuals continue to identify with national or ethnic communities?
4. Does recognising the existence of genocide entail recognising the existence of collective rights? If so, is this a good thing?
5. Which legal instruments in IHRL provide for a community's right to exist?
6. Within IHRL, to what does a right to self-determination entitle peoples?
7. To what extent does conceiving of national identity as an 'imagined community' help explain the power of nationalism?
8. Is liberal nationalism ultimately an oxymoronic concept?
9. Must a human right to national or ethnic identity exist only as a remedial instrument for overcoming oppression and injustice?
10. In what ways does the recognition of minority rights complicate the defence of personal autonomy?

Setting the scene

This book is committed to examining the complex relationship between two positions: respecting universal human rights norms as enshrined within international human rights law (IHRL) and recognising the value and importance of cultural belonging to countless millions, if not billions, of human beings. The preservation of existing culturally based identities is a core concern for many peoples across the world. The gradual eradication of diverse cultural communities has been recognised by many human rights agencies and human rights instruments as being entirely at odds with the objective of preserving and promoting cultural diversity as a means for upholding people's enjoyment of their human rights. The interdependency between respecting IHRL and recognising the importance of cultural belonging is enshrined within, amongst others, the UNESCO Universal Declaration on Cultural Diversity (2001). Article 4 of the Declaration states:

> the defence of cultural diversity is an ethical imperative, inseparable from respect for human dignity. It implies a commitment to human rights and fundamental freedoms, in particular the rights of persons belonging to minorities and those of indigenous peoples. No one may invoke cultural diversity to infringe upon human rights guaranteed by international law, nor to limit their scope.

While Chapter 6 will focus upon indigenous peoples, this chapter analyses what is arguably the most problematic of all minority rights claims: the claims of national and ethnic minorities to protect and preserve their collective identities against the claims of other minorities or majority populations to their identities. These claims are so problematic precisely because of the all-important stipulation contained in the final sentence of Article 4 of the UNESCO Declaration and the extent to which claims to protect existing national and ethnic communities can sometimes challenge the alliance between human rights and cultural diversity.

Anyone even vaguely familiar with the 'slaughter-bench' of relatively recent human history will be aware of the awful contributions which nationalism and the pursuit of ethnic purity have made to countless murderous human conflicts. Systematic violence and wholescale genocide have characterised a succession of nationalist and ethnically based political campaigns since the emergence of nationalism as a populist ideology in the early to mid-nineteenth century. While some nationalist and ethnic conflicts can be explained as expressions of interest-based disputes over valuable territory or resources, others seem to defy the instrumentally rationalist explanations which scholars of human conflict typically offer. Sometimes, the specific appeal to nationalist and ethnic identity appears to offer a purported justification for what is actually nothing more than an apparently persistent human impulse to inflict severe suffering upon others for the sake of doing so. As I stated earlier in Chapter 1, while the modern human rights movement was not the result of any single event and actually emerged out of a complex political environment, there can be no doubt that the Holocaust exercised a compelling moral motivation for many who sought to re-establish a global order after the catastrophe which resulted from Nazi Germany's pursuit of ethnic purification and an ever-expanding *Lebensraum* for the 'German people'. More recently, Europe has witnessed the unexpected return of ethnic cleansing during the Balkans war of the 1990s, which influenced another landmark development in IHRL with the establishment of the International Tribunal for the Former Yugoslavia and the subsequent establishment of the International Criminal Court in accordance with the 2001 Rome Statute.

Beyond Europe, ethnic cleansing was also central to the Hutus' genocidal attacks upon Tutsis in Rwanda in 1994 and to the extremely bloody conflict in Sri Lanka between the Sinhalese and the Tamils, which only recently concluded. Numerous nationalist and ethnic conflicts continue to rage across parts of Africa, the Middle East and Asia. Nationalist aspirations have taken a more political form within Europe in recent years, epitomised by the political gains made by overtly xenophobic, nationalist political parties in numerous regional, national and European elections. The protection of national frontiers appears to have re-emerged as a priority and concern for many European voters with very worrying consequences for the many refugees fleeing the identity-based conflicts in the Middle East and North Africa. It is reasonable to claim, therefore, that over the past sixty years or so, nationalism and ethnicity have exerted a persistent influence upon the development of IHRL as institutions and instruments have been created which have overtly sought to restrict the expressions of these particular forms of identity politics. Nationalism and ethnicity have all too often provided the vehicles for the very forms of gross inhumanity and barbarism which human rights exist to prevent and transcend.

The persistence of ascribed identity

The re-emergence of national and ethnic conflict directly contradicts the general trend which many had argued history would take with the demise of the Soviet system and the apparent triumph of liberal-democratic capitalism towards the end of the twentieth century. Beginning with Francis Fukuyama's somewhat timely (1989) proclamation that human history had effectively ended with the triumph of the 'West' and continuing with numerous commentators arguing that collective forms of conflict would gradually be replaced by a global pull towards various forms of individualism, it seemed reasonable, for a brief moment at least, to assume that nationalism and ethnicity would wither and die as more and more people would seek to embrace burgeoning opportunities to change their fate and pursue new life choices and 'experiments in living'. The celebration of individualism included an important element, which is best seen in Thomas Franck's highly important work, *The Empowered Self* (1999). Franck argued that domestic and international law had effectively become instruments for the protection and promotion of individuals' opportunities to autonomously pursue their own paths. He insisted that the normative legitimacy of law depended upon the law's ability to enable individuals to reject claims made upon them by class, nationality, ethnicity and the like. He considered such forms of ascribed identity as at odds with the realisation of individualism and an obstacle to individual empowerment. He focused particular attention upon nationalism and ethnicity. He stated that 'nationalism is in retreat . . . individualism has emerged . . . as an increasingly preferred alternative to self-determination imposed by nationalism's genetic, territorial imperatives' (1999: 1). In respect of any persisting forms of ascribed identity, Franck argued that the individualist challenge to nationalism and ethnic chauvinism 'consists of two related claims: first, that each individual is entitled to choose an identity reflecting personal preference; and, second, that in composing that identity, each may select more than one allegiance' (1999: 39). The emerging and triumphant form of global individualism which Franck discerned was embodied by the spread of rights-based legal systems, committed to protecting and promoting individuals' liberty to ultimately fashion their own communal allegiances and interests.

On the face of it there appears to be a great deal of common ground between Franck's laudable individualism and the normative spirit which underlies IHRL. Nationalism and ethnicity have all too often been the direct enemies of IHRL. One may reasonably question whether human rights would even have emerged as a dominant global discourse without the terrible impetus of national and ethnic hatred. Human rights exist, in large part, to protect individuals against such potentially harmful collective forces. Thus, human rights are deeply committed to protecting the moral and physical sovereignty of separate individual human beings. As we have discussed above (and will return to again below) human rights have been conventionally applied only to individual human beings and have been explicitly denied as capable of belonging to a collective, as such. Finally, for many defenders and critics alike, human rights have been consistently defended on the grounds that they provide the means by which oppressive (because collective) ways of being and believing can be challenged and changed as the spirit of Enlightenment individualism diffuses across the globe. For many, human rights are a doctrine which is utterly incompatible with the kinds of forces which underpin the allegedly waning appeal of national and ethnic forms of belonging and identity. On this view, supporting human rights necessarily commits one to defending the kind of individualism which Franck espoused. Human rights is founded, in large part, upon the ideal of individual liberty. Ascribed identities are considered by many to be incompatible with the ideal of individual liberty and so human rights should not, so the argument runs, be used to prop up or promote any such claims to identity.

Human rights have been the subject of repeated and pervasive misinterpretation and misunderstanding. Defenders and critics of human rights alike have persistently misattributed a common normative identity and purpose to IHRL in arguing that the doctrine is singularly committed to, for example, a specific form of, what I shall refer to as, naïve individualism. As I argued in Chapter 1, the specific content of IHRL has not unfolded, and does not unfold, in accordance with the dictates of a single philosophically normative vision. IHRL is not solely the offspring of Kant, or Locke, or liberal-democracy, or Enlightenment individualism. IHRL reflects and is directly shaped by multiple forces, which have no single and unifying objective or purpose in common. We might conceivably seek to fundamentally reshape the content of IHRL to better fit the kind of individualism espoused by the likes of Franck but, if we were successful, what we would be left with would be very different to what IHRL currently consists of. We would also, despite Franck's (and many others') claims to the contrary, be left with a body of IHRL which simply ignored the continuing concerns and interests of vast swathes of humankind across the globe. Whatever one thinks of the normative appeal of Franck's understanding of individualism, it is simply empirically wrong to claim that human beings have rejected the appeal of ascribed forms of national and ethnic identity and have turned resolutely towards the ethic of making and remaking one's self in defiance of communal and social expectations. The existence and development of a distinct body of IHRL that is directly concerned with protecting and promoting individuals' access to their own national and ethnic communities testifies to the extent to which nationalism and ethnicity remain central to the lives of countless numbers of human beings. The persistence of national and ethnic interests does not signal the defeat or superfluity of individualism, but does signal the extent to which any analysis of this area of human rights has to proceed without the support of simplistic dogma. Naïve individualism, which is principally characterised by a refusal to recognise the persistence and force of ascribed forms of identity, is not helpful in enabling human rights to engage with the actual world and the ways in which actual human beings pursue their manifest interests. Human rights are a multifaceted doctrine and IHRL continues to respond to a variety of deeply complex phenomena, which prevent reducing the doctrine to a single substantively normative vision or perspective.

The entire project, if we can name it so, of a human rights-based espousal of cultural diversity entails conceiving of the basis of individuals' identities in more sophisticated terms than those which merely insist upon the allegedly and infinite malleability of any individual's personal identity. Much, perhaps even the majority, of humankind does not embrace the vision of individuals' capacity to persistently experiment with their own lives in emulation of some Modernist European intellectual or artist. While the espousal of cultural diversity is clearly incompatible with mass social conformism (in its various manifestations), human rights institutions and instruments have consistently sought to uphold the value of existing communities, whose differences, in part, are precisely based upon their rejection of a purportedly 'Western' brand of individualism. The human rights mantra insists that no culture can claim rights to ways of being and believing that pose a threat to others' human rights. However, the promotion of cultural diversity extends to include recognition for communities in which individual members' identities are more accurately considered to be ascribed, rather than voluntary, in nature. To simply denounce all and any ostensibly ascribed forms of identity would greatly reduce the size of the human rights 'tent' within which diverse communities are invited to co-exist and would make a mockery of the espousal of cultural diversity. However, as I shall discuss in greater detail below, the recognition of ascribed identities by IHRL is very problematic.

Minority rights have become a central component of IHRL and have significantly influenced human rights theorising. In many respects, the justification for minority rights rests upon a premise which naïve individualism rejects, and, in so doing, exemplifies a core area of concern for a human rights-based approach to identity. The need for minority rights arises out of a combination of individuals' deep identification with a specific community and others' hostility towards said community. It seems entirely absurd to suggest that passionate supporters of opera should be accorded minority rights protection in an age where mainstream cultural tastes are increasingly less 'sophisticated' and opera-goers have become an endangered minority in many places. Minority lifestyle choices should not be compensated for by rights protection for the simple reason that, all other things being equal, the adverse effects of such choices can be avoided by individuals pursuing less costly lifestyles. Minority rights claims can only emerge under conditions where individuals' core 'choices' cannot so easily be altered and where it is somehow wrong to imagine the costly identification can be readily exchanged for a more instrumentally rational cultural allegiance. Many of us have come to intuitively think that it is simply wrong to ask a member of a discriminated-against ethnic minority to renounce his or her identity in order to avoid the discrimination. Some aspects of many individuals' identities are not amenable to such manipulation. The existence of minority rights indicates the extent to which IHRL has encompassed an acknowledgement of some forms of identity which cannot be changed with the ease with which one's clothes can be changed.

Following on from the above point, naïve individualism would really only require the existence of one human right: freedom of association as broadly encompassed within Article 22 of the ICCPR to ensure the protection of forming, de-forming and reforming communities of individuals. As Chandran Kukathas (2003) has argued, when we conceive of individual identity as based upon voluntary choices and commitments, we are bound to reject a number of claims which advocates of rights to cultural identity typically make. For Kukathas, freedom of association (and its necessary correlate, dissociation) accords the tasks of forming, maintaining and altering the identity of communities entirely to the individual members of those communities. Kukathas insists that while opportunity costs may differ for different individuals, each individual will always retain the capacity to leave any community they are a member of. On this view, no identity is entirely ascribed and the duty of the state extends only to include preventing communities from formally denying individuals' right to leave. Other cultural rights are not, for Kukathas, justifiable since no community ultimately exists separately from its individual members and no individual is formally compelled to remain a member of any community. Individuals should not thereby be entitled to specific rights to national or ethnically based ways of being and believing. On Kukathas's reading, no community has a distinct right to exist and individuals who continue to identify with 'impoverished' communities must bear the costs of their choice. Minority rights are thereby rejected for seeking to provide unwarranted compensation for avoidable costs.

The promotion of cultural diversity, the establishment of minority rights and the extension of rights protection to more than simply a single right of freedom of association all testify to the extent to which human rights cannot be simply condemned for postulating a form of naïve individualism, nor can human rights be easily accused of ignoring the social context, or ground, upon which and out of which IHRL is founded and develops. Human rights has responded and continues to respond to identity-based claims to an extent which belies the attempts by the likes of Makau Mutua (2002) to characterise the doctrine as beset by the limitations of naïve individualism. However, the prevailing approach within much human rights thinking and legislating seeks to walk a very difficult path, between recognising that rights to identity are apparently required precisely because many individuals inherit much of what makes them who they are from their national and ethnic communities, whilst insisting that all human rights must ultimately comply with the ideal of individual liberty. The remainder of this chapter examines whether it is possible to coherently square this circle.

Rights in question

This section will present and analyse the existing and extensive body of IHRL which is specifically concerned with the rights of national and ethnic minorities. I will do so by drawing upon the detailed framework which Patrick Thornberry (1991) has provided in his highly influential study of minority rights. Thornberry identified three categories of such rights:

1. A national and ethnic minority community's right to freely exist.
2. A national and ethnic minority community's right to express their collective identity.
3. A national and ethnic minority community's rights to non-discrimination and equality.

A right to freely exist

The establishment of a community's right to freely exist does not, necessarily, imply the need for collective rights (which I shall discuss below). However, it does depart from the kind of naïve individualism I discussed above and which is exemplified by Kukathas's (2003) discussion of rights. A right to exist as a national or ethnic minority unequivocally entails recognising that such communities exist in ways which cannot be merely reduced to the individual characteristics of their individual members. The first clear formulation of the right of a community to freely exist can be found in the 1948 UN Convention on the Prevention and Punishment of the Crime of Genocide. Specifically, Article 2 states:

> in the present Convention, genocide means any of the following acts committed with intent to destroy, in whole or in part, a national, ethnical, racial or religious group, as such:
> (a) Killing members of the group;
> (b) Causing serious bodily or mental harm to members of the group;
> (c) Deliberately inflicting on the group conditions of life calculated to bring about its physical destruction in whole or in part;
> (d) Imposing measures intended to prevent births within the group;
> (e) Forcibly transferring children of the group to another group.

In identifying genocide as the attempt to destroy national, ethnic, racial or religious groups, Article 2 establishes a right of such groups to freely exist as such. Absent the existence of the group and one is left with mere acts of criminal assault and murder against individuals, whose identity may be dismissed as immaterial to the offence.

After the Genocide Convention, Article 1 of the ICCPR provides another legal expression of the right of a community to freely exist. The article states, 'all peoples have the right of self-determination. By virtue of that right they freely determine their political status and freely pursue their economic, social and cultural development.' The reference to 'peoples' rather than individuals, or persons, is particularly important and is intended to refer to communities of individuals. The treaty body of the ICCPR underlined the fundamental importance of Article 1 through their issuing of General Comment 12 (1984), which offered the following interpretation of the scope and significance of the article:

> in accordance with the purposes and principles of the Charter of the United Nations, Article 1 of the International Covenant on Civil and Political Rights recognizes that all peoples have the right of self-determination. The right of self-determination is of particular importance because its realization is an essential condition for the effective guarantee and observance of individual human rights and for the promotion and strengthening of those rights.

In essence, a people's right to self-determination is a necessary condition for individuals' enjoyment of all other human rights.

An individual's right to a nationality is recognised in several international and regional instruments, such as Article 15 of the UDHR. It is also protected by Article 24(3) of the ICCPR, which is specifically concerned with children's right to acquire a nationality. Clearly, a right to nationality generally entails the legal recognition of existence of nationalities in the first instance.

Beyond UN treaties, a people's right to freely exist is also recognised in the African Charter on Human and Peoples' Rights. Thus, Article 20 declares that:

1. All peoples shall have the right to existence. They shall have the unquestionable and inalienable right to self-determination. They shall freely determine their political status and shall pursue their economic and social development according to the policy they have freely chosen.
2. Colonized or oppressed peoples shall have the right to free themselves from the bonds of domination by resorting to any means recognized by the international community.

3. All peoples shall have the right to the assistance of the States parties to the present Charter in their liberation struggle against foreign domination, be it political, economic or cultural.

The African Charter has particularly spearheaded the promotion of national and ethnic minorities' rights to freely exist as distinct groups. However, it is reasonable to claim, particularly given the continuing ethnic and tribal conflict which rages through several nation-states in Africa, that Article 20 was not agreed upon by member states of the African Union in order to encourage successionist attempts to break away from some of those self-same states.

Within the European context, the Council of Europe has developed the Framework Convention on the Protection of National Minorities, which is widely recognised as the world's most detailed and comprehensive legal framework for minority rights. Article 1 states that 'the protection of national minorities and of the rights and freedoms of persons belonging to those minorities forms an integral part of the international protection of human rights, and as such falls within the scope of international co-operation'.

From the above, it is clear that national and ethnic communities possess a right to exist through several instruments of international and regional human rights law.

A right to express collective identity

The principal source of the right of national and ethnic communities to express their collective identities is Article 27 of the ICCPR, which declares:

in those States in which ethnic, religious or linguistic minorities exist, persons belonging to such minorities shall not be denied the right, in community with the other members of their group, to enjoy their own culture, to profess and practise their own religion, or to use their own language.

Note that the right is framed in distinctly negative terms, which requires of states not to *deny* such groups the enjoyment of their culture. On the face of it, Article 27 does not impose more positive duties upon states to actively support national and ethnic minorities' opportunities to practise their customs and traditions.

The Council of Europe's Framework Convention on Minorities formulates the right of communities to express their collective identity in terms which do impose positive duties upon states parties. Thus, Article 5 states that 'the Parties undertake to promote the conditions necessary for persons belonging to national minorities to maintain and develop their culture, and to preserve the essential elements of their identity, namely their religion, language, traditions and cultural heritage'. Article 15 extends this right to include minority communities' engagement in the broadly public sphere by stipulating that 'the Parties shall create the conditions necessary for the effective participation of persons belonging to national minorities in cultural, social and economic life and in public affairs, in particular those affecting them'.

The most detailed formulation of national and ethnic communities' right to express their identities in the private and public spheres is found in the albeit non-legally binding UN Declaration on the Rights of Persons Belonging to National or Ethnic, Religious and Linguistic Minorities (1992). Specifically, Article 2 provides a comprehensive stipulation of what a right to identity covers. Thus:

1. Persons belonging to national or ethnic, religious and linguistic minorities (hereinafter referred to as persons belonging to minorities) have the right to enjoy their own culture, to profess and practise their own religion, and to use their own language, in private and in public, freely and without interference or any form of discrimination.
2. Persons belonging to minorities have the right to participate effectively in cultural, religious, social, economic and public life.
3. Persons belonging to minorities have the right to participate effectively in decisions on the national and, where appropriate, regional level concerning the minority to which they belong or the regions in which they live, in a manner not incompatible with national legislation.
4. Persons belonging to minorities have the right to establish and maintain their own associations.

5. Persons belonging to minorities have the right to establish and maintain, without any discrimination, free and peaceful contacts with other members of their group and with persons belonging to other minorities, as well as contacts across frontiers with citizens of other States to whom they are related by national or ethnic, religious or linguistic ties.

Article 4(2) of the same declaration acknowledges the need to identify clear limitations to any community's expression of its identity and declares that:

States shall take measures to create favourable conditions to enable persons belonging to minorities to express their characteristics and to develop their culture, language, religion, traditions and customs, except where specific practices are in violation of national law and contrary to international standards.

It is clear that national and ethnic communities do enjoy rights to express their collective identities through numerous international and regional human rights law and instruments.

Rights to non-discrimination

IHRL accords fundamental rights of non-discrimination to individuals through many core instruments. The specific rights of national and ethnic communities to non-discrimination are fewer in number but are an established feature of IHRL. Thus, Article 20(2) of the ICCPR states that 'any advocacy of national, racial or religious hatred that constitutes incitement to discrimination, hostility or violence shall be prohibited by law'. Article 1 of the UN International Convention on the Elimination of All Forms of Racial Discrimination states:

in this Convention, the term 'racial discrimination' shall mean any distinction, exclusion, restriction or preference based on race, colour, descent, or national or ethnic origin which has the purpose or effect of nullifying or impairing the recognition, enjoyment or exercise, on an equal footing, of human rights and fundamental freedoms in the political, economic, social, cultural or any other field of public life.

Within regional human rights systems, Article 14 of the European Convention on Human Rights (ECHR) explicitly prohibits discrimination in the following terms:

> the enjoyment of the rights and freedoms set forth in this Convention shall be secured without discrimination on any ground such as sex, race, colour, language, religion, political or other opinion, national or social origin, association with a national minority, property, birth or other status.

Article 19 of the African Charter declares that 'all peoples shall be equal; they shall enjoy the same respect and shall have the same rights. Nothing shall justify the domination of a people by another'.

Having established the existence of distinct rights of national and ethnic minorities to exist, to express their collective identities and to be free from discrimination, I shall now analyse this body of IHRL. Specifically, I shall answer two distinct questions: (1) who possesses national and ethnic minority rights? and (2) how can these rights be justified?

Who possesses national and ethnic minority rights?

The obvious answer to the above question is, of course, that national and ethnic minorities possess the rights which I outlined in the previous section. A more substantial answer, however, requires a more complex and detailed analysis.

The phrase 'peoples' is typically found within those covenants, treaties, instruments and declarations that are directly concerned with the rights of national and ethnic minorities. Interestingly, there is no definitive, legally authoritative understanding of what constitutes a 'people'. Article 1 of the International Convention on the Elimination of All Forms of Racial Discrimination (ICERD) and Article 2 of the Genocide Convention explicitly include national, ethnic and racial groups under the category of 'peoples'. The Council of Europe's Framework Convention on Minorities acknowledges that the convention does not include a definition of what constitutes a 'national minority'. The International Court of Justice's (1975) *Western Sahara* Advisory Opinion extended the category of who could rightfully claim statehood from a nation to a 'people'. In its General Comment 23

(1994) on Article 27 of the ICCPR (the 'minority rights' article) the Committee for Civil and Political Rights (CCPR) offered the following view on who could legitimately claim protection under the right: 'the terms used in Article 27 indicate that the persons designed to be protected are those who belong to a group and who share in common a culture, a religion and/or a language'. The reference to the term 'belong' in General Comment 23 is deeply significant and frequently recurs in other instruments. Thus, Article 2(1) of the UN Declaration on the Rights of Persons Belonging to National or Ethnic, Religious and Linguistic Minorities (1992) identifies the terms of the declaration as applying to 'persons belonging to national or ethnic, religious and linguistic minorities (hereinafter referred to as persons belonging to minorities)'. Similarly, Article 1 of the Council of Europe's Framework Convention on Minorities states, 'the protection of national minorities and of the rights and freedoms of persons belonging to those minorities forms an integral part of the international protection of human rights'.

The rights of national and ethnic minorities are typically intended to apply only to members of such communities. Rights to practise a community's traditions and customs, or to exclusive use of land and territory, or to speak the native language are rights which are intended to be possessed and enjoyed only by identifiable members of the communities which enjoy such legal protection. Minority rights are intended to benefit members of minority communities. It is therefore imperative that the legal bodies charged with upholding access to these rights are able to correctly identify who rightfully belongs to any such community. It is fair to say that no such definitive criteria for community membership generally have been identified within IHRL and this whole area may be described as 'work in progress'. There is no single, legally agreed upon definition of what a 'sense of belonging' must comprise and the entire area of legally determining the membership criteria for any legally recognised community is deeply problematic. An obvious example of this can be seen in respect of the criteria for determining nationality.

There is no single basis for acquiring citizenship within international law. Thus, in respect of determining a child's right to a nationality under Article 24(3) of the ICCPR there are two quite different approaches which different states endorse: *jus sanguinis* (the law of the state of nationality of the parents(s) or earlier ancestry), and *jus soli*

(the child's state of birth). Beyond the rights of a newborn child, some
states allow for the acquisition of citizenship through naturalisation,
whereas others do not. Similarly, some states recognise the dual or
multi-citizenship entitlements of their citizens while other states do
not. Given the complexities for determining membership of the foremost bounded community within international law, it should come
as little surprise that the field of minority rights lacks clear criteria for
determining any individual's legitimate claims to belong to a national
or ethnic minority.

The task of identifying criteria for membership of a community
extends to the very heart of the larger issue surrounding the very
basis for identity claims and, specifically, the enduring concerns over
voluntary as opposed to ascribed identities. An individual's membership of a national or ethnic community is not typically like his
or her membership of many other associations. To give an example,
Myanmar/Burma is one of the most ethnically diverse countries
in the world. The 2008 constitution formally recognises that there
are six different nations and 135 different ethnic groups that reside
within the sovereign territory of that country. The importance which
the constitution accords to national and ethnic identity reflects the
sheer weight and significance which many citizens accord to their
own (and others') identity. Many people in Myanmar/Burma define
themselves and their interests in accordance with the collective attributes and characteristics of the national or ethnic community they
have been born into. A broad range of other associations and group-
ings are constituted along national and ethnic lines, such as political
parties, cultural clubs, development projects and the like. Changing
one's national or ethnic identity is utterly inconceivable for most, as is
the idea that outsiders may be able to unilaterally claim membership
of another community. Identity is, thus, quintessentially ascriptive in
character.

Myanmar/Burma's experience of national and ethnic identity can
be found in many other parts of the world and is certainly not unique
or particularly extreme in this respect. One obvious conclusion to be
drawn from this is the following: membership of a national or ethnic
community may be voluntarily renounced by individuals but it cannot
be acquired through the mere exercise of an individual's will. I personally have German and Irish parentage. No matter how much I will it
to be so, I will never be legitimately accepted as rightfully belonging to

any of the myriad ethnic communities which populate the African continent, for example. Nor, as a white-skinned male, will I ever be able to legitimately claim protection by US federal employment laws intended to protect the employment opportunities of African-Americans. All of this will appear self-evidently true and uncontroversial to many. The common-sense usage and understanding of national and ethnic identity is, I think it is fair to say, best understood as generally ascriptive in character and does not support the view that anyone can claim membership of any national or ethnic community that catches their fancy, so to speak. More importantly perhaps, nor is it typically possible for many members of national and ethnic minority communities to avoid discrimination and hostility by simply renouncing their association with the vilified group.

The body of IHRL concerned with national and ethnic minority rights is not so clear on this issue. As I discussed in Chapter 1, human rights generally is based upon the ideal of individual liberty. The ideal of individual liberty is enshrined in various minority rights instruments. For example, Article 3(1) of the Council of Europe's Framework Convention on Minorities states:

> every person belonging to a national minority shall have the right freely to choose to be treated or not to be treated as such and no disadvantage shall result from this choice or from the exercise of the rights which are connected to that choice.

On this basis, IHRL cannot be used to force any individual member of a national or ethnic community to remain a recognised member of the community or, one assumes, to be forced to share in any of the benefits and protections which may be afforded the community. However, the sense in which 'every person belonging to a national minority' is to be understood does not reduce to the mere discretion of individuals' preferences. The recognition of one's membership of a national minority precedes any individual member's state of consciousness. Ascribed identity, generally, is central to IHRL's engagement with national and minority rights.

The existence of ascribed forms of national and ethnic identities also figures in a wider concern with the general capacity of individualist-based constitutional systems to adequately provide for the specific interests of many national and ethnic communities. Some authors, such as Vernon Van Dyke, have gone so far as to argue that 'liberalism cannot be trusted to deal adequately with the question of status and rights for ethnic communities' (1995: 32). Like other authors whose arguments I shall consider in greater detail below, Van Dyke (1995) argues that liberalism's normative adherence to an account of the individual agent as ultimately capable of voluntarily acquiring and affirming any and all identity-based commitments is empirically false and renders any such liberal rights-based approach incapable of effectively understanding and providing for many ethnic communities' interests and needs. Van Dyke insists that many members of many ethnic communities do not conceive of themselves as morally separable from or independent of their communities. The established presence of ethnic communities within states requires, he argues, the legal recognition that there exists an intermediate level of agency between that of the state and the individual. Providing adequately for the core interests of individual members of many ethnic communities requires the state's protection of the collective rights of such ethnic communities. These rights should extend, he argues, to degrees of self-determination over those areas of the communities' collective life, so to speak, that are central to sustaining the core and collective identity of the community. He is careful, however, to insist that rights to collective self-determination do not amount to a right to succession.

   Van Dyke's position takes literally the collective category of a 'people' as enshrined within IHRL and draws the conclusion that national and ethnic minority rights must therefore be collective rights if they are to perform the task they are intended for: protecting the members of vulnerable communities. The meaning of 'collective right' here is precisely a right which is possessed by the collective and which is not ultimately reducible to individual members of the community who otherwise would separately possess the right. As I discussed in Chapter 3, the concept of collective rights is deeply problematic within human rights thinking. Despite the conceptual challenges, there are clear precedents for some form of acceptance of collective rights within IHRL. Most notably, the African Charter on Human and Peoples' Rights explicitly acknowledges the need for collective rights in its very title. Peoples' rights are simultaneously human rights but also possessed by a group of human beings qua group. Similarly, collective human rights have been recognised by the European Parliament through a

Parliamentary Recommendation to the European Court of Human Rights which stated:

> national minorities [have the rights] to be recognized as such by the states in which they live; to maintain their own educational, religious and cultural institutions; to participate fully in decision-making about matters which affect the preservation and development of their identity and in the implementation of those decisions.[1]

Some authors (e.g. Jovanović 2005) have argued that the Genocide Convention rests upon a necessary commitment to the notion of a community possessing a collective right since it is not the singular and separate rights of each individual member which genocide violates, but the collective rights of the community qua community. As Joseph Raz has argued in respect of any group's claims to a right to self-determination, 'the interest of any one of them is an inadequate ground for holding others to be duty-bound to satisfy that interest. The right rests on the cumulative interests of many individuals' (1986: 209).

Against this, the Council of Europe's Framework Convention on Minorities explicitly rejects the claim that minority rights entail the recognition of collective rights. Thus, in the background and explanatory notes to the terms of the Convention, it is stated that Article 3(2) 'does not imply the recognition of collective rights. The emphasis is placed on the protection of persons belonging to national minorities, who may exercise their rights individually and in community with others'. In this highly significant respect, the Convention is in line with many other international instruments which directly address minority rights. For example, the CCPR's General Comment 23 clarifies that, while minority cultures are protected by Article 27 of the ICCPR, individual members of minority cultures and not those cultures themselves are the bearers of the right.

It is reasonable to conclude that, in actual fact, the answer to what looks like a simple enough question – who possesses national and ethnic minority rights? – is rather complex and unclear. What is generally agreed is that the right is possessed by a people who exist as a national or ethnic minority. Any individual member's legitimate claim to enjoy the benefits of minority rights protection is dependent upon their membership of the community in question. Numerous legal instruments refer to a sense of belonging as crucial to determining membership criteria but there are no agreed upon criteria for what any such sense of belonging must objectively, or even phenomenologically, consist of. While members retain the right to exit or renounce their membership, the ascribed nature of much national and ethnic identity complicates individuals' claims to belong to any particular community. Finally, international legal instruments take different positions upon the question of whether national and ethnic minority rights can be secured without the need for collective rights.

How can these rights be justified?

The mere existence of a human community does not, by itself, justify protecting and promoting those elements of the community that are considered to constitute the collective identity of the community by those who are ostensibly most affected by the community: its members. Individual members of any community will continue to possess their fundamental human rights entitlements, irrespective of the additional rights protections offered to their communities through IHRL. However, a core aspect of the entire justification for national and ethnic minority rights is precisely that the conventional exclusion of any legal consideration for factors such as national and ethnic identities is harmful to those individuals whose core interests and well-being are directly affected by their national and ethnic identities. Put simply, that IHRL cannot adopt a position of principled blindness to those forms of identity since others' targeting of them can have such devastating effects upon those who bear them and their enjoyment of their human rights. This argument is central to all identity-based rights claims. In many cases, the argument appears morally benign when it is applied to overt communities of victims, whose fate has been exacerbated by the generally 'colour-blind' commitments of many legal instruments. It becomes far more problematic when it is applied to communities whose moral value is less clear. After all, many rightly see nationalism and ethnic pride as containing a terrible potential for causing great harm to others: an appeal to protecting national and ethnic identity has often been at the heart of many instances of gross and systematic human rights violations.

The twentieth-century intellectual Karl Popper spoke for many when he characterised nationalism in the following terms: it appeals 'to our tribal instincts, to passion and to prejudice, and to our nostalgic desire to be relieved from the strain of individual responsibility which it attempts to replace by a collective or group responsibility' (1962: 49). Another towering intellectual figure of the twentieth century, Isaiah Berlin, warned against the danger of failing to distinguish between collective self-determination and individual self-rule by projecting himself into the position of someone who seeks collective emancipation. Berlin wrote:

> I wish for the emancipation of my entire class, or community, or nation, or race, or profession. So much can I desire this, that I may, in my bitter longing for status, prefer to be bullied and misgoverned by my own race or social class. (Berlin 1969: 157–8)

Popper and Berlin committed their professional and intellectual lives to the defence of a form of individualism which, they thought, would counter collectivist forces and prevent more terrible acts of collective murder from taking place.

The hopes of Popper and Berlin appeared to have been encouraged by later, albeit more sober, statements regarding the waning appeal of national and ethnic ties of belonging. Thus, leading contributors to cosmopolitanism described the world as becoming increasingly 'post-national' in character (Habermas 2001). Based in part upon the diffusion of the legal institutions of human rights and the apparent successes of regional political and trading blocs, such as the European Union, many accepted the premise that national and ethnic forms of identity would become largely irrelevant to an ever-expanding, globalised community of human beings. Whatever one's opinion of the moral appeal of post-nationalism, predictions of the necessary demise of national and ethnic identity have clearly proven to be, at best, premature for many peoples across the world. It is well beyond the scope of this book to offer an account for why the 'post-national constellation', as Habermas referred to it, has not materialised. However, it is necessary to consider the basis of national and ethnic identity construction in order to explain the persisting attraction of such identities for so many.

Many sociologists and historians of nationalism and ethnicity have argued that all such forms of identity are ultimately constructions and fabrications. This way of thinking corresponds to a wider anti-essentialist trend within broader academic analyses of cultural identity, which I have discussed above. Thus, Ernest Gellner (1983) argued that nations and nationalism were material constructions which owed their existence and appeal to broader, structural forces of modernisation which have been driving many human developments since the late eighteenth and early nineteenth centuries in Europe. Nationalism does not originate in the *Blut and Boden* (blood and soil) of many who defended it. Benedict Anderson (1991) developed upon the materialist and anti-essentialist analysis of nationalism in his study of how various developments (the creation of newspapers, for example) enabled peoples to begin to imagine the existence of purportedly unified national communities. For Anderson, the nation is a thoroughly 'imagined community'. Finally, Fredrik Barth (1989) identified what he considered to be the situational basis to many forms of ethnic identity. Against those who discerned primordial constituents of some forms of ethnicity, Barth argued that the basis and boundaries of many ethnic identities are persistently shifting and changing. Ethnicity is a fabricated reality.

Much of the scholarship underlying such writings has been meticulous and worthy of deep professional respect. However, the precise account of the constructed and malleable basis of national and ethnic identity which this scholarship provides bears little resemblance to the ways in which those who endorse their 'imagined communities' actually think of their own identities. The academic task of deconstructing these specific collective forms of identity departs significantly from the self-perceptions and phenomenology of many of those human beings who bear and sustain their national and ethnic identities. One may be tempted to simply dismiss the persistence of such commitments as mere false consciousness, but this is unlikely to diminish the pull of nationalism and ethnicity for many.

An alternative account of the basis for national and ethnic identity has been provided by Anthony Smith (1986, 1996). Smith's account has attracted a significant amount of academic criticism. However, his account more closely resembles the phenomenology of national and ethnic identity for many and, as such, may also be thought of as providing a more compelling defence of some forms of national and ethnicity minority rights claims.

Smith's account of the basis for national and ethnic identity rejects the constructivist arguments offered by the likes of Anderson and Barth, which he criticises for presenting national and ethnic identity as 'plastic and malleable' (1996: 446). He also rejects what he considers to be the instrumentalist account defended by the likes of Gellner. Smith argues that such forms of identity pre-date the emergence of the kind of structural forces and conditions which Gellner views as underlying nationalism. Smith's account may also be contrasted with other accounts which are more sympathetic to some forms of nationalism and ethnicity but which posit an entirely inter-subjectivist basis to such identities. Thus, Hugh Seton-Watson defines a nation as existing where 'a significant number of people in a community consider themselves to form a nation, or behave as if they formed one' (1977: 7). Seton-Watson's definition excludes any reference to purportedly objective elements underlying the formation of a shared sense of national identity and appears to anticipate Anderson's later characterisation of nations as 'imagined communities'. For his part, Smith argues that forms of shared national identity originate in and appeal to what he refers to as an 'ethnie', which he presents as a substrate of many nations. He defines an ethnie as 'a named human population of alleged common ancestry, shared memories and elements of a common culture with a link to a specific territory and a measure of solidarity' (1996: 447). Smith argues that the appeal of national and ethnic identities would never have been so effective (and often so terribly damaging) if they had been merely based upon forms of false consciousness and utterly contingent conditions and constructs.

Smith's essentialist account of the basis and appeal of national and ethnic ties explicitly presents an objectivist alternative to those accounts which posit a subjective basis to any such forms of collective identity. Other contributors to the literature on the justification of collective identity rights-based claims have defended a similarly objectivist account. For example, the foremost advocate of so-called liberal nationalism, Yael Tamir, has argued that 'a group is defined as a nation if it exhibits both a sufficient number of shared, objective characteristics – such as language, history, or territory – and self-awareness of its distinctiveness' (1993: 66). One may also consider Margalit and Raz's (1990) account of national identity (which I discussed in Chapter 3) as comprising objectivist components, which precede the subjective experience of individual members of the community.

For present purposes, the claims of Smith, Tamir, Margalit and Raz offer stronger phenomenological justification for the rights-based claims of those who understand their own national and ethnic identities as

based upon ascribed, and not contingent, characteristics. As such, they
also resonate forcefully with the broader tradition of thinking, referred
to as the 'politics of recognition', which I discussed in an earlier chapter
and which has been central to the entire project of identity-based rights
claims. Specific rights of national and ethnic minorities to exist and to
prosper can only be justified on grounds which include the practical
difficulty or sheer unreasonableness of requiring that discriminated-
against individuals simply renounce their identities in order to avoid the
discrimination and hostility to which they are subjected. Demanding
that minorities assimilate into the majority community utterly fails to
recognise the depth and significance of many people's commitment to
their specific identities. Even if it is practically possible or legally permissible to do so, many people consider the possibility of changing their
national or ethnic identity to be literally inconceivable. David Horowitz,
a leading political scientist of ethnicity, expresses this point eloquently:

> Ethnic affiliations typically fulfil needs that might otherwise go
> unmet. What some such functions might be is hinted at in a general
> way by the conception of an ethnic group as a greatly extended
> family, a unit that provides blood solidarity and personalistic help
> in an increasingly impersonal environment – in short, ascription in
> an ostensibly nonascriptive world. (Horowitz 2001: 74)

Minority rights claims to national and ethnic identities are justified
on the grounds that many such forms of identity cannot be simply
renounced or rejected by those who bear them. Many individuals experience discrimination and hostility precisely because of the attitudes
which others hold towards them: for the law to ignore identity is merely
to ignore the harms which are inflicted upon many by those who target
their identities. Identity-based rights claims have a deeply remedial
(or protective) function to the extent that they exist in order to protect
potential victims from systematic and identity-based discrimination
and hostility. The protective motivation for such rights is intended,
in part, to deny similar rights claims to those groups who would then
use their rights to harm others. Recall that one of the core maxims of
IHRL is that no right can be justifiably possessed if its exercise violates
the human rights of others. The fundamental normative motivation for
the entire promotion of a human rights-based commitment to cultural
diversity is, after all, to defend communities' human rights, not to

enable some to deny others' their equal right to recognition. For those who support the spirit of promoting cultural diversity, it seems reasonable to conclude that national and ethnic minorities are thoroughly entitled to rights-based protection and that there remains little more to be said on the subject. However, having summarised the content of the relevant IHRL in this area and discussed both who can claim identity-based rights and how these claims may be normatively justified, I must now turn to consider several areas of the IHRL of national and ethnic minorities which are typically overlooked but which nevertheless affect understandings and implementations of these rights.

Conceptual and practical concerns

I argued in Chapter 1 that there are few, if any, good reasons to seek to fundamentally revise or reshape the content of IHRL, in spite of the fact that many philosophical analyses of IHRL would have precisely that effect. One suspects that any reduction in the content of IHRL would have little impact upon those academic authors who propose such a course of action and would have far greater consequences for many of those who are more exposed to the abuse of power and privilege. I take the same approach in respect of the IHRL of national and ethnic minorities and thus generally endorse existing international and regional provisions. However, there are several areas which warrant a closer analysis in order to strengthen existing instruments. Each of these areas is effectively integral to the theory and practice of the existing IHRL of national and ethnic minorities. I begin with an enduring question concerning individualism.

Individualism and ties that bind

The philosophy of individualism has exerted a profound influence upon the emergence and development of IHRL. Generally speaking, the greater part of IHRL aims to protect and promote the purportedly inherent rights of individual human beings. Since the emergence of the modern human rights movement in the immediate aftermath of the Second World War decades passed without any concertedly critical analysis of the universal appeal of ethical individualism. However, ethical individualism within human rights is increasingly questioned and scrutinised, particularly by those who aim to achieve a better reconciliation between cultural diversity and human rights. Many communities across the world do not embrace individualism. Indeed, many emancipatory projects have been based upon an appeal to collective forms of self-determination, as was abundantly clear from many of the anti-colonial movements of the 1960s and 1970s. Individualism has often not been the driving force for oppressed peoples' pursuit of emancipation. The continuing appeal of national and ethnic minority rights for many groups of people represents a continuation of this emancipatory spirit. As the phrase goes, 'I cannot be free, unless we are all free.' The inclusion of such rights within IHRL may be partially justified precisely by this appeal to emancipation but it also has the effect of incorporating some collectivist spirit within what is otherwise a largely individualist doctrine. There are many implications of this, ranging from relatively abstract considerations of the basis of human rights through to far more practical concerns over the implementation of such rights in particular contexts.

At the most abstract level, the inclusion of national and ethnic minority rights within IHRL entails a reconsideration of the largely contractarian assumptions upon which many philosophical justifications of human rights have been based. Broadly speaking, a contractarian account of human rights, exemplified by the work of, for example, Thomas Scanlon (1998), argues that an institutional framework of human rights can be derived from the bottom up by identifying what sufficiently rational and free individuals would agree to. Political and legal systems, on this approach, fundamentally reflect the core interests of those who are subject to the jurisdiction of any political community. Central to the thoroughly hypothetical vision which contractarians trade upon is the myth of the rational individual agent who is sufficiently unencumbered by commitments and partial affiliations and thus capable of determining his or her own will prior to any socialisation. On the contractarian approach, all identity is voluntarily acquired and there can be no such thing, really and truly speaking, as ascribed identities.

Whatever its normative appeal to its supporters, it is clear that the contractarian approach has little to commend it to the advocates of national and ethnic minority rights. Such communities are not phenomenologically experienced by many of their members as mere associations of entirely unencumbered and voluntary agents. National and ethnic minorities do not, in any sociologically sound sense, emerge out of quasi-contractual negotiations between otherwise unrelated individuals. Indeed, one could drive this point further and question the broader appeal of the contractarian vision of any political community. One may reasonably speculate whether mutually reciprocal legal and ethical commitments between individual members of any given political community or society are better served by the promotion of some more effective and substantive social glue or cement. I shall return to this important point towards the end of this chapter.

On a slightly less abstract level, national and ethnic minority rights also raise important questions over some of the arguments which liberal authors, in particular, have presented in support of minority rights. Arguably the foremost advocate of a liberal theory of minority rights is Will Kymlicka. In a number of works now spanning four decades, Kymlicka has sought to remedy liberalism's apparent insensitivity towards the importance for individuals of cultural belonging and has extended this to include a detailed formulation of minority rights. To simplify an extensive body of work, Kymlicka places the ideal of the autonomous individual at the heart of his account of minority rights. For Kymlicka, the moral value of any given community can be broadly measured by how well it serves to promote its individual members' pursuit of an autonomous life. He states that the 'link between societal cultures and liberal values provides one of the yardsticks for assessing the claims of ethnocultural groups' (Kymlicka 2001: 54). Ethnocultural communities which do not support individuals' purportedly core interests in autonomy are not deserving of support and should be encouraged to change over time.

Kymlicka's highly important contributions to the liberal understanding of minority rights has been deeply significant and has drawn attention to a number of highly problematic and, as yet, unresolved issues which undoubtedly impact upon a human rights-based approach to national and ethnic minority rights.

Kymlicka's prioritisation of the autonomy ideal has been criticised from within liberalism (Kukathas 1992; Galston 1995) and from outside of liberalism in the form of Bhiku Parekh's (2006) communitarian critique. Interestingly, both approaches converge on the claim that Kymlicka's theory of minority rights effectively and illegitimately requires all ethnocultural communities to become substantively liberal in character by, first and foremost, reformulating their core values around that of personal autonomy. Kymlicka's model has been accused of seeking to promote liberal hegemony over diverse cultural communities. Kymlicka has sought to dampen these accusations and concerns through a series of responses. Thus, he denies that actual cultures can be classified as entirely 'liberal' or entirely 'illiberal' in character. He argues:

> to assume that any culture is inherently illiberal, and incapable of reform, is ethnocentric and ahistorical. Moreover, the liberality of a culture is a matter of degree . . . All cultures have illiberal strands, just as few cultures are entirely repressive of individual liberty. (Kymlicka 1995: 94)

While his point seems sociologically sound, it is clear that it does not attempt to renounce or refashion his theory's commitment to the autonomy ideal.

Parekh's specific criticisms of Kymlicka are contained within a broader body of work which has consistently counterposed what he presents as the reality of many established ethno-cultural communities (to continue with Kymlicka's term) with the values and ideals found within the dominant political and legal philosophies upon which laws are based. Parekh's alternative vision of what he considers to be a genuinely *multicultural* approach to legislating for national and ethnic minority rights raises some important issues and questions for the IHRL of national and ethnic minority rights, specifically in respect of the continuing influence of individualism within that body of law. Thus, Parekh insists that most non-individualist and ostensibly illiberal communities are worthy of respect and legal recognition. Cultures provide phenomenological frameworks in which individuals fashion and shape their lives. Cultures create sources of meaning and value for their members. As I discussed in an earlier chapter, Parekh argues that cultures should not be able to prevent members from seeking to exit the community, but they need not be committed to upholding personal autonomy as a condition of their legitimacy.

Indeed, Parekh argues that the important contributions which cultural belonging can make to their members' well-being sometimes justifies the claim that individuals may be said to owe a sense of allegiance and commitment to those communities which they do not wish to leave. Parekh declares:

> our culture gives coherence to our lives, gives us resources to make sense of the world, stabilizes our personality, and so on . . . We

then feel and should feel a sense of loyalty to our culture because of its profound contribution to our lives. (Parekh 2006: 159–60)

This specific aspect of Parekh's position closely resembles the argument presented by Ronald Dworkin and his formulation of so-called associative obligations (1986: 200), which pertain to mutually reciprocal commitments between individual members of any political community. Unlike the more contractarian vision of reciprocal rights and duties, this understanding of cultural loyalty is, to quote another defender of this position, Yael Tamir, 'not grounded on consent, reciprocity, or gratitude, but rather on a feeling of belonging and connectedness' (Tamir 1993: 137). It seems ostensibly reasonable to at least raise the question of whether obligations may be accorded to individual members of existing communities in order to help ensure the continuing existence of those communities. The IHRL of national and minority rights, given its focus upon the role of nation-states as the principal duty-bearers, has yet to adequately engage with this question.

The suggestion that individuals may be accorded responsibilities or duties within the broader legal framework of human rights protection typically raises real concerns within human rights circles. Human rights-based duties and responsibilities are attributed to the international system, individual states and even some 'other organs of society' (UDHR Preamble), but IHRL has consistently baulked at extending such duties to routinely include individuals themselves. The greatest fear in this regard is that the establishment of such a category of duties and responsibilities will be used by states and others to deny human rights to those who are, in some sense, considered to be too irresponsible or feckless to justify possessing their rights in the first instance. This would, of course, fundamentally contradict a core tenet of entitlement to distinctly *human* rights: they are possessed by virtue of being human and are not based upon meritorious behaviour. I believe that one can develop a defensible account of associative obligations along the lines outlined above, whilst remaining committed to the human rights-based objective of ensuring that national and ethnic minorities are able to survive and provide the resources their members look to them for. After all, many individuals' commitments to their communities are not coercive. Countless numbers of members of national and ethnic minorities routinely behave in the ways proposed by the likes of Parekh, Dworkin and Tamir. Such communities are, in part, sustained precisely by their members opting to speak the native languages, or choosing to reside on or close to the community's long-established territory. Whilst the community can only survive and prosper if a sufficient number of its members comply with the community's core traditions, customs and practices, to describe such compliance as discharging a duty or obligation is to misconceive and misrepresent the nature of the relationship. Authorities are all too often driven towards using the language of 'duties' and 'obligations' when members of a community grow reluctant to continue upholding the community's collective identity. This undoubtedly has occurred in many such communities, but it clearly is not true of all.

The concerns about the potentially coercive basis and effects of associative obligations reflect, in some cases, the continuing effect of naïve individualism and the failure of many naïve individualists to appreciate the powerful forces which bind collectives and communities together. Indeed, psychological research has repeatedly identified human beings' powerful disposition towards forming groups and identifying with others on the basis of shared cultural attributes and characteristics. Many of us consistently display very strong impulses towards in-group favouritism and preferences for fellow group members (Tajfel 1975). This body of research also offers detailed explanations for why forms of national and ethnic identity can turn towards violence and hostility. As I noted in an earlier chapter, the formation of a collective identity requires the existence of some specific 'other' who is both external to, but also constitutive of, another group's identity. Put simply, in-group favouritism is often accompanied by discrimination against and hostility towards outsiders. Typically, this hostility is not directed against everyone who does not belong to a group, but to a specific group of others (Hutus and Tutsis, Catholics and Protestants, etc.) As Horowitz (2001) notes, this distinction of insiders and outsiders very often includes pejorative comparisons between 'advanced' and 'backward' customs, traditions, practices and entire peoples. Many group identities are formed and maintained in this way. As Kwame Appiah has written, 'cultural norms are, after all, constituted not only by what they affirm and revere, but also by what they exclude, reject, scorn, despise, ridicule' (2005: 139). Across the world, many communities' identities are based, in part, upon the denial of equal respect for pejoratively defined and significantly other communities.

This feature of collective identity formation constitutes, arguably, one of the greatest challenges to the implementation of the IHRL of national and ethnic minority rights claims. Typically, the communities which attract such rights-based protections are themselves the weaker party within some bipartisan community conflict. In such instances, extending such protection will attract little controversy. However, the human rights-based approach to rights to cultural identity must remain ever vigilant of the potential of any community's pursuit of its identity to fall foul of this dynamic.

This feature of collective identity formation also provides one of the strongest justifications for a human rights-based approach to protecting national and ethnic minorities. Some will be inclined to raise a well-oiled objection to the manner in which I am depicting national and ethnic minorities. Thus, as I discussed in an earlier chapter, countless contributors to this field of studies have rejected the vision of any cultural community being an entirely discrete, closed-off and fundamentally static entity. In contrast, cultural communities are depicted as constructed, malleable, permeable and ever changing. This anti-essentialist depiction of culture is, on occasion and somewhat ironically perhaps, itself insensitive to the specific characteristics of some cultural communities. Clearly, not all cultural communities are the same, either substantively or, more importantly, formally. This is particularly the case with many national and ethnic cultural communities, for whom boundedness and closure are particularly important to the collective sense of self the community is committed to maintaining. As Benedict Anderson has written, 'no nation imagines itself to be universal' (1991: 16). The importance of the human rights-based approach in this respect consists precisely in the establishment and protection of core values and norms, which underpin the very possibility of separate communities being able to co-exist in a mutually reciprocal and sufficiently respectful manner. While many defend minority rights generally as a means for preventing electoral majorities tyrannising minorities within otherwise notionally electorally democratic systems, another crucial role minority rights must play is to ensure the establishment of generalisable criteria out of which and in accordance with which minority communities can co-exist with majorities and other minorities. On this basis, no community has a right to practise those customs and traditions which aim at or result in fundamentally undermining other communities' equal right to enjoy their cultural traditions and practices. The philosopher Thomas Pogge expresses this well when he writes, 'base any claims you make for your own ethnic group on principles that you would be

prepared to extend to any other ethnic group' (1997: 188). A commitment to a human rights-based approach thereby affords individual,
multi-ethnic states the grounds upon which the rules of engagement
between otherwise competing communities can be negotiated in ways
which fundamentally seek to avoid conflict and hatred becoming the
driving forces for collective identity formation.

Concluding thoughts and tying off some loose ends

The human rights-based protection of national and ethnic minorities requires an important revision to some of the individualist
assumptions which the doctrine of human rights has rested upon.
Specifically, recognising the need for such rights entails a simultaneous recognition of the limits of some individuals' capacity for making
choices over who they are. National and ethnic minority rights are
required precisely because many individuals who bear these identities
cannot simply leave or renounce their national or ethnic communities
in order to avoid discrimination. There are some aspects of some of
us which exert deeper influences upon us than many forms of naïve
individualism recognise. However, the IHRL of national and ethnic
minorities also remains deeply committed to norms and values which
are at the heart of human rights and which seek to ensure that any
such rights are exercised and enjoyed in a manner which does not
jeopardise the fundamental human rights of other individual human
beings.

The IHRL of national and ethnic minorities does not abandon the
individual to collective forces. Rather, it calls for what is still yet to
be completed within human rights circles: a more sophisticated
understanding of the relational character of individual agency and an
acknowledgement that we all of us form our identities through our
relations with others. In far too many cases, some individuals' national
and ethnic identities have been formed through hateful and discriminatory relations with others. A commitment to human rights offers an
institutionally robust alternative to such damaging relations.

Acknowledging the relational character of specifically national and
ethnic identity formation also draws attention to another area which
requires far more detailed scrutiny and discussion within human rights
circles and which I referred to earlier when criticising the contractarian model of political community formation. When they do so at all,

communities of people reflect upon core political and legal institutions and norms from within long-established social contexts, many of which will be significantly influenced by national and ethnic features. The invaluable importance of existing human rights norms is that these forms of collective reflection can be exercised in accordance with values and norms which are capable of being recognised and accepted by all of those who are subject to the authority of the political community. A commitment to human rights offers the possibility of providing a form of normative glue, analogous to the kind of social glue which collective rituals and customs have been seen to provide for national and ethnic communities (Durkheim and Mauss 1963). More recent authors (e.g. Tamir 1993; Habermas 2001) have similarly sought to reconcile the recognition of the sheer importance of community belonging with respect for universalisable, normative rules. As Tamir writes, such an approach 'celebrates the particularity of culture together with the universality of human rights, the social and cultural embeddedness of individuals together with their personal autonomy' (1993: 79). I will return to consider the implications of this approach in the conclusion to this book. For the time being, I believe that the IHRL of national and ethnic minorities makes an essential contribution to the broader doctrine of human rights precisely through reminding us of the need for human rights to better relate to cultural community and cultural belonging. The inclusion of minority rights recognition on such terms also offers a powerful response to those who argue that human rights is only suited to so-called Western, utterly individualised, societies in which, allegedly, there exists little appreciation for the value of community.

Suggested reading

- Robert Fine, 'Cosmopolitanism and Human Rights', in Thomas Cushman (ed.), *Handbook of Human Rights* (New York: Routledge, 2012), pp. 100–9.
- Steven Grosby, *Nationalism: A Very Short Introduction* (Oxford: Oxford University Press, 2005).
- Will Kymlicka, 'Introduction', in Will Kymlicka (ed.), *The Rights of Minority Cultures* (Oxford: Oxford University Press, 1995), pp. 1–30.
- Yael Tamir, *Liberal Nationalism* (Princeton: Princeton University Press, 1993).

Note

1. <https://wcd.coe.int/com.instranet.InstraServlet?command=com.instranet.CmdBlobGet&InstranetImage=2517175&SecMode=1&DocId=2038966&Usage=2> (last accessed 27 August 2016), p. 11.

6

The Rights of Indigenous Peoples

Key questions

1. Why is there so little existing IHRL covering indigenous peoples?
2. Why are claims to the possession of tribal land so important for many indigenous peoples?
3. Can you identify three examples of where law has defended indigenous peoples' human rights?
4. Why is the ruling in *Endorois v Kenya* so significant?
5. Why do some of the ways of being and believing found amongst many indigenous peoples create such difficult challenges for the human rights doctrine?
6. Why are indigenous peoples' oral traditions so problematic for many 'modern' legal systems?
7. What does indigenous peoples' right to self-determination entitle them to?
8. In what ways does extending rights to indigenous peoples challenge 'naïve individualism'?
9. Why is modern constitutionalism so problematic for indigenous peoples?
10. How has the need to respond to indigenous peoples influenced our understanding of economic development?

Introduction

Some criticisms of human rights have long reminded me of the ironic quote attributed to the early twentieth-century car manufacturer, Henry Ford, who is reputed to have said that a customer could have any colour of Model T car so long as it was black. Some critics, I believe, conceive of human rights in similar terms. Human rights, it is argued, originate in and necessarily reflect a set of partial ideals and values, which are not recognised by all peoples everywhere. On this understanding, when human rights defenders ostensibly proclaim that cultures are entitled to their own practices and beliefs, what they really mean is that members of other cultures can make their own choices only so long as they opt for 'black', so to speak. Human rights-based commitments to espousing cultural diversity are, for such critics, not to be taken seriously. I do not, needless to say, agree with the critics' depiction of the scope of the human rights doctrine, but the concerns they raise cannot and should not be dismissed out of hand. While the metaphorical colour kaleidoscope of human rights undoubtedly extends beyond the monochrome, just how multicoloured is IHRL?

The preceding chapters have identified a broad range of culturally based identities which are not only compatible with human rights norms, but draw heavily upon IHRL for their continuing survival. This chapter focuses upon a rather different group of identities. Indigenous peoples and their increasing claims to human rights-based protection raise very significant questions for IHRL and the entire doctrine of human rights. Indeed, I consider indigenous peoples as posing the greatest challenge to a human rights-based espousal of cultural diversity for a number of reasons.

First, the character of many indigenous peoples' ways of being and believing is, in some cases, arguably the most alien to the ways of being and believing out of which the spirt of human rights emerged. A human rights-based espousal of the value of cultural diversity clearly cannot only include ways of being and believing which broadly comply with a historically and geographically limited industrialised and bureaucratically managed set of societal structures. A commitment to the idea of humanity cannot only include those peoples who have succumbed to the lure of instrumental rationality and who, like so many of 'us', can only truly claim to be sure about the distinctly material value of things. The establishment and protection of human rights to indigenous peoples generally, requires reimagining how forms of human life can be collectively organised in ways which fundamentally challenge dominant forms of economic and political rationality. Protecting the rights of indigenous peoples requires abandoning the kind of criteria which pertain only to so-called Western, conventionally 'liberal' cultures. If this can be achieved within a human rights-based perspective, a great deal of the criticism alleging that human rights are purely 'Western' constructs will be finally silenced.

Second, extending human rights to many indigenous peoples requires reworking conventional ways of thinking within human rights circles. For example, many indigenous peoples do not conceive of human agency in the individualist terms which have exerted such a deep influence upon much human rights thinking. If we are to avoid demanding of indigenous peoples that they comply with our ways of being and believing (choosing 'black') we (advocates of IHRL) will need to give greater credence to, for example, communities' need for distinctly collective rights to such things as language and territory. Indigenous peoples therefore afford the possibility of developing more genuinely universal forms of legal instrument within IHRL.

Third, according sufficient respect towards many indigenous peoples will require abandoning any remaining assumptions which are based upon what James Tully refers to as a 'stages view of history' (1991: 64). From the beginnings of the European voyages of discovery into the utterly ethnocentrically named 'New World', indigenous peoples have suffered terribly as Europeans sought to export their respective versions of 'civilisation' across the globe. The hard power of gunboat colonialism was accompanied by a collection of no less deadly soft-power weapons, which sought to justify stealing others' lands and destroying others' ways of life as a necessary consequence of 'civilising the natives'. As if genocide could ever be justified by an appeal to the demands of history and so-called progress. Anyone who seeks to argue that human rights can be justified by the purported logic of history's modernising progression is, unwittingly perhaps, evoking the kind of reasoning which has underpinned the destruction and degradation of countless communities of indigenous peoples. Indigenous peoples are, therefore, not to be understood as modernity's recalcitrant other. Thinking of them in this way serves to place them outside of the 'logic' of a way of thinking which can only conceive of human rights as core manifestations of a thoroughly 'modernised' form of civilisation. Responding effectively to the claims of indigenous peoples will require an acknowledgement of the extent to which normative ideals have been abused and could still be abused in the name of a very partial but prevalent understanding of 'progress'. Thus, understanding the claims of indigenous peoples requires the development of a more reflexively critical perspective upon the ways in which human rights norms and concepts have aided and abetted domination and oppression in order to ensure that they no longer continue to do so.

Fourth, IHRL is tied to a state-centric international system, which is fundamentally based upon a commitment to the legal myth of state sovereignty. In the real world, the de facto sovereignty of states is limited and unequally enjoyed in a multitude of ways. However, international law (and IHRL as a sub-set of international law) is tied to a way of thinking about the basis and scope of state legitimacy which has its origins in the Treaty of Westphalia (1648) and Europe's attempt to solve the problem of sectarian conflict. According rights to indigenous peoples challenges many of these notions of state sovereignty. In some cases, states have refused to even recognise the existence of indigenous peoples residing within their sovereign territory precisely because of indigenous communities' refusal to be assimilated within the state's population. Many indigenous peoples have sought not so much legal recognition by the state as to be left alone by it. While most such claims have not been motivated by indigenous peoples' desire for sovereignty (in the Westphalian sense of the term), states have typically responded to them as if they were rebelling against the state and its rule of law. Responding to the claims of indigenous peoples entails the development of alternative conceptions of self-determination within IHRL and, I shall argue, a potentially radical reformulation of the purpose of some elements of IHRL.

Finally, indigenous peoples represent one of the, if not the most, important sources of genuine cultural diversity in the world. Protecting them through the mechanism of human rights thus provides one of the most important means by which IHRL can truly protect and promote cultural diversity. For all of the above reasons (no doubt further reasons could be added to my list), protecting the rights of indigenous peoples is one of the most urgent and important objectives of IHRL. I shall proceed to consider the complex relationship between IHRL and indigenous peoples' rights in due course. However, before I do so, it is important to be clear on precisely who is included within the category of indigenous peoples and to consider what might be termed the demographics of indigeneity.

Definition of indigenous peoples

As with most other forms of identity-based rights claims, IHRL does not provide a single, legally authoritative definition of who can be legitimately defined as 'indigenous'. The closest we have to a definition is the following, which was first presented by the first UN Special Rapporteur on indigenous peoples, José Martínez Cobo. I reproduce it here in its complex and detailed entirety:

> Indigenous communities, peoples and nations are those which, having a historical continuity with pre-invasion and pre-colonial societies that developed on their territories, consider themselves distinct from other sectors of the societies now prevailing on those territories, or parts of them. They form at present non-dominant sectors of society and are determined to preserve, develop and transmit to future generations their ancestral territories, and their ethnic identity, as the basis of their continued existence as peoples, in accordance with their own cultural patterns, social institutions and legal system. (Martínez Cobo 1986/7: paras 116–18)

This historical continuity may consist of the continuation, for an extended period reaching into the present of one or more of the following factors:

   a. Occupation of ancestral lands, or at least of part of them
   b. Common ancestry with the original occupants of these lands
   c. Culture in general, or in specific manifestations (such as religion, living under a tribal system, membership of an indigenous community, dress, means of livelihood, lifestyle, etc.)
   d. Language (whether used as the only language, as mother-tongue, as the habitual means of communication at home or in the family, or as the main, preferred, habitual, general or normal language)
   e. Residence in certain parts of the country, or in certain regions of the world
   f. Other relevant factors.

On an individual basis, an indigenous person is one who belongs to these indigenous populations through self-identification as indigenous (group consciousness) and is recognized and accepted by these populations as one of its members (acceptance by the group).

This preserves for these communities the sovereign right and power to decide who belongs to them, without external interference. (Martínez Cobo 1986/7: paras 379–82)

Indigenous peoples, then, are bound to a specific territory, which pre-exists the subsequent formation of a 'modern' nation-state. They need not necessarily constitute a minority of the existing population (see, for example, present-day Bolivia), but they do not occupy positions of social, political or legal power within the broader society. They are committed to maintaining and preserving their collective identity through a variety of relevant practices, customs and beliefs.

Indigenous peoples' sense of belonging is based upon a combination of self-identification and acceptance by the wider indigenous community. Self-identification is highlighted in the legally non-binding UNDRIP. Thus, Article 33 states, 'indigenous peoples have the right to determine their own identity or membership in accordance with `their customs and traditions'. Self-identification is also highlighted in the legally binding ILO Convention 169, Article 1 of which states that 'self-identification as indigenous or tribal shall be regarded as a fundamental criterion for determining the groups to which the provisions of this Convention apply'. This article also includes a statement of whom the Convention applies to, which includes the following:

   (a) tribal peoples in independent countries whose social, cultural and economic conditions distinguish them from other sections of the national community and whose status is regulated wholly or partially by their own customs or traditions or by special laws or regulations;

   (b) peoples in independent countries who are regarded as indigenous on account of their descent from the populations which inhabited the country, or a geographical region to which the country belongs, at the time of conquest or colonization or the establishment of present state boundaries and who irrespective of their legal status, retain some or all of their own social, economic, cultural and political institutions.

Demographics and suffering of indigenous peoples

Having established a set of criteria or characteristics by which indigenous peoples can be identified as such, it is important to also know how many peoples in the world are indigenous and to achieve a clear picture of the extent to which they have suffered.

Indigenous peoples account for most of the world's cultural diversity.

Amnesty International estimate that there are approximately 370 million indigenous peoples occupying 20 per cent of the world's territory.[1] It is also estimated that there are currently some 5,000 different indigenous cultural communities located in some seventy countries across the world. The Inter-Parliamentary Union further estimate that indigenous peoples comprise some 5 per cent of the world's population but constitute 15 per cent of the world's most disadvantaged peoples.[2]

Indigenous peoples have suffered systematic persecution and discrimination over several centuries. The sufferings of indigenous peoples are far too numerous to list in a single chapter but some of the 'highlights' include the effective genocide perpetrated against the North American Indian tribes; the concerted destruction of indigenous peoples' habitat and environment in many parts of the world, including Central and South America; the forced relocation of many indigenous peoples in parts of Eurasia and Central Asia; the systematic removal of Aboriginal children from their families in Australia, which was part of a broader policy to prevent the preservation of Aboriginal culture; and countless other policies and acts which all aimed at the suppression or outright destruction of indigenous peoples.

Lest one imagine that the suffering of indigenous peoples is primarily of historical interest, volumes of statistics continue to highlight the effects of long-standing discrimination and oppression. For example, in the United States, a Native American is 600 times more likely to contract tuberculosis and 62 per cent more likely to commit suicide than a non-indigenous US citizen. In Australia, an indigenous child can expect to die twenty years earlier than a non-native Australian. In New Zealand, the life expectancy gap is eleven years, in Nepal it is twenty years and in Guatemala it is thirteen years.

Successive UN Special Rapporteurs for indigenous peoples have identified a continuing and detailed set of human rights violations from which indigenous peoples suffer. These include issues of violence and brutality; continuing state assimilation policies; the marginalisation of indigenous cultures; the dispossession of land; forced removal or relocation from native lands; the systematic denial of land rights; the adverse impact of large-scale economic development projects; abuses by military and other state security and law enforcement officials; and a multitude of other systematic abuses. Many indigenous peoples are highly mobilised and politically active in seeking to overcome their own suffering. However, as a former UN Special Rapporteur noted, 'in many countries, indigenous people are persecuted because of their work in defence of their human rights and fundamental freedoms, and are the victims of extrajudicial executions, arbitrary detention, torture, forced evictions and many forms of discrimination' (UN Commission on Human Rights 2006: para. 6).

Another recurring feature of successive UN Special Rapporteur reports on the violations suffered by indigenous peoples is the systematic and institutionalised discrimination and racism they suffer at the hands of state and public officials, including government officials, police officers, health-care workers and even teachers. Many states refuse to document complaints made against state and public officials, or do not disaggregate documented complaints, thereby effectively hiding the extent to which indigenous peoples (and other ethnic minorities) suffer discrimination.

Finally, and in respect of the plight of native languages, it has been estimated that 90 per cent of all languages will disappear within the next 100 years. Typically, there are thought to be between 6,000 and 7,000 oral languages in the world today. Most of these languages are spoken by very few people, while a handful of them are spoken by an overwhelming majority of the world. Some 97 per cent of the world's population speaks only 4 per cent of its languages, while only 3 per cent speaks 96 per cent of them. A great majority of these languages are spoken by indigenous peoples, and many (if not most) of them are in danger of becoming extinct.

The development of an international set of standards and legal instruments

The relationship between indigenous peoples and the law generally is complex. One can forgive many indigenous peoples for not placing a great deal of faith in the law as a means for protecting their human rights. After all, generations of indigenous peoples have lost and unwittingly forfeited access to their lands and livelihoods through successive treaties, beginning with the United States Indian Treaties and the Removal Act of 1830, which legally authorised the mass displacement of Native Americans from their tribal lands. In Canada, a succession of treaties was signed between the British Crown and subsequent Canadian governments and the so-called First Nations peoples, through which settled lands in Ontario, Manitoba, Saskatchewan and Alberta were transferred from the stewardship of indigenous peoples to exclusive possession by the state. The law has all too often served as one of the most powerful weapons against indigenous peoples and the enjoyment of their human rights.

In other instances, the content of IHRL has offered a powerful tool for communities of people seeking to achieve their human rights entitlements through changing domestic legislation. This route is complicated in the case of indigenous peoples for the simple reason that precious little established IHRL exists that specifically aims to protect the human rights of indigenous peoples. (I shall shortly turn to consider why there is so little IHRL in this area.) Generally, the international community has enjoyed some success in producing normative standards for indigenous peoples' rights, but these have yet to materialise into a formal instrument of IHRL, such as a legally binding UN convention. What is the extent of existing IHRL in this respect?

The only legally binding international treaties which deal specifically with indigenous peoples' rights are two Conventions of the ILO: the Indigenous and Tribal Populations Convention, 1957 (No. 107) and the Tribal Peoples Convention 169 (1989). Convention 169 effectively revised the earlier Convention 107 and extended the terms and scope of the legal protection provided. Convention 169 recognises indigenous peoples' right to self-determination within a nation-state and sets standards for national governments concerning indigenous peoples' economic, socio-cultural and political rights. The Convention is legally binding within the (as of April 2016) twenty-one member states that have ratified it, most of which are located in Latin America. The Convention comprises forty-four articles which are arranged into ten categories that outline the minimum standards of the rights of indigenous peoples. These articles, among other things, recognise 'the aspirations of [indigenous] peoples to exercise control over their own institutions, ways of life and economic development and to maintain and develop their identities, languages and religions, within the framework of the States in which they live' (Article 7). The Convention guarantees indigenous peoples the right to participate in decision-making on activities that may impact their own societies and territories, such as natural resource extraction, while maintaining the integrity of their societies, territories and cultures. The Convention further recognises the right to indigenous peoples to prioritise their own development needs (Article 7). The Convention calls upon governments to uphold these rights and to recognise indigenous peoples' unique historical and socio-economic position within the state and their integral connection to their territories, and protects them against displacement. The Convention further guarantees indigenous peoples' rights to equal and fair employment opportunities (Articles 20–3), rights to health care (Article 25) and education (Article 27), including education in one's own language (Article 28). The Convention has been consistently criticised for its weak enforcement record. Despite the Convention's low number of signatories and serious shortcomings in its enforcement, many indigenous peoples have welcomed the Convention for establishing an important precedent in their ongoing attempts to secure international recognition of indigenous peoples' human rights as legal rights, rather than as normative standards and aspirations.

Beyond IHRL there have also been a number of significant domestic and regional rulings, which afford specific protections to indigenous peoples. The majority of these are concerned with collective land title claims and I present the key details of four such examples below:

1. **Canada:** *Calder v British Columbia (1973).* The *Calder* case reviewed the existence of 'aboriginal title' claimed by the Nisga'a people of British Columbia, Canada. The Nisga'a argued that they possessed land rights over their traditional territories and had never surrendered or lost their rights to the land. Chief Frank Arthur Calder lost the case, based on a procedural point, but the decision of the Supreme Court effectively set a precedent for legally recognising that Aboriginal title to land existed prior to the colonisation of the continent and was not merely derived from statutory law. This resulted in the Government of Canada's overhauling its land claim negotiation processes.

2. **Australia:** *Mabo v Queensland (1992).* In 1992, the Australian High Court held that the common law of Australia recognises native title to land, rejecting the doctrine that Australia was *terra nullius* (land belonging to no one) at the time of European settlement. The decision established that native title can continue to exist where Aboriginal and Torres Strait Islander people have maintained their connection with the land through the years of European settlement and that the content of native title is to be determined according to the traditional laws and customs of the Aboriginal and Torres Strait Islander people

involved. The case had been led by Eddie Mabo of the Meriam people from the Mer (Murray) Islands of the Torres Strait. Sadly, Mr Mabo died before the Court's decision was rendered.

3. **Botswana:** *Sesana v Botswana (2006).* In December 2006, the Botswana High Court ruled that the 2002 eviction and displacement of indigenous San peoples from their ancestral lands in the Central Kalahari Game Reserve (CKGR) was unlawful and unconstitutional, as was the government's decision to terminate the provision of basic services to the San peoples within the CKGR. The Court recognised that the San, as indigenous peoples, have the right to live, hunt and gather on their ancestral land inside the CKGR and that they should not have to apply for permits to enter it.

4. **Kenya:** *Endorois v Kenya (2010).* One of the most recent of the relevant rulings was set by the African Commission on Human and Peoples' Rights, which ruled that Kenya's eviction of a native people from their traditional land constituted a violation of their human rights under the African Charter. The Kenyan government evicted the Endorois people, a traditional pastoralist community, from their homes at Lake Bogoria in central Kenya in the 1970s, to make way for a national reserve and tourist facilities. In the first ruling of an international tribunal to find a violation of the right to development, the Commission found that this eviction, with minimal compensation, violated the Endorois' right as an indigenous people to property, health, culture, religion and natural resources. It ordered Kenya to restore the Endorois to their historic land and to compensate them. It is the first ruling to determine who are indigenous peoples in Africa, and what are their rights to land.

While there is little existing IHRL specifically concerned with indigenous peoples, since the early 1970s there has been a continuous stream of UN-based institutional initiatives in this area. Thus, in 1972, the United Nations Sub-Commission on Prevention of Discrimination and Protection of Minorities commissioned a study into the discrimination suffered by indigenous peoples. The main author of the study was the above-mentioned José Martínez Cobo, who was to become the first UN Special Rapporteur for indigenous peoples. The study coincided with the emergence and rapid growth of the international indigenous movement across various continents. The study's focus upon human rights significantly influenced the development of the indigenous peoples' movement and was reflected in the extent to which many of the key objectives of the movement were framed in the language of human rights.

The 'Martínez Cobo Study', as it was to become known, established a momentum which led, in 1982, to the creation of the first United Nations mechanism on indigenous peoples' issues, namely the Working Group on Indigenous Populations of the Sub-Commission. In 1983 the Working Group decided to allow the participation of representatives of indigenous peoples and their organisations, thereby ensuring the direct representation of victims of human rights violations in the institutional machinery. At that time, this was an unprecedented move.

Between 1984 and 1993 indigenous issues gained increased international attention, through the establishment of the UN Voluntary Fund for Indigenous Populations (1985), the adoption of ILO Convention No. 169 on Indigenous and Tribal Peoples in Independent Countries (1989), the proclamation of the International Year of the World's Indigenous People (1993) and, subsequently, the proclamation of two separate International Decades of the World's Indigenous People (1995–2004 and 2005–14).

In 2000 a UN Permanent Forum on Indigenous Issues (the UNPFII was created. This followed a process of international consultation following the Vienna Conference of 1993. The UNPFII has a broad mandate, namely to discuss economic and social development, culture, the environment, education, health and human rights, and to advise the Economic and Social Council and the United Nations system on all matters pertaining to its mandate, promote the coordination and integration of indigenous issues in the United Nations system, raise awareness about indigenous issues and produce information materials on indigenous issues.

The Working Group on indigenous populations was abolished in 2007 and replaced with the Expert Mechanism on the Rights of Indigenous Peoples. The Expert Mechanism is a subsidiary body of the HRC, composed of five experts, which provides thematic expertise on the rights of indigenous peoples to the Council, focusing mainly on studies and research-based advice. The mandate of the Special Rapporteur is currently occupied by Victoria Tauli-Corpuz. The Special Rapporteur's mandate is based upon several IHRL standards, which include the ILO Resolution (169), ICCPR, ICESCR, ICERD, CEDAW, CRC and the UN Convention on Biological Diversity.

Finally, and arguably, the most significant institutional development was the formulation of the UNDRIP, which was adopted by the UN General Assembly in September 2007. As a Declaration, the UNDRIP is not legally binding upon member states, although it offers the most comprehensive normative framework for identifying the rights of indigenous peoples as human rights.

Prevailing obstacles to the legalisation of indigenous peoples' rights

There has been no shortage of institutional initiatives and the special mandate draws upon a comprehensive body of IHRL standards. However, the fact remains that the legal machinery for the international protection of specifically indigenous peoples' rights effectively rests upon a single ILO Convention, which has been ratified by only twenty-one member states. Why is this the case?

There are undoubtedly many institutional and specifically political explanations for this parlous state of affairs. However, given the specific focus of this book, I shall concentrate upon more conceptual obstacles and barriers, which, I argue, are more intractable and difficult to overcome and which thereby provide a more robust explanation for the lack of IHRL in this area. There are several core areas in which the development of a body of IHRL for indigenous peoples is problematic. As I said at the beginning of this chapter, some of the recurring and distinguishing elements of indigenous identity challenge long-established conceptualisations of human rights and IHRL. Successfully addressing the concerns in order to better address the needs of indigenous peoples requires rethinking some core elements of the normative basis of IHRL. The disconnect between indigenous peoples' rights and IHRL reveals the degree to which the latter remains unduly influenced by partial norms and conceptualisations.

Oral traditions and alternative paradigms

Reconciling respect for human rights with a commitment to cultural diversity must include the establishment of a right to *think* differently about the world. So much is recognised in a huge body of jurisprudence underpinning freedom of speech and expression. However, many indigenous peoples have traditionally represented reality in ways which differ fundamentally from what might be broadly defined as the rational-scientific paradigm of thinking and representation. Indeed, it was precisely indigenous peoples' refusal to think in such terms, which typically led to them being labelled as 'backward' by many outsiders. The importance of what has been termed 'traditional knowledge' has been recognised within the UNDRIP and the Convention on Biological Diversity (1992). For example, Article 8(j) of the latter requires contracting member parties to:

> respect, preserve and maintain knowledge, innovations and practices of indigenous and local communities embodying traditional lifestyles relevant for the conservation and sustainable use of biological diversity and promote their wider application with the approval and involvement of the holders of such knowledge, innovations and practices and encourage the equitable sharing of the benefits arising from the utilization of such knowledge innovations and practices.

Article 31 of UNDRIP states:

> indigenous peoples have the right to maintain, control, protect and develop their cultural heritage, traditional knowledge and traditional cultural expressions, including human and genetic resources, seeds, medicines, knowledge of the properties of fauna and flora, oral traditions, literatures, designs, sports and traditional games and visual and performing arts. They also have the right to maintain, control, protect and develop their intellectual property over such cultural heritage, traditional knowledge, and traditional cultural expressions.

Indigenous peoples' right to conceive of the world in paradigmatically different ways to those which so many of the rest have succumbed to appears to have been at least normatively recognised. However, there are limits to what might be termed this state of paradigmatic pluralism.

One of the most intractable and problematic areas of difference concerns the importance of oral traditions for many indigenous peoples. In many communities, knowledge has been contained in oral narratives and rituals, which have been formally passed from generation to generation. In itself, the distinctly oral, rather than documented, form of collective knowledge should pose no particular obstacle to developing a body of IHRL for indigenous peoples. However, the oral tradition has been a recurring factor in many legal disputes between indigenous peoples and outsiders. For example, indigenous land title was rarely, if ever, established through the drawing up of written deeds. Many indigenous peoples simply knew where their land began and ended. The lack of written deeds in many legal disputes resulted in indigenous peoples losing their title claims simply because they could not document their claims in the form required by the courts.

The oral tradition was also a significant factor in the radically differing understandings of precisely what had been agreed to in a succession of Canadian treaties with the First Nations peoples. In some cases, verbal agreements between the parties were not reflected in the subsequent documents resulting in representatives of the First Nations peoples wrongly assuming that the spoken word was the bond between the two parties. These recurring 'lost in translation' incidences remain a long-standing grievance amongst contemporary descendants of the native Canadians who lost the enjoyment of their native lands through many of these treaties.

Self-determination

The paradigmatically different ways of thinking about and perceiving the world also extend to what is the most significant element of international law: the right to self-determination. Under international law, self-determination is considered to be *jus cogens* or a peremptory norm. The UN Special Rapporteur's mandate includes a specific reference to Article 1 of the ICCPR, which, as I discussed in the previous chapter, establishes a people's right to self-determination. Indigenous peoples' normative right to self-determination is also established through several articles of UNDRIP. Thus, Article 3 states that, 'indigenous peoples have the right to self-determination. By virtue of that right they freely determine their political status and freely pursue their economic, social and cultural development.' Subsequent articles specify the application of this right of self-determination. Article 9 states:

indigenous peoples and individuals have the right to belong to an indigenous community or nation, in accordance with the traditions and customs of the community or nation concerned. No discrimination of any kind may arise from the exercise of such a right.

Finally, Article 34 declares that 'indigenous peoples have the right to promote, develop and maintain their institutional structures and their distinctive customs, spirituality, traditions, procedures, practices and, in the cases where they exist, juridical systems or customs, in accordance with international human rights standards'.

International lawyers have typically focused upon the likely implications of such rights to self-determination for the existing sovereign member states within which indigenous peoples reside. Not surprisingly, there has been no appetite amongst member states to consider the possibility of indigenous peoples seceding from those states. Article 46(1) of UNDRIP thus asserts:

> nothing in this Declaration may be interpreted as implying for any State, people, group or person any right to engage in any activity or to perform any act contrary to the Charter of the United Nations or construed as authorizing or encouraging any action which would dismember or impair, totally or in part, the territorial integrity or political unity of sovereign and independent States.

This interpretation of self-determination resonates with the oft-cited 1840 Treaty of Waitangi, signed by the UK Crown and over 500 Maori Chiefs, in which the Maori were recognised as having equal rights to British subjects but which also established the right of the Crown to rule over New Zealand.

Rather than further add to an already well-served debate, I shall focus upon a different area of concern, which has more radical implications for IHRL generally: how self-determination is conceptualised.

As I discussed in Chapter 1, human rights thinking has been heavily influenced by liberalism. In many respects, liberalism has exerted a profoundly positive influence upon human rights norms and the development of IHRL. However, one crucial area which has been problematic is the continuing effect of what I referred to in the previous chapter as 'naïve individualism', which is exemplified by a set of assumptions that all human beings do or ought to think of themselves and their interests in individualist terms. Naïve individualism has undoubtedly influenced many liberal conceptions of self-determination. In some instances, this has been particularly relevant for how we might reformulate our human rights-based understandings of self-determination for peoples who, like many indigenous peoples, conceive of their interests in distinctly collectivist terms.

For example, some highly respected contractarian liberal theories of consent have explicitly rejected the claim that individuals could rationally consent to conventionally 'traditional' ways of being and believing, such as those which particularly characterise many indigenous peoples. The contractarian liberal philosopher David Gauthier exemplifies this positon. He writes:

> we begin by formulating four criteria for classifying one way of life as more advanced than another, as exhibiting a higher stage of development. The first, and perhaps least important, is density of population . . . The second is duration of life . . . The third is material well-being: other things being equal A is a more advanced way of life than B if it enables those who practise it to enjoy, on average, a greater abundance, and more varied kinds, of material goods. And fourth and most important, is breadth of opportunity: other things being equal A is a more advanced way of life than B if those who practice it enjoy, on average, a choice among more diverse and varied vocational and avocational roles. (Gauthier 1986: 28)

Gauthier exemplifies a form of constitutional thinking which James Tully has labelled 'modern constitutionalism' (1991: 29). Tully argues that liberal political and legal philosophy has been deeply influenced by modern constitutionalism since its emergence in the political philosophy of John Locke and Thomas Hobbes in the seventeenth century. As Gauthier's words indicate, modern constitutionalism is based upon a hierarchical mode of thinking and evaluation which is utterly incompatible with the genuine recognition of significant cultural differences. It also simply assumes the a priori validity of certain principles and criteria and then applies these to everyone subject to the authority of the state. For example, many indigenous peoples do not conceive of advanced ways of life as necessarily consisting of greater material prosperity. Not doing so, on Gauthier's criteria, ostensibly justifies labelling them as 'less advanced' and less worthy of mutual respect and recognition.

A constitution based upon a commitment to human rights norms obviously entails the prior establishment of substantively normative criteria. The significance of Tully's specific contribution to understanding the implications of indigeneity for constitutionalism is to highlight the extent to which human rights norms may be unduly restrictive towards some, in this instance non-acquisitive and non-materialistic, ways of being. Tully proposes that constitutions need to dispense with unduly partial commitments and presumptions if they are to be better placed to legislate for genuine diversity. He states:

> a contemporary constitution can recognize cultural diversity if it is reconceived as what might be called a 'form of accommodation' of cultural diversity. A constitution should be seen as a form of activity, an intercultural dialogue in which the culturally diverse sovereign citizens of contemporary societies negotiate agreements on their form of association over time in accordance with the three conventions of mutual recognition, consent and cultural continuity. (Tully 1991: 30)

Tully argues that modern states' engagement with specifically indigenous peoples has typically been devoid of mutual recognition, consent and cultural continuity. In the name of the presumed superiority of immigrant cultures, states have imposed alien laws upon indigenous peoples, flatly denied the value and worth of indigenous cultures, and finally, often sought to suppress traditions and practices which have been deemed to be 'less advanced'. In response, some indigenous peoples have seen no option but to pursue secessionist objectives in the face of authorities which refuse to recognise their right to exist as they collectively desire. An overly partial conception of self-determination, ironically perhaps, can generate precisely the kind of alienation and estrangement which leads some groups to challenge state sovereignty.

The human rights-based claims of indigenous peoples thus have a vital contribution to make to the normative development of IHRL. I do not think that IHRL is any longer entirely influenced by the kind of intellectual partiality of what Tully refers to as 'modern constitutionalism'. Nor, as I shall argue in the concluding section to this chapter, can the human rights community grant a blank cheque to indigenous communities to pursue what ever-present practices and customs they consider to be authentically theirs. However, the need for human rights to respond to identity-based claims and to become generally more sensitive towards cultural diversity has been crucial in drawing human rights away from, what was previously, a far too close relationship with the abstract uniformity of much liberal thinking.

The ongoing development of how self-determination is conceptualised and, one hopes, finally achieved by indigenous peoples will further positively influence human rights thinking in this area.

Conceptions of property – what's mine is ours?

The relationship between human rights and economics is deeply complex and far too large a topic to engage with in sufficient detail here. However, some background observations are necessary in order to make sense of the importance of differing conceptions of property and their impact upon IHRL.

During the Cold War, many assumed that civil and political rights were broadly consistent with, if not significantly influenced by, market-based economic systems and theories, whereas economic, social and cultural rights were broadly in line with economic systems and theories which advocated significant degrees of state intervention in the market or outright command economies, such as those found within the Soviet sphere of influence. It was also often assumed that civil and political rights required little direct financial support from states, whereas their economic, social and cultural rights counterparts required the kind of financial support which could only be provided by states committed to relatively high levels of public expenditure and some degree of redistributive taxation. While traces of this overly simplistic way of thinking are still sometimes found in contemporary writings, human rights thinking has moved steadily towards a far more holistic understanding of what human rights are and an understanding of the interdependency of civil and political and economic, social and cultural rights. As Amartya Sen (1981) demonstrated some time ago, famines do not occur in democratic countries. Conceiving of human rights and IHRL in holistic terms entails the development of a more sophisticated and subtle analysis of the relationship between economics and human rights than this topic has often been graced with.

IHRL most certainly includes substantial commitments which require of states that they provide far more for their citizens than merely minimal public provision. The ICESCR certainly cannot be thought of as a capitalist manifesto. More broadly, the entire doctrine of human rights is normatively incompatible with any economic system which reduces human beings to mere forms of human capital and which seeks to legitimise the wholesale denial of liberty, equality and human dignity to many. In recent years, there have emerged a number of scholarly contributions to this area which are more sensitive towards the potential of capital to alleviate, rather than cause, wholescale human rights violations (e.g. Pogge 2002; Ruggie 2014). The UN is also slowly developing a draft convention covering the human rights-based responsibilities of transnational corporations, developing upon the so-called Ruggie Principles of 2008. Conceptions of property are a potentially very important element in understanding how economics and human rights can be reconciled.

Many indigenous peoples have not traditionally conceived of property in what might be generally referred to as materialistic, market-oriented terms. The character of many indigenous communities has typically prevented their members from conceiving of material prosperity, economic development and the ownership of land in the terms which, for example, have been central to structural adjustment interventions by the World Bank in many developing economies. In terms which closely resemble what the anthropologist Marshall Sahlins (1972) ironically referred to as 'stone age economics', many indigenous peoples have been traditionally economically motivated to produce only for their own finite and fixed needs. Self-subsistence, and not the generation of an economic surplus, has been central to many indigenous peoples' economic behaviour and rationality. Self-subsistence forms of economic rationality are, of course, entirely incompatible with market-based industrialisation which, as Marx (1978) famously demonstrated in his 1857 *Das Kapital*, is fundamentally based upon workers producing a surplus, which they do not own and which constitutes the business owner's all-important profit.

Development economics has been undergoing radical changes over the past three decades. Human rights norms have infiltrated their way into the principles and objectives of many development and aid projects. In contrast to the former, largely consequentialist-based, models which aimed at generating increased gross domestic product (GDP) for national economies or increased income for individuals and communities, the so-called human rights-based approach to development (HRBA) insists that projects must both respect human rights and fundamentally aim at increased protection and promotion of human rights as their central objective. While it is far from universally supported and lauded within the development world, the HRBA exerts a significant influence upon how the UN measures development (through the UN Development Programme Human Development Index) and how countless development projects are designed.

The specific character of indigenous peoples' traditional modes of production has been recognised within several UN development initiatives, which aim at environmental sustainability and greater levels of self-sufficiency. One may go so far as to claim that, specifically in respect of indigenous peoples, a new paradigm is emerging within development institutions, typically referred to as 'development with identity'. This new paradigm is being promoted by several UN agencies, including the International Fund for Agricultural Development (IFAD), the Inter-American Development Bank (IDB) and UNESCO. In its Operational Policy on Indigenous Peoples and Strategy for Indigenous Development adopted in 2006, IDB defines 'development with identity' as referring to:

> a process that includes strengthening of indigenous peoples, harmony and sustained interaction with their environment, sound management of natural resources and territories, the creation and exercise of authority, and respect for the rights and values of indigenous peoples, including cultural, economic, social and institutional rights, in accordance with their own worldview and governance. (IDB 2006)

One of the core challenges for this new approach consists of supporting and promoting development initiatives and organisational systems which are unique to indigenous peoples in order to improve their living conditions in accordance with their own aspirations and in a manner which is thoroughly consistent with each community's specific socio-cultural situation and vision. This entails greater access, with gender equality, to socio-economic development opportunities that strengthen identity, culture, territoriality, natural resources and social organisation, and reduce material poverty and marginalisation.

The development with identity paradigm offers a model by which indigenous communities may be able to avoid and overcome their exposure to far more market-oriented development projects which have had devastating effects upon them. The model also requires a subtler approach to integrating environmental considerations into economic planning. The tendency to conceive of indigenous peoples as somehow rooted in the past serves to overlook the potential lessons their ways of being might hold for a world which is confronted by the consequences of relating to the environment as merely an infinitely exploitable storeroom for human desire.

The final area of interest in respect of indigenous conceptions of property is land. Land title claims have been a recurring source of legal dispute between indigenous communities and freeholders or the state. For the vast majority of indigenous peoples, the land constitutes a vital element of their collective identity, and loss of their tribal lands has been one of the most pronounced and damaging forms of abuse which indigenous peoples have suffered from.

There are various examples of indigenous peoples' loss of access to their land. One of the most revealing is statistics on the extent to which indigenous peoples have relocated to urban areas. A growing number of indigenous peoples are today living in urban areas. This is the result of, among other things, the deterioration in and dispossession of lands, the forced evictions and the lack of local employment opportunities that many indigenous people experience. The Economic Commission for Latin America and the Caribbean (ECLAC) estimates that in Guatemala and Mexico, one in three indigenous individuals now live in urban areas. The same report states that in Bolivia, Brazil and Chile, more than half of the indigenous population lives in urban areas. Cases studies from a UN-Habitat–OHCHR report reveal that indigenous peoples in urban settings live in dismal conditions, frequently experiencing extreme poverty (UN-Habitat and OHCHR 2005).

Despite some potential benefits of living in urban areas, such as closeness to public facilities, in most cases indigenous peoples experience substantial difficulties. They typically experience racism and discrimination from the wider urban population. They often lack employment and income-generating opportunities. Most are living in inadequate housing or are homeless. In general, disrespect for a wide range of human rights and fundamental freedoms of indigenous peoples is often a main underlying cause for persisting poverty among urban indigenous communities.

The loss of access to their lands (and the consequences which follow) directly contradicts numerous international standards. Thus, Article 26 of UNDRIP states:

1. Indigenous peoples have the right to the lands, territories and resources which they have traditionally owned, occupied or otherwise used or acquired.

2. Indigenous peoples have the right to own, use, develop and control the lands, territories and resources that they possess by reason of traditional ownership or other traditional occupation or use, as well as those which they have otherwise acquired.

3. States shall give legal recognition and protection to these lands, territories and resources. Such recognition shall be conducted with due respect to the customs, traditions and land tenure systems of the indigenous peoples concerned.

This article is not, of course, a legal instrument since the UNDRIP is not legally binding. Indeed, as I have been arguing above, far too many harms inflicted upon many indigenous peoples are not, strictly speaking, violations of the legally binding, internationally recognised human rights, given the lack of existing IHRL specifically concerned with protecting and promoting the human rights of indigenous peoples.

Key lessons to be learnt

As I have demonstrated above, the IHRL of indigenous peoples falls far short of the normative standards which have been developed and which provide a key impetus and source for what one hopes will be the subsequent development of an established and comprehensive body of legal protections. The mere passing of human rights law is not, of course, sufficient to ensure people's enjoyment of their human rights, but it is, I believe, a necessary condition for such enjoyment. I have sought to show how the disparity between normative standards and established law derives, in part, from specific but essential elements of indigenous peoples' collective identity. From the ways in which many indigenous peoples traditionally conceive of the world to the characteristically collectivist nature of their ways of conceiving of such 'goods' as land, many indigenous peoples' ways of being and believing challenge long-standing and often rather tacit conceptions and assumptions found within IHRL. In this respect, indigenous peoples afford an opportunity to reconsider and reformulate important areas of human rights thinking in order to better accommodate the kind of diversity which indigenous peoples potentially provide for.

As I discussed in the previous chapter in respect of national and ethnic identities, indigenous peoples serve to remind us that many

human beings do not conceive of their cultural identifications and affiliations as based upon, in any sense, private choices. Many members of
indigenous communities have suffered precisely because they are not
able to simply walk away from or renounce their identities. They cannot
be other than who they are, so to speak, despite the fact that the indigenous communities which many members continue to identify with
have been systematically discriminated against or persecuted.

Normative justifications for human rights are invariably based upon
some form of cosmopolitanism and my approach is no different in that
regard. At the heart of any cosmopolitan vision is a commitment to
what I shall term the inherently transformative potential of humankind. Human rights exist, in large part, to afford individuals the opportunity to, so to speak, become different to how they are. To pursue
goals and aspirations which depart from and even directly challenge
established ways of being and believing. However, advocates must
also recognise that not everyone esteems and desires personal and
collective change. We must also recognise that a desire to maintain
established ways of being and believing is not always and everywhere
evidence of coercion and what I referred to earlier as cultural harm. The
case of many indigenous peoples perfectly exemplifies this phenomenon. Many indigenous peoples are, after all, seeking rights against the
encroachments of an ever-changing 'outside world'. Many indigenous
peoples are, in effect, seeking a right *not* to change.

Contributors to discussions of rights to cultural identity typically
depict culture as an infinitely malleable and inherently fluid phenomenon. On this view cultural communities are constantly changing and
evolving. I have already discussed in earlier chapters both the strengths
and the weaknesses of this conception of culture. Certainly conceiving
of culture in such terms sits comfortably with a broader understanding
of freedom as necessarily entailing a consistent striving to be different,
or to gain more 'stuff'. Many formulations of individual freedom in
political philosophy can be described as oriented towards the future
and as entailing the necessity for change as a measure of the exercise
of individual freedom. Indigenous peoples typically defy this set of
assumptions. Many indigenous peoples are seeking to preserve and
protect long-standing traditions and customs from their exposure to
external forces of change. Many indigenous peoples' claims are therefore based upon what Kwame Appiah (2005: 130) refers to as the 'preservationist ethic'. Many indigenous peoples can be said, I believe, to be

acting freely in their attempts to preserve their heritage. A large part of this may be due to the influence of cyclical conceptions of time within many indigenous peoples' belief systems. Whatever the cause, indigenous peoples draw attention to our need to pay far greater attention to the possibility of a community possessing a right not to change and what this may mean in practice. What any such set of demands and desires cannot extend to, of course, are attempts to justify human rights violations under the name of tradition.

Indigenous peoples' rights must remain compatible with the equal human rights of all. In respect of indigenous peoples, this proviso is enshrined in Article 46(2) of UNDRIP, which states:

> in the exercise of the rights enunciated in the present Declaration, human rights and fundamental freedoms of all shall be respected. The exercise of the rights set forth in this Declaration shall be subject only to such limitations as are determined by law and in accordance with international human rights obligations. Any such limitations shall be non-discriminatory and strictly necessary solely for the purpose of securing due recognition and respect for the rights and freedoms of others and for meeting the just and most compelling requirements of a democratic society.

Article 44 of UNDRIP also states that 'all the rights and freedoms recognized herein are equally guaranteed to male and female indigenous individuals'.

While many indigenous peoples continue to suffer systematic abuse and discrimination, recent studies have identified the extent to which many female members of indigenous communities have been experiencing what I referred to in an earlier chapter as forms of cultural harm. Thus, the most recent (2015) report of the UN Special Rapporteur for Indigenous Peoples explicitly highlighted the vulnerabilities of indigenous women. The report points to the extent to which indigenous communities have responded to outsiders' attacks against their self-determination by subjugating the rights of women. To quote the report directly:

> in the battle for indigenous communities to assert their right to self-determination, women's rights have often been considered divisive and external to the indigenous struggle and connected to

'external values' or 'Western values' that privilege individual over communal rights. Such a false dichotomy between collective and women's rights has, paradoxically, further entrenched the vulnerability of indigenous women to abuse and violence. Indigenous women are therefore stripped of their right to self-determination by both violations against their collective rights, as members of indigenous communities, and violations against their individual rights, as sub-collectives within those communities. (UN HRC 2015: 5)

Similar concerns were raised by an earlier UN Special Rapporteur report in respect of violence against women in the name of traditional values. The report identified numerous forms of violence against women which occur within some indigenous communities. These include FGM and child marriage. As the report stated:

the fact that those traditional practices cut across religious, geographical and ethnic characteristics demonstrate that there are multidimensional causal factors and that no one factor attributed to the identity of women makes them vulnerable. Violations suffered by indigenous women and girls must be viewed within the context of the broad spectrum of violations experienced and their specific vulnerabilities as members of indigenous communities. (UN Special Rapporteur 2007: 15)

A commitment to uphold the human rights of indigenous peoples must obviously extend to include all members of all such communities.

Suggested reading

- James Anaya, *Indigenous Peoples in International Law* (New York: Oxford University Press, 2004).
- Elvira Pulitano, *Indigenous Rights in the Age of the UN Declaration* (Cambridge: Cambridge University Press, 2014).
- Colin Samson, *A World You Do Not Know: Settler Societies, Indigenous Peoples and the Attack on Cultural Diversity* (London: Institute for the Study of the Americas, 2014).
- James Tully, *Strange Multiplicity: Constitutionalism in an Age of Diversity* (Cambridge: Cambridge University Press, 1991).

Notes

1. <https://www.amnesty.org/en/what-we-do/indigenous-peoples/> (last accessed 27 August 2016).
2. <http://www.ipu.org/splz-e/bolivia14.htm> (last accessed 27 August 2016).

7

Religion and Human Rights

Key questions

1. Why is the distinction between holding and manifesting a religious belief so important?
2. Why is the right of religious freedom a fundamental component of IHRL?
3. Why do some argue that human rights cannot be justified on secular grounds?
4. Why have various world religions felt the need to espouse human rights as being consistent with their teachings?
5. What are some of the key areas of incompatibility between many religions and human rights norms?
6. Does a state's commitment to human rights require that separate religions adopt more liberal values and beliefs?
7. Why is defining 'religion' so problematic?
8. Does respecting the right to religious freedom of diverse groups require state neutrality on the question of religion?
9. What is 'hate speech' and to what extent should religious communities be protected from it?
10. To what extent are states justified in banning the manifestation of religious commitments in public spaces?

Introduction

I now turn my attention towards religiously based forms of identity and commitment. While the IHRL covering religion also extends to include non-religious beliefs and conscience, I shall focus almost exclusively upon distinctly religiously based ways of being and believing. Even with this limitation, the potential scope of relevant material is huge and far exceeds what could be sufficiently well covered in a single chapter. As such, this is the longest chapter in the book. I shall consider several areas, including the complex relationship between religion and human rights, the extent to which differing world religions can be shown to be compatible with core human rights norms and, finally, how it might be possible to ensure that a fundamental right to religious freedom can be secured within a diverse world in which religion continues to play a key role in both the protection and the violation of human rights.

The persistence of religion

While 'God' may have died for Friedrich Nietzsche, the late-nineteenth-century German philosopher, it should be abundantly clear to anyone even vaguely familiar with life in the early twenty-first century that religion continues to exert a profound influence upon billions of people and many state and public authorities and officials. The European Enlightenment's objective of restricting the influence of religious faith to the private sphere of home or place of worship has proven to be only partially successful. Indeed, in many parts of the globe, continuing to express a commitment to the Enlightenment-derived ideals of public reason is the preserve of a small, sometimes much maligned, minority. The continuing, if not growing, appeal and authority of organised religions across the globe problematises the thesis that the world would necessarily succumb to the power and liberating charms of secularism. In a somewhat ironic manifestation of the adage of needing to be careful of what you wish for, the worries of many secularists concerning the disenchanting consequences of a potentially rationally organised world, are proving to be somewhat exaggerated given the continuing influence of religion upon the private and public domains.

For some theorists and activists, the continuing power of religion raises particular problems for the global defence of human rights. The most news-worthy example of this since the terrible events of 9/11 has, of course, been the use which murderous terrorists have made of an entirely partial and manifestly eccentric reading of the Quran. Less news-worthy, although probably just as harmful, have been the effects of the Catholic Church's ban on birth control and abortion in many parts of the world, including upon those currently afflicted by the Zika virus in which severely deformed babies are being born into a life which will be short and painful. Finally, for those who consider Buddhism as epitomising norms of pacifism and tolerance, it will no doubt come as a great surprise to learn of the existence of Buddhist monks who advocate systematic violence against other religious communities in countries such as Myanmar, Sri Lanka and Thailand. The annual report of the US Commission on International Religious Freedom catalogues the extent to which religiously fuelled conflict directly results in large-scale human rights violations. Thus, the most recent, 2015 report identified a cluster of countries in which religious freedoms are being systematically denied and in which religious conflict underpins broader social and political turmoil and instability. Countries in which severe violations of religious freedom that are systematic, ongoing and egregious are occurring include China, Eritrea, Iran, Myanmar, North Korea, Saudi Arabia, Sudan, Turkmenistan and Uzbekistan. Below this tier of the worst-offending countries are others in which systematic, though slightly less severe, violations of religious freedom are occurring. These countries include Afghanistan, Azerbaijan, Cuba, India, Indonesia, Kazakhstan, Laos, Malaysia, Russia and Turkey. The US Commission was established by the International Religious Freedom Act (1998) and thus its determinations have direct consequences for US foreign and overseas trade policies. Given the recurring presence of religious conflict within many human rights violations, it is not surprising that many simply accept that a commitment to human rights is, in various ways, incompatible with a more partial commitment to any specific religious doctrine.

Some who endorse the assumption that human rights and religion are, at root, basically incompatible with each other have directed their criticisms towards what they perceive as a purposefully hostile attitude which pervades human rights' engagement with religion. Take, for example, the words of Werner Menski, a respected academic authority upon South Asian legal systems, who writes, 'Putting itself on a pedestal, human rights jurisprudence as a new form of secular religion has turned out to be rabidly intolerant of religion and generates negative responses to its own intolerance' (Menski 2012: 81). This characterisation of the allegedly militantly secularist underpinnings of human rights norms has been an established feature of discourse in this area for some considerable time. As a characterisation of the relationship between human rights (both human rights norms and IHRL) it is, however, entirely wrong. In actual fact, the relationship between human rights and religion(s) is far more complex, nuanced and, in places, contradictory than any single characterisation can allow for.

Human rights and religion: one side of the coin

A commitment to the doctrine of human rights has often been considered and denounced as the latest expression of faith-less secularism. To assume, or to argue, that human rights are fundamentally incompatible with religious faith(s) entails a corresponding claim that human rights are incompatible with the requirements of recognising cultural diversity, given the persistence of extremely diverse religious faiths across the globe. At this point, it should be acknowledged that the human rights doctrine and broader movement would be in deep trouble if those of religious faith were effectively alienated from human rights. Thankfully, they are not. Or, rather, the relationship is a complex one and consists of compatible and incompatible elements. Before I discuss the latter, I shall consider the extent to which religion has been, and continues to be, an integral component of human rights norms and IHRL.

To begin with, IHRL includes a fundamental right of individual freedom of religion and conscience under Article 18 of the ICCPR, which draws upon its earlier incarnation within the UDHR. Article 18 states:

1. Everyone shall have the right to freedom of thought, conscience and religion. This right shall include freedom to have or to adopt a religion or belief of his choice, and freedom, either individually or in community with others and in public or private, to manifest his religion or belief in worship, observance, practice and teaching.
2. No one shall be subject to coercion which would impair his freedom to have or to adopt a religion or belief of his choice.
3. Freedom to manifest one's religion or beliefs may be subject only to such limitations as are prescribed by law and are necessary to protect public safety, order, health, or morals or the fundamental rights and freedoms of others.
4. The States Parties to the present Covenant undertake to have respect for the liberty of parents and, when applicable, legal guardians to ensure the religious and moral education of their children in conformity with their own convictions.

Subsequent rights of religious freedom and conscience are also protected within various regional human rights instruments (such as Article 9 of the ECHR, Article 12 of the American Convention on Human Rights and Article 10(1) of the African Charter). The adoption and manifestation of religious belief are also protected under many domestic legal systems.

In addition to the ICCPR, the UN body of human rights instruments also includes the Declaration on the Elimination of All Forms of Intolerance and of Discrimination Based on Religion or Belief (1981) which, though not legally binding, provides a more detailed formulation of what constitutes discrimination and intolerance than is found within Article 18 of the ICCPR.

The fundamental right of religious freedom is, therefore, an essential component of IHRL. It is also highly important to note that the existence of the right is not entirely due to the efforts of the secularly minded, who, some might imagine, were motivated to offer the right as a begrudging concession to those who continued to be enthralled by an epistemologically inferior body of beliefs.

Reading back from the present moment, religion has exercised a profound influence upon the development of human rights thinking and successive UN instruments. As human rights philosophers continue to struggle in their efforts to definitively ground the doctrine upon intellectually sound, secular foundations, a constituency of theorists have consistently argued that the secularist approach to normatively justifying human rights is destined to fail. Philosophers such as David Novak (2012), Nicholas Wolterstorff (2008) and Michael Perry (1998) have argued that secular reasoning is ultimately incapable of justifying a belief in the inherent dignity of human beings and that, in the words of Perry (1998: 39), human rights are 'finally (and unavoidably) a theological project'. I shall consider and challenge such claims below.

Notwithstanding contemporary appeals to the alleged necessity of theological reasoning in any attempt to ultimately justify the normative foundations of human rights, religion has also exerted a prominent influence upon the framing of the foundational document of the modern human rights movement: the UDHR. Several world religions were represented by principal members of the UN Commission on Human Rights, which was tasked with drafting the UDHR. Thus, René Cassin was Jewish, Pen-chun Chang was Confucian, Charles Malik was a Maronite Christian and Jacques Maritain was a Catholic philosopher.

Lest some imagine that such members of the Commission left their faith at the door, so to speak, of the drafting process, René Cassin explicitly connected human rights to religion when he wrote:

> the concept of human rights comes from the Bible, from the Old Testament, from the Ten Commandments ... Thou shalt not murder is the right to life. Thou shalt not steal is the right to own property ... We must not forget that Judaism gave the world the concept of human rights. (Cited in Ishay 2004: 19)

Micheline Ishay, a historian of human rights, has written that 'while human rights force us to think about universality in political and economic terms, they benefit from such portrayals of brotherly love one finds in Micah (the Hebrew bible), Paul (the New Testament), the Buddha, and others' (Ishay 2004: 19).

A core element of human rights thinking is also deeply indebted to earlier theological deliberations. As I discussed in earlier chapters, the idea of universality is indispensable to the normative underpinnings of IHRL. The concept of moral universality arguably achieved its most unequivocal and self-confident expression in the natural law tradition, which has been extensively analysed within the literature on the theory of human rights. Emerging in Greek and Roman political and legal philosophy, the natural law tradition posits the existence of a pre-social realm, accessible through the exercise of reason, in which genuinely universal principles of justice can be identified and brought to bear upon the regulation of actual human relations. This way of thinking persisted (albeit with some twists and turns along the way) within Christian theology well into the period immediately prior to the emergence of the European Enlightenment. Philosophers such as John Locke and Jean-Jacques Rousseau then reformulated the idea of natural law in the seventeenth and eighteenth centuries respectively and derived from it the concept of natural rights, which were conceived of as pre-social, pre-political moral instruments designed to enable the establishment of just political and legal systems. Natural rights have continued to attract their supporters during the modern day, most notably perhaps through the attempt by John Finnis (1980) to refashion a natural rights foundation for the human rights doctrine. Through the appeal to natural law and natural rights, theology has undeniably exerted a profound influence upon the development of human rights norms.

In addition to the existence of fundamental rights to religious freedom and the demonstrable influence of religion upon the development of the human rights doctrine, over the past fifty years several world religions have made authoritative statements affirming human rights. The first of these was the Papal Vatican Decree, December 1965: Declaration on Religious Freedom, which affirmed the Catholic Church's recognition of numerous fundamental human rights, including individual rights to life, to the enjoyment of a sufficient standard of living, of a right to labour, to education, health care, religion, assembly and association. The Vatican Decree also recognised the legitimacy of the separation of church from state within nation-states. In 1990 the Organization of the Islamic Conference issued its so-called Cairo Declaration on Human Rights in Islam. In its Preamble the Cairo Declaration states:

> fundamental rights and universal freedoms in Islam are an integral part of the Islamic religion and that no one as a matter of principle has the right to suspend them in whole or in part or violate or ignore them in as much as they are binding divine commandments, which are contained in the Revealed Books of God and were sent through the last of His Prophets to complete the preceding divine messages thereby making their observance an act of worship and their neglect or violation an abominable sin, and accordingly every person is individually responsible – and the *Ummah* collectively responsible – for their safeguard.

The Cairo Declaration was subsequently followed by the World Council of Churches committing itself to affirming the UDHR in 1999.

Official religious pronouncements on the compatibility between the moral basis of human rights and various world religions have also been complemented by a steady stream of recent academic studies into the similarities between various religious concepts and ideals and core human rights norms (see Witte and Green 2012).

In respect of Christianity, I have already briefly considered the significance of natural law theology upon the development of human rights. In addition, numerous scholars have identified core precedents of many fundamental human rights contained within Scripture. Thus, Wolterstorff (2012) identifies correlative rights contained within the Ten Commandments, so that, for example, the Sixth Commandment's 'thou shalt not kill' is correlated with a fundamental right to life. Wolterstorff then develops upon the Christian concept of *imago dei* as a key normative element of subsequent natural rights and then human rights thinking. The concept of *imago dei* refers to the idea first expressed in the book of Genesis that human beings are made in the image of God. Because we are made in the image of God, there are a multitude of things which we cannot do to each other and a multitude of things which we ought to do for each other. As each and every one of us is conceived of as made in God's image, we are also prohibited from acting partially towards some others. The concept of non-discrimination is, it is claimed, prefigured in Genesis. A great number of Christians have committed their lives to the defence of causes which are unequivocally concerned with the protection of human rights. Thus, the German pastor, Dietrich Bonhoeffer, whose opposition to the Nazis in his native Germany resulted in his murder, stated that 'it is for Christ's sake, and the sake of his coming kingdom, that the rights of every person are to be recognized and respected' (cited in Reed 2012: 236). More recently, Archbishop Desmond Tutu played a central role in South Africa's relatively peaceful transition from Apartheid through his championing of a non-retributive, reconciliatory approach to transitional justice. In Latin America, numerous Catholics contributed to the struggle against military dictatorships and authoritarian regimes during the 1970s and 1980s. In some cases, such as the brutal murder of Archbishop Oscar Romero in San Salvador in 1980, such acts of courage cost many their lives.

Against the widespread Islamophobia which has emerged within many societies of late, numerous scholars have also clearly identified unequivocal similarities between elements of Islamic teaching and human rights. Thus, Irene Oh (2012) has reiterated the fundamental importance to Muslims of overcoming social and economic injustice through the Quran's insistence upon the duty of *zakat*, which requires acts of benevolence and giving amongst Muslims. Referring to a similar set of Quranic duties, Ishay has stated that 'the doctrine of social service, defined in terms of alleviating suffering, and healing the needy, constitutes an integral part of Islamic teaching' (Ishay 2004: 40). The Quran also contains numerous precepts, or *Surah*, which directly correlate with existing human rights. For example, protection against defamation is found within *Surah* 24: 16, the denunciation of poverty as a form of injustice is contained within *Surah* 22: 7–8, individuals' rights of residence are found within *Surah* 2: 85 and a right to asylum from oppression is found within *Surah* 4: 97–9. Many Muslims have affirmed the independent value of human rights and the compatibility between Islam and human rights. Thus, Islamic scholars such as Abdullahi Ahmed An-Na'im (2008), Fatima Mernissi (1975) and Abdolkarim Soroush (2000) 'espouse views that tend to align with Western notions of free speech and women's rights, and they vigorously denounce Islamic extremism' (Oh 2012: 262). Beyond what Hilary Putnam (1987: 60) refers to as the 'Jerusalem-based religions', others have also identified strong precedents for human rights thinking in other world religions.

Hinduism, which is practised by over one billion human beings worldwide, has often been associated with ways of being and believing that are fundamentally incompatible with core human rights. For example, the notorious Hindu caste system is a reflection of the Hindu notion of moral order, referred to as *dharma*. The Hindu caste system is a hierarchical whole within which individuals are not accorded equal moral worth. Furthermore, like other so-called Eastern religions, the cosmology of Hinduism envisages a single moral universe in which all are related and no one is, in a sense, fundamentally separate or morally sovereign. Individuals achieve merit through their actions and no one possesses inherent entitlements. Against this, some Hindu scholars, such as Arvind Sharma (2004), have sought to identify areas in which human rights and Hinduism are more compatible than the conventional view typically allows for. For example, while the Indian constitution is a secular document, it is important to acknowledge that it was largely drafted by an untouchable, B. R. Ambedkar. It is also important to acknowledge that the current Indian constitution, which aims to ultimately regulate a state comprising some 950 million Hindus, contains more rights than those found within the US Bill of Rights, including a right to equality, a right against exploitation, a right to freedom of religion, cultural and educational rights and a right to constitutional remedies. Finally, Mahatma Gandhi, who considered himself to be an orthodox Hindu, has been widely lauded as one of the twentieth century's most outstanding defenders of human rights.

Although it is less of an organised religion and more a philosophy of life, elements of Confucianism have been identified as central to human rights thinking. Confucianism, which dates back some 2,500 years, is a complex and multifaceted doctrine. However, core elements include a focus upon the interdependency of human life, the need to establish harmony, rather than conflict, and a view of political power as existing to serve the interests of the people and not the elite. In her study of Confucius' contribution to the development of human rights, Micheline Ishay writes:

> Confucius elaborated, over two millennia ago, an ethical posi-
> tion that encompassed aspects of current views on human
> rights. Indeed, he believed that all individuals, even commoners,
> possessed rational, aesthetic, political, social, historical, and tran-
> scendental qualities that could be cultivated through education.
> (Ishay 2004: 22)

Finally, in my admittedly somewhat selective survey of religious per-
spectives, Buddhism has attracted a significant degree of interest from scholars seeking to identify core similarities between the religion and modern-day human rights thinking. Like all world religions, Buddhism is extremely internally diverse and comprises a multitude of different perspectives and traditions. However, at its core, Buddhism is fundamentally concerned with overcoming sickness, anguish and suffering in peaceful and compassionate ways. Buddhism espouses the value of various freedoms including *ahimsa* (freedom from violence), *asteya* (freedom from want), *aparigraha* (freedom from exploitation), and *arm-
ritatva* and *arogya* (freedom from early death and disease respectively). Buddha famously rejected the prevailing caste system of his native India of the sixth century BCE. A core element of Buddhist ethics consists of the so-called Five Lay Precepts: do not kill, do not steal, do not lie, do not commit sexual misconduct and do not ingest intoxicants. Some scholars have argued that these precepts necessarily entail and are consistent with correlative rights (Keown 1992) and that Buddhism can thereby substantively contribute to determining the content of human rights. Finally, the Dalai Lama has consistently written of what he considers to be the fundamental compatibility between human rights and Buddhism. In one such pronouncement, he wrote:

> no matter what country or continent we come from we are all
> basically the same human beings. We have the common human
> needs and concerns. We all seek happiness and try to avoid suffer-
> ing regardless of our race, religion, sex, or political status. Human
> beings, indeed all sentient beings, have the right to pursue hap-
> piness and live in peace and in freedom. (Cited in King 2012: 113)

King herself proceeds to claim that 'Buddhist social and political activities universally embrace human rights' (King 2012: 116).

Human rights and religion: the other side of the coin

As has been stated many times, all organised religions are deeply diverse and are typically characterised by internal divisions and discord. Quite apart from the countless numbers of human beings who have died or have killed in the name of their religious faith, countless others have also suffered terribly at the hands of fellow believers who otherwise uphold a different interpretation of a single sacred text or figure. Thus, it is a statement of fact to state that human rights and religion are simultaneously both compatible and profoundly incompatible. The sheer, confusing diversity of any specific religious belief system and community serves to refute any such assertions that all followers of X religion are either peace-loving or filled with zealous hatred of those who do not espouse the same beliefs. For example, take the quote above concerning the alleged commitment of Buddhist activists to embracing human rights. As stated, the claim is quite simply false. In Myanmar, a Buddhist monk, U Wirathu, has been calling for the violent persecution of non-Buddhists, particularly the ethnic Rohingya who are predominantly Muslim and largely found in the north-eastern Rakhine state of Myanmar. The Rohingya are not recognised as one of the 135 officially recognised ethnic groups in Myanmar and are considered by the UN to be one of the most persecuted minorities in the world. This particular manifestation of Buddhism, in the form of U Wirathu and his many followers, is undoubtedly contributing to the plight of the Rohingya. Of course, the actions of some Buddhists do not justify an alternative, negative characterisation of the entire religion, but it does serve to remind us that those who self-identify with any given religion are capable of interpreting the demands of their faith in a multitude of ways.

The same, of course, can be said of Islam. Islamic states have, despite the Cairo Declaration, consistently acted in ways which fall significantly short of a satisfactory commitment to international human rights norms. Witness the sheer number of reservations which Islamic states have issued against the CEDAW, as I discussed in Chapter 4. Some individual Islamic states have also pursued distinctively harsh policies in the treatment of offenders and religious minorities, as is the case with Saudi Arabia's penal code and the punishment of cutting off a thief's hands. Other Islamic states, such as Iran, have criminalised homosexuality, which carries a maximum penalty of the death sentence. Beyond sovereign states, there is also the terrible human rights toll resulting from the actions of numerous terrorist groups, such as *Da'esh* and *Boko Haram*, which draw upon their own Islamist readings of the Quran and Shari'a in their otherwise clearly nihilistic campaigns across parts of the Middle East and Africa.

Many other overt human rights violations and forms of systematic persecution and discrimination have been perpetrated in the name of Christianity. In many parts of Africa, leading members of the Anglican Church have been actively supporting state laws which criminalise homosexuality. In recent months, there has also been a spate of news reports detailing a growing homophobic mood among many Christians in some southern states of the United States. It is important to acknowledge that these campaigns have been organised not by extreme outsiders, so to speak, but by established and authoritative figures within the respective churches. For these followers of Christ, God's love is not boundless, apparently, and certainly does not extend to those who choose same-sex partners.

Clearly none of the above examples can be described as compatible with human rights, even where, in the case of some of the recent legal cases in the United States, the protection of homophobic attitudes is provided by appeals to the First Amendment of the US Constitution. The countless incidents of religiously fuelled violations of human rights obviously pose the greatest challenge to any attempt to somehow square the circle between respecting religious diversity and a commitment to upholding all human beings' equal human rights. Having considered the two sides of a deeply complex relationship between human rights and religion, I turn now to the formidable task of attempting to square the circle.

In pursuit of commensurability

The task before us is daunting. IHRL must exist within and respond to the world as it is. The global human rights movement would never have achieved as much as it has if its norms and ideals were militantly opposed to, or intolerant of, religion. Human rights cannot be the perfectionist creed of the militantly secular. *The Washington Times* reported on 23 December 2012 that some 84 per cent of the world's adult population affiliate with some religious faith. As a constituency of people, secularists, atheists and agnostics comprise a very small minority. If human rights are to achieve a sufficient degree of normative respect amongst sufficient numbers of the peoples across the world, they cannot set themselves against the moral beliefs and commitments of the vast majority of the world's population. This is a pragmatic truth, but it also has far deeper and more substantial philosophical underpinnings.

The first of these underpinnings concerns the extent to which IHRL reflects and is fundamentally indebted to a substantive moral doctrine or philosophy. Against those who prefer to ignore the essentially normative character of IHRL, I have consistently argued that IHRL is based upon and is normatively shaped by core norms and ideals. Responses to the various challenges levelled against the legitimacy of IHRL are best fashioned, not by an exclusive appeal to the realities of state sovereignty and state interests, but by appeal to the universal moral authority of a doctrine which seeks, at the very least, to fashion a world in which inhumanity is securely contained. By means of a commitment to recognising the moral authority of the ideals of liberty, equality and human dignity, human rights must be understood as requiring the establishment of a normative order, which upholds these ideals. Describing human rights as a normative doctrine does not, however, mean that it amounts to a separate (and rival) moral philosophy of life. One can understand this point more clearly by comparing it with a long-standing debate within political philosophy, that between so-called perfectionists and anti-perfectionists.

Many, if not all, religious belief systems can be understood as being essentially perfectionist conceptions of the moral good. In their differing ways, religious belief systems typically espouse a substantive and detailed vision of the moral good and an account of how true believers should conduct their lives. I have already shown the extent to which each religion comprises very different interpretations of and perspectives upon those core elements or sacred texts which each religion is based upon. The internal diversity of each religious community testifies to the limitations of imposing a single authority upon even a single community of believers. This effect is greatly amplified, of course, in multi-faith societies, which I shall consider in greater detail below.

Interestingly, some have sought to downplay the diversity of religious communities by arguing that it is possible (and for the purposes of regulating multi-faith societies, positively desirable) to fashion an ecumenical vision in which most of the world's major religions can be shown to exhibit a core set of commitments, so that it may be possible to identify an overlapping consensus of fundamentally religious ideals which all faiths can commit to alongside their continuing adherence to their own faith. Personally, I think the ecumenical approach only works if we overlook areas of fundamental disagreement, such as those found between religious doctrines which accord a unique and distinct value to human beings and those which extend fundamental value to all sentient beings. The resulting partiality of the 'ecumenical' vision negates its objective. The incompatibilities between different religious doctrines prevent seeking to re-establish the human rights doctrine upon an overlapping consensus of religious commitments. This does not mean that human rights are thereby incapable of respecting religious communities.

It is undoubtedly true that the morality of human rights has been deeply influenced by religious elements, as I have demonstrated above. However, I think it is essential that IHRL remain doctrinally independent of the substantive content of any and all specific religious doctrines if it is to remain capable of providing the fundamental basis for regulating core areas of human life amidst diversity. If IHRL is to be capable of legislating for all, it must, so to speak, belong to no single or partial constituency of peoples. In this sense, to resume the engagement with the terminology of political philosophy, human rights must not be defended as another perfectionist doctrine. As I shall discuss further below and specifically in respect of defending human beings' right to religious freedom, this does not mean that human rights must militantly uphold a form of secularism which tends towards viewing religion as a mere 'opiate of the people'. The tendency to view religion as being profoundly and irredeemably at odds with humanism all too often results in the persecution of religious communities, which is manifestly a violation of a fundamental right to religious freedom. Human rights must thereby be reconciled with a world in which the vast majority of human beings seek guidance from a bewildering range of belief systems. Of course, this process of reconciliation will always be shaped by the necessity that no human right can be claimed and exercised in order to systematically and intentionally violate others' human rights. Secularists cannot compel the religious to renounce their faith and separate faiths cannot compel adherents of other faiths to convert.

A second area of consideration concerns the depth to which religious commitments can influence many people's very sense of self. As

I have argued at various points throughout this book, one of the areas in which human rights thinking has often failed to adequately engage with the sheer diversity of human life concerns the models of agency which much of human rights thinking has drawn upon. The extent to which many individuals perceive themselves as fundamentally connected to their religious commitments raises significant challenges to much conventional human rights thinking on the nature of what I shall refer to as religiously constituted agency and identity. I explore this point in greater detail below. For the time being, a quote from the previously mentioned Islamic defender of human rights, Abdullahi An-Na'im, should serve to illustrate the point I am making. In considering the respective moral claims made upon individuals by human rights on the one hand and religion on the other, An-Na'im writes, 'if I am faced with a choice between being Muslim or a commitment to human rights, I will choose being Muslim without any hesitation . . . no conception of human rights can possibly compete with my religion as such' (An-Na'im 2012: 57).

This point speaks to the above concern also, in respect of the need for human rights to draw upon normative sources which do not reduce to or compete with any specific religious doctrine. However, it also draws attention to the constitutive power of religious commitment for many. The sheer importance of religious commitment for many a believer's identity and very sense of self is also well expressed by a member of the South African Constitutional Court. In his ruling upon *Christian Education, South Africa v Minister of Education (2000)*, Justice Albie Sachs wrote:

> for many believers, their relationship with God or creation is central to all their activities. It concerns their capacity to relate in an intensely meaningful fashion to their sense of themselves, their community and their universe. For millions in all walks of life, religion provides support and nurture and a framework for individual and social stability and growth. Religious belief has the capacity to awake concepts of self-worth and human dignity which form the cornerstone of human rights. (Cited in Van der Vyer 2012: 249)

The phenomenological significance of religious belief for many serves to problematise an understanding of religious conviction as ultimately merely one of a potentially infinite number of entirely discretional individual choices and commitments. This raises serious issues for how the right of religious freedom has been variously interpreted and implemented in many jurisdictions.

The right to religious freedom lies at a highly important juncture at which many competing forces converge, cross and, on occasion, collide. The object of the right necessarily raises the potential of individuals and communities claiming dispensation from the need to recognise others' rights to pursue interests and objectives which are taboo or roundly condemned amongst those claiming their religious rights. In this way (I consider specific examples of this below) the morality of human rights can sometimes clash with the specific morality of a religious belief system which some of its adherents claim cannot tolerate some others' lifestyle choices. IHRL has a stock response to such instances of conflicting rights: that no right can be exercised in order to violate or significantly abridge others' enjoyment of the same or different rights. Some people's claims to the enjoyment of their specific religious beliefs place great strain on this response. Setting to one side the manifestly illegitimate resort to death and destruction which some have pursued in the name of their respective faiths, instances in which an individual's conscience is extended beyond their own immediate sphere and into the lives of others through changes in public policy or legal rulings raise particular challenges to my pursuit of identifying a sufficiently comprehensive and commensurate relationship between the morality of human rights and diverse religious communities' right to manifest their beliefs and traditions within the framework of IHRL. As I have repeatedly indicated in the last few pages, I shall consider specific instances of this challenge throughout the remainder of this chapter. Before I proceed to this, however, it is important to be clear on what the normative basis is for my attempt to negotiate those challenges.

IHRL comprises a body of positive law with distinct parameters and boundaries. This is no less the case with the specific right of religious freedom. Considerations upon the basis and limits of anyone's legitimate claims to the exercise of religious freedom typically entail engaging with the normative underbelly of IHRL. The doctrine of human rights cannot hope to compete with the vast multitude of separate religious belief systems which it seeks to regulate through the protection of a fundamental right to religious freedom. In this sense, the normative basis and content of human rights must refrain from endorsing a single, characteristically secular, perfectionist moral vision of how human life can best be led. Refraining from seeking to compete with substantive moral and religious doctrines and visions does not entail that human rights are fated to be re-established as a primarily pragmatic, political project. The ultimate normative objective does not merely consist of hoping to prevent the mass spilling of blood. Human rights are also, and far more ambitiously perhaps, concerned with establishing and upholding systems in which recurring expressions of humanity, rather than inhumanity, can proliferate. Philosophers have suggested various ways in which human beings differ fundamentally from other animals. I think it is reasonable to claim that one of the key differences between 'us' and other species is our capacity for spiritual and religious conviction: the capacity for the religious experience is a distinctive, unique constituent of humanity. It is also, I believe, an indispensable feature for many human beings' sense of their own dignity.

Philosophically astute readers may be slightly surprised at my appeal to human dignity as providing a key normative criterion for grounding and determining the limits of a right to religious freedom within diverse environments. As a philosophical ideal, dignity has typically been associated with a Kantian form of moral philosophy. My appeal to dignity might therefore appear to contradict my earlier insistence upon the urgent need for human rights thinking to begin to take seriously non-Kantian perspectives upon the basis and formation of identity. Typically, Kant's philosophy has been associated with a way of thinking which explicitly excludes any concern for what he refers to as the 'phenomenal' realm from that in which the principles of constitutional governance are framed. The Kantian tradition views dignity as an inherent property of individual, morally autonomous human beings. By stressing the sheer importance of recognising and engaging with the interpersonal constituents of forming human identities, my approach calls into question the efficacy of assuming the existence of some impregnable inner citadel of human moral worth and accords far greater power to the potential of interpersonal relations to thwart or prevent the development of the capacity for, in this instance, any human being's enjoyment of human dignity. The realisation of the ideal depends upon the opportunity to enjoy a dignified life. A dignified life, in turn, depends, to a significant extent, upon the opportunity to contribute to and benefit from acting in accordance with the idea of humanity, as I outlined in Chapter 1. Living under the protection of human rights is, in turn, one of the core legal and political manifestations of acting in accordance with the idea of humanity. In this sense, dignity is an achieved status and anyone's enjoyment of a minimally dignified life is therefore vulnerable to how others treat one. Jeremy Waldron phrases this well when he writes, 'a person's dignity is not just some Kantian aura. It is their social standing, the fundamentals of basic reputation that entitle them to be treated as equals in the ordinary operations of society' (2012: 5). In arguing that dignity must be secured, Waldron then states that 'as a social and legal status, it has to be established, upheld, maintained, and vindicated by society and the law, and this . . . is something in which we are all required to play a part' (2012: 60). Human dignity, understood in this way, therefore provides for Waldron and for me a core normative ideal by which it is possible to distinguish between legitimate and illegitimate claims to the protection of a right to religious freedom.

Defining religion amidst diversity

Like many others who have written on the subject of religion, I have been referring to the phenomenon as if its meaning is clear and well defined. In actual fact, one of the many challenges which legislating for religious freedom raises concerns how religion itself is defined. It seems reasonable to imagine that deliberations over the right require a shared definition of the object of the right. Legislators and theorists alike have consistently had to confront the troubling fact that there is no single, universally endorsed definition of what even constitutes a 'religion'. Defining religion is obviously complicated by diversity. The sheer range of communities and congregations claiming the title of a religious group within most multi-faith societies and more broadly across the globe complicates the search for some alleged essence of religion. However, the definitional challenge is not merely the consequence of quantitative factors and emerges, instead, out of the phenomenological realities of many people's lives. Thus, writing against the backdrop of what was then a largely homogenous community, James Madison first raised doubts over the specific ability of legislators to define 'religion' in his 1785 tract, *Memorial and Remonstrance*, in which he condemned the view that the 'Civil Magistrate is a competent Judge of Religious Truth' ([1785] 2010). Madison may have been only dimly aware of how his words would echo across centuries of US Supreme Court deliberations over what or who might legitimately claim the protection of religious speech in a vast body of primarily First Amendment jurisprudence.

Successive generations of US Supreme Court justices have con-fronted the challenge of having to define what constitutes a 'religion' in a range of legal cases covering, amongst others, the status of employ-ment contracts (*The Church of the Holy Trinity v United States, 1895*), the denial of employment on religious grounds (*Torcaso v Watkins, 1961*), the right to conscientious objection against military service (*United States v Kauten, 1943; United States v Seeger, 1965*) and the parental rights of parents over their children's education (*Wisconsin v Yoder, 1972*). In *Holy Trinity*, the Court espoused a theistic definition of reli-gion in which a belief in the existence of God (in this case specifically a Christian God) was a necessary and objective element of a legitimate religion. Beginning with *Kauten*, however, the theistic, purportedly objective, definition was gradually replaced with a far more subjec-tive understanding of what constitutes religious experience from the perspective of believers themselves. The resulting approach takes its bearings from Paul Tillich's (1948: 57) emphasis on what is of 'ultimate concern' to believers and is expressed in *Seeger* where the ruling estab-lishes the following criteria for determining whether an action or belief is entitled to legal protection: 'the test is whether a given belief that is sincere and meaningful occupies a place in the life of its possessor parallel to that filled by the orthodox belief in God of one who clearly qualifies for the exemption' (*United States v Seeger, 1965*: 166). A similar position was also finally adopted by the UK Supreme Court in its ruling over *Hodkin v Registrar (2013)*, which recognised Scientology as a bona fide religion. Drawing upon a non-theistic understanding of religion, which places the greatest emphasis upon the significance of the said belief system for a plaintiff, Lord Toulson stated at paragraph 57:

> I would describe religion in summary as a spiritual or non-secular belief system, held by a group of adherents, which claims to explain mankind's place in the universe and relationship with the infinite, and to teach its adherents how they are to live their lives in conformity with the spiritual understanding associated with the belief system. (*Hodkin v Registrar, 2013*: 18)

In other European jurisdictions, such as Germany and Russia, Scientology has been denied legal protection as a religion on the grounds that it fails to meet their respective criteria for determining what constitutes a legitimate religion in those countries.

It is reasonable to conclude then that above-discussed signatories of the ICCPR (the US, UK, Germany and Russia) do not share a single understanding of what constitutes a religion for the purposes of upholding Article 18. The question of what constitutes a religion has been addressed by the treaty body overseeing the ICCPR in its General Comment 22. It is, however, reasonable to conclude that the criteria the CCPR offered are so broad as to provide little real tangible assistance in attempts to settle such issues. Thus, General Comment 22, paragraph 2 states:

> Article 18 protects theistic, non-theistic and atheistic beliefs, as well as the right not to profess any religion or belief. The terms 'belief' and 'religion' are to be broadly construed. Article 18 is not limited in its application to traditional religions or to religions and beliefs with institutional characteristics or practices analogous to those of traditional religions. The Committee therefore views with concern any tendency to discriminate against any religion or belief for any reason, including the fact that they are newly established, or represent religious minorities that may be the subject of hostility on the part of a predominant religious community.

Thus, one may reasonably agree with one commentator's view that:

> so many definitions of religion have been framed in the West over the years that even a partial listing would be impractical. With varying success they have all struggled to avoid, on the one hand, the Scylla of hard, sharp, particularistic definitions and, on the other hand, the Charybdis of meaningless generalities. (King 1995: 282)

I now turn my attention to analysing specific examples of the challenges which confront the protection of a right to religious freedom within diverse environments. I shall restrict my discussion to what are conventionally recognised as established religious belief systems and communities, whilst acknowledging the unresolved question of how anything can be singled out as 'religion' in the first case.

A right to religious freedom in practice

Suffice it to say that there are countless examples of religious freedom in practice, covering a vast range of human affairs and interests. No single chapter in a volume of this nature could hope to provide a sufficiently comprehensive survey or analysis of this particular area of concern. I have chosen then, in keeping with the broader focus upon the challenges raised by reconciling human rights with cultural diversity, to focus upon a selection of issues which are most pertinent to protecting a right to religious freedom in the context of a commitment to diversity. I align my discussion along three distinct axes. The first can be thought of as a largely vertical relationship between state authorities and the rights of religious believers which fall under the state's jurisdiction. The second is a far more horizontal relationship and concerns the relations between different religious communities within the same jurisdiction who are, on occasion, competing over claims to the exercise of the same right. The final axis is also a horizontal relationship and consists of the relationships between believers and non-believers, both of whom make rights-based claims which appear to threaten some important interests of the other. Thus, my analysis of the right of religious freedom in practice focuses upon both the requirements for granting the right and when the right can be legitimately limited. Before I dive into these somewhat murky waters, it is important to first be absolutely clear what the ICCPR has to say about granting and limiting Article 18.

The IHRL of religious freedom establishes a fundamental distinction between the holding and the manifesting of religious belief. This distinction is also included in a wide range of regional and domestic legal instruments which protect religious freedom. The legal source of the distinction is found in Article 18 of the ICCPR. By way of a reminder, Article 18(1) states:

> everyone shall have the right to freedom of thought, conscience and religion. This right shall include freedom to have or to adopt a religion or belief of his choice, and freedom, either individually or in community with others and in public or private, to manifest his religion or belief in worship, observance, practice and teaching.

Article 18(1) cannot be limited or suspended. In its General Comment 22, paragraph 3, the CCPR reaffirmed this interpretation of 18(1). Thus:

Article 18 distinguishes the freedom of thought, conscience, religion or belief from the freedom to manifest religion or belief. It does not permit any limitations whatsoever on the freedom of thought and conscience or on the freedom to have or adopt a religion or belief of one's choice. These freedoms are protected unconditionally, as is the right of everyone to hold opinions without interference in Article 19.1.

As the CCPR's words indicate, the freedom to *manifest* one's religion can be subject to limitations as provided for under Article 18(3) which states:

freedom to manifest one's religion or beliefs may be subject only to such limitations as are prescribed by law and are necessary to protect public safety, order, health, or morals or the fundamental rights and freedoms of others.

The distinction between holding and manifesting religious beliefs may be compared to the broader distinctions often drawn between the private and the public spheres and that between negative and positive liberty. Such distinctions are necessary and credible, but one should be wary of assuming that neat, hard and fast dividing lines can always be identified and upheld in practice.

First axis – state and religious believers

Within international law states bear the principal duty to uphold individuals' human rights. One of the great paradoxes of IHRL, however, is that states constitute the single worst violators of human rights. Political scientists have developed an extensive body of research into the causes and effects of states' violations of human rights (see Landman and Carvalho 2009). Some states are essentially totalitarian or authoritarian in character and engage in systematic violations of human rights. Other states are profoundly impoverished or suffering from widespread corruption and their ability to provide for the material well-being of their citizens is severely limited. Another group of states are established liberal-democracies and have cultivated a reputation for systematically respecting human rights at home and abroad. Some of these states are broadly justified in the claims they make for themselves. Others are less justified. Interestingly, the right of religious freedom is often threatened and undermined in a range of states spanning those which routinely violate human rights and those which claim to uphold IHRL. One of the key explanatory factors in states' violation or protection of religious freedom consists of the extent to which any given state is officially committed to a single religious doctrine, or, indeed, the extent to which a state may seek to prohibit the manifestation of religious beliefs in the public sphere.

Nazila Ghanea (2012) has identified three separate categories of relationship between state and religion. The first consists of states whose legal and political system is based upon or accords specific protections to an established religion. Examples of such include the various Islamic republics and some other non-Islamic states in which the head of state must belong to a specific religion as is the case in the UK, Denmark, Norway, Sweden, Lebanon, Bhutan and Thailand. The second comprises states in which there are established systems of cooperation between the state and a single religious community. Such cooperation can take many forms and include, for example, the legal requirement of the payment of so-called church taxes, which exists in several European states, such as Austria, Croatia, Germany, Iceland and Switzerland. Interestingly, in several states of the US, atheists are prohibited from holding public office, including in Arkansas, Mississippi, North and South Carolina, Tennessee and Texas. Finally, there are nation-states in which the church and state are entirely separate. In some of these nation-states, this separation is based upon the state's commitment to a particular form of state secularism, as is the case in France and Turkey, but which, as I shall consider below, has raised specific problems for those who adhere to religious communities within those countries.

Irrespective of a state's relationship to a given religious community, the principal domain in which the state is able to directly influence religion comprises those spaces in which religious belief is manifested. All state signatories to the ICCPR are, in this respect, committed to a policy of non-interference or non-intervention concerning individuals' *holding* to any religious doctrine. There are, however, innumerable ways in which states can support or obstruct the *manifestation* of religious beliefs.

Many secularists argue that religious freedom requires the separation of church from state. Interestingly, the CCPR does not agree.

General Comment 22, paragraph 9 presents the Committee's position on the legitimacy of state religions. Thus:

> the fact that a religion is recognized as a state religion or that it is established as official or traditional or that its followers comprise the majority of the population, shall not result in any impairment of the enjoyment of any of the rights under the Covenant, including articles 18 and 27, nor in any discrimination against adherents to other religions or non-believers.

Paragraph 10 adds the following stipulation:

> if a set of beliefs is treated as official ideology in constitutions, statutes, proclamations of ruling parties, etc., or in actual practice, this shall not result in any impairment of the freedoms under article 18 or any other rights recognized under the Covenant nor in any discrimination against persons who do not accept the official ideology or who oppose it.

The key issue, then, is not so much whether the state accords particular importance to a single religious community under its jurisdiction, but whether, in doing so, other religions are thereby prevented from enjoying the protections afforded by Article 18 generally. Article 18(2) of the ICCPR expressly prohibits the use of coercion in compelling or preventing individuals' adherence to religious belief by stating that 'no one shall be subject to coercion which would impair his freedom to have or to adopt a religion or belief of his choice.'

While the mere existence of states' preferential treatment in the religious sphere does not necessarily result in placing undue burdens upon followers of minority religions, this state of affairs often extends to include provisions and practices which have precisely this effect. For example, many states which uphold a single religion also ban or criminalise apostasy. Apostasy, the giving up or renouncing of one's former religious commitments, is a crime in twenty-three countries across the Middle East, South Asia and South East Asia. In some of these countries, such as Afghanistan, Brunei, Saudi Arabia, Sudan and Yemen, the maximum sentence is death. Clearly, apostasy laws amount to an overt form of coercion and are thus entirely at odds with Article 18(2) of the ICCPR.

A slightly less dramatic instrument for undue state interference in religious freedom is to be found in those states which have established laws against blasphemy. Blasphemy is a highly complex and oft-debated issue (see Dacey 2012). Defenders of specific religious communities have argued that many religions are in need of legal protection, specifically through limiting what others can say about religion in general, or more typically, concerning a specific religious community. Blasphemy laws typically seek to restrict forms of speech or expression which may be shown to be particularly harmful to the character and standing of a community of religious believers. As such, they entail a broader engagement with the whole issue of defamatory speech, which I consider in greater detail below. Opponents of blasphemy laws typically argue that such laws accord states far too much licence to directly intervene in the religious sphere and typically in ways which accord undue protection to a single, often state-sanctioned religion. In effect, blasphemy laws unduly shield already powerful bodies from criticism and external scrutiny. In 2012 a Pew research study indicated that 22 per cent of states across the globe have blasphemy laws on their statute books (Pew Research Center 2012). In many of these states, such as Algeria, Egypt, Iran, Malaysia, Saudi Arabia and Sudan, these laws are used to further bolster the power of already very powerful religious bodies. Each of these countries has been consistently criticised by various inter-governmental and non-governmental bodies for their persistent persecution of religious minorities.

In respect of states in which a specific religion is accorded particular legal significance, one can broadly conclude that, whilst this state of affairs often reflects the social dominance of a specific religious community, it can be deeply restrictive towards the rights of those who would choose either to renounce their religion or convert to another religion and those religious minorities who are effectively denied equal standing or even face systematic restrictions upon their attempts to exercise their religious beliefs. The CCPR's refusal to condemn state religions attempts to maintain a precarious balance between recognising both state sovereignty and the realpolitik of existing state practice and the need to ensure that the protections afforded by Article 18 are genuinely enjoyed by all in a non-discriminatory way. The CCPR might, conceivably, have staked out a more uncompromisingly principled position by, for example, restricting any state intervention in the affairs of any religious community. It might, in other words, have offered unequivocal support for state secularism as the basis for ensuring the implementation of Article 18. Were that things could be so simple and straightforward.

Having shown that states' favouring a specific religious community often adversely impacts religious freedom, it might seem ostensibly reasonable to endorse the alternative position which calls for state neutrality in all religious matters.[1] Neutrality can take many different forms. It can, for example, resemble the kind of freedoms afforded by the First Amendment of the US Constitution, as previously discussed. Such forms of neutrality often allow for overt manifestations of religious commitment in a broad range of private and public spaces. Other interpretations of neutrality are more complex insofar as they draw directly upon philosophical understandings which require not so much equal or impartial state provision for all recognised religious communities, as the deliberate exclusion of the manifestation of religious belief from particularly sensitive state or public spaces. This is the case with the French commitment to *laïcité* and the Turkish Constitution's provision of state secularism. The former is particularly pertinent and illustrative of the issues this approach can raise.

The so-called *Foulard Affaire* (or headscarf question) in France has been extensively debated and discussed (see, for example, Benhabib 2008). Following a succession of challenges to the long-standing exclusion of the conspicuous display of religious symbols in French schools, the French Parliamentary Assembly finally passed a law in 2004 which expressly forbids students' attending school whilst wearing, for example, Islamic headscarves, the veil, the Jewish yarmulke or large crucifixes. In 2010, an additional law was passed which expressly banned the wearing of the burqa in all public places. The 2004 law appeals directly to the long-standing French adherence to a form of secularism which seeks to exclude religion from public life. The 2010 law appeals more directly to the felt need to protect purportedly vulnerable women from certain forms of Islam whilst also appealing to the need to uphold public order and morality. Both laws have been subsequently upheld by separate rulings of the European Court of European Rights (ECtHR). Thus, in *Dogru v France (2009)* the Court upheld the French law and reaffirmed an earlier ruling concerning the same issue in respect of Turkey's ban of Islamic dress in Turkish universities (*Sahin v Turkey, 2007*). The intention of both rulings is to restrict the expression of messages purportedly associated with certain forms of Islam. In the view of the ECtHR, these messages uphold a form of religious fundamentalism which threatens public order and gender equality. The *Sahin* decision refers explicitly to the need to support Turkey's commitment to protecting state secularism. France's banning of the burqa was upheld in *S.A.S. v France (2014)*.

It is interesting to note that the position of the ECtHR differs from the CCPR's stated position on the right to manifest one's religious beliefs through dress and other visible symbols. Thus, General Comment 22, paragraph 4 states:

> the freedom to manifest religion or belief in worship, observance, practice and teaching encompasses a broad range of acts. The concept of worship extends to ritual and ceremonial acts giving direct expression to belief, as well as various practices integral to such acts, including the building of places of worship, the use of ritual formulae and objects, the display of symbols, and the observance of holidays and days of rest. The observance and practice of religion or belief may include not only ceremonial acts but also such customs as the observance of dietary regulations, the wearing of distinctive clothing or head coverings, participation in rituals associated with certain stages of life, and the use of a particular language customarily spoken by a group.

The CCPR, to be fair, does not stipulate whether the display of religious symbols may be restricted to specific places or excluded from other spaces in which those of other religious convictions or the non-religious are also to be found. Merely restricting the manifestation of any human custom does not, in itself, constitute a violation of one's right to engage in the custom, after all. The question I shall address, however, is whether the kind of restrictions introduced under the type of state secularism which the likes of France and Turkey uphold constitute an undue violation of some people's religious freedom.

Put bluntly, I agree with the many commentators who have denounced particularly the French approach and the ECtHR's support for this position (see Elver 2012). The French position exemplifies a form of militant state secularism which unduly restricts the manifestation of some people's deep religious commitments whilst simultaneously fuelling a widespread perception amongst many of the estimated six million French citizens who are Muslim that their faith is incompatible with the core values of the French state. The militant secularist position fails to recognise the extent to which religious faiths differ profoundly from each other and the respective laws disproportionately impact only some religious communities. It also often results in legislative measures which are not proportional to the issue they address. Underlying my position is a deeper conviction that diversity is not best served by purportedly 'colour-blind' approaches which require individuals' alienating themselves from their own identities in order to continue to enjoy their fundamental rights. These are large claims and I need to defend them in finer detail.

I have argued at various points throughout this book that a principled, human rights-based commitment to recognising the value of diversity does not require that states grant full internal autonomy to all of those communities over whom they exercise legal authority. My analysis of the potential for cultures to harm particularly some women and girls should suffice to demonstrate my sensitivity towards some of the particularly French feminist objections to specific aspects of Islam. As I argued in Chapter 4, some women and girls are effectively trapped within profoundly patriarchal and harmful cultural conditions. However, as I argued above, human rights cannot engage in open conceptual warfare with world religions. A more effective strategy is to remain focused upon supporting the development of individuals' own capacities to seek to initiate progressive change within their own communities. There have been, and continue to be, many reformist women's groups comprising Muslim women who are drawing upon elements of their own religion to establish a momentum for change. Madhavi Sunder (2012) has sought to challenge more conventional feminist denunciations of culture and religion as being inherently 'bad for women' by cataloguing various Islamic women's movements which draw inspiration from their readings of their religion. One example of such is the so-called *Musawah* women's movement, which was initiated by a meeting in 2009 of over 250 Muslim women's activists from forty-seven countries.[2] The activism of groups such as this enables others to deconstruct forms of cultural essentialism, which continue to infect so much discussion and practice, particularly concerning Islam. While they may not intend to have this effect, militant forms of secularism often serve to bolster the attempts by fundamentalists and traditionalists through attributing precisely the kind of collective identity to a community (i.e. as being essentially oppressive towards women) as the patriarchal leaders of such communities seek to uphold against internal reformists.

The French law explicitly seeks to prevent the display of 'conspicuous' forms of religious symbolism. Given that the law cannot begin to engage with religious beliefs as forms of mere consciousness and can only limit manifestations of religion, this seems ostensibly reasonable enough. However, its effect is to disproportionately impact those religious belief systems for which adherence to the religion requires overt manifestations of faith, such as clothing requirements. Other religions, various forms of Anglicanism for example, may exert just as powerful an influence upon the values of their adherents but do not require any conspicuous display of religious conviction. The effect of the law is thus discriminatory towards some religions.

States can obstruct and actively violate many people's fundamental right to religious freedom, particularly in respect of the innumerable ways in which religious belief is manifested. Very few, if any, states are genuinely single-faith societies. IHRL requires states to respect, protect and fulfil individuals' fundamental right to religious freedom. There are many ways in which states can variously fail to discharge this core obligation. Not all of the states which fail to do so are necessarily Islamic republics or authoritarian regimes.

Second axis – across communities and individuals

States exert the greatest influence upon individuals' and communities' right to religious freedom. However, states are not alone in this regard. The actions and commitments of other people can also have a profound effect upon establishing or obstructing the kinds of social and cultural environments which are conducive to the equal enjoyment of a right to religious freedom. The general influence of others is apparent in a myriad of ways. In narrowing my frame of reference, I shall examine this particular axis by focusing upon a single phenomenon: religious defamation.

There are many examples of laws against defamation across the globe. They comprise a diverse range of definitions and elements. Most, however, recognise defamation as necessarily including a statement which causes serious harm to the reputation of some other party. Thus, the UK Racial and Religious Hatred Act (2006) is specifically concerned with religious (and racial) hatred which it defines as 'hatred against a group of persons defined by reference to religious belief or lack of religious belief' (29A). The act of religious hatred under the UK Act consists of the expression of threatening words or behaviour, or written material intended to stir up religious hatred. The Act does not include a precise definition of what constitutes 'hatred', nor does it specify what actions amount to the 'stirring up' of religious hatred. Many advocates of free speech are, on these and more principled grounds, often deeply troubled by defamation laws. Arguably the most concerted opposition is to be found in the US, where free speech and even various forms of what some inside and outside the US consider to be 'hate speech' are protected by the First Amendment to the US Constitution. Those opposed to defamation laws typically argue that even allowing for the fact that many consider some forms of speech directed towards them to be harmful speech, for the purposes of law it is objectively impossible to determine what constitutes genuinely 'harmful speech' and that free speech is absolutely essential for any democratic society. Within highly diverse societies, it is often argued, we must each of us be able to express and to receive opinions about ourselves and others. The content of these expressions may be considered by some to be deeply 'unpleasant', but such is the price we must pay in order to ensure the free exchange of ideas and viewpoints. Defamation laws serve to obstruct the objective of securing the cherished 'free market' of ideas and opinion (Lewis 2010). This general aversion to the legal protection provided by defamation laws is also endorsed within many human rights circles, including various UN bodies. This is particularly the case with respect to the specific concept of the defamation of religion.

IHRL does contain a fundamental provision for the legal prohibition of religious hatred. Thus, Article 20(2) of the ICCPR states, 'any advocacy of national, racial or religious hatred that constitutes incitement to discrimination, hostility or violence shall be prohibited by law.' This has been affirmed by the CCPR's General Comment 22, paragraph 7 of which states:

> in accordance with Article 20, no manifestation of religion or belief may amount to propaganda for war or advocacy of national, racial or religious hatred that constitutes incitement to discrimination, hostility or violence. As stated by the Committee in its General Comment 11 [19], states parties are under the obligation to enact laws to prohibit such acts.

While paragraph 1 of the same General Comment expressly recognises that religious beliefs are manifested by individuals and communities of individuals, the typical interpretation of the protections afforded by Article 20(2) tend to reserve these protections to individuals alone and explicitly exclude the possibility that religions as collective entities might be protected by defamation laws. Nazila Ghanea expresses this position clearly when she contends that 'the claim for equal treatment should relate to an individual or group of individuals not to a religion or other belief system' (2012: 212).

The individualist position on defamation has figured prominently in various UN bodies and initiatives. For example, for a number of years, the HRC and the General Assembly were the centres of a sustained effort by the Organisation of Islamic Cooperation (OIC) and some of its members in their attempt to establish an international legal norm restricting speech that defamed religions, particularly Islam, and not merely Muslims as individual believers. The most recent HRC Resolution on the issue of religious defamation (Resolution 16/18) recognises the existence of forms of religious intolerance, hatred and negative stereotyping which many religious *communities* experience and focuses upon developing positive measures to counter religious intolerance and protect individuals from discrimination or violence, rather than on criminalising expression. In 2009, and against the backdrop of the concerted attempt to establish specific protections against Islamophobia, three UN Special Rapporteurs (on religion, racism and speech) publicly expressed their worries over the growing emphasis placed upon the need to protect against religious group defamation. They stated:

> the difficulties in providing an objective definition of the term 'defamation of religions' at the international level make the whole concept open to abuse. At the national level, domestic blasphemy laws can prove counterproductive, since this could result in de facto censure of inter-religious and intra-religious criticism. Many of these laws provide different levels of protection to different religions and have often proved to be used in a discriminatory way. (Cited in Evans 2012: 194)

As Carolyn Evans comments on this statement, 'the extension beyond hate laws to the concept of defamation of religions, however, may be used to shore up the power and authority of the religious majority and its political and religious hierarchy' (2012: 194).

There is a wealth of evidence supporting many people's worries over the potential for group religious defamation laws to bolster policies and legal instruments which directly violate others' human rights, specifically in respect of freedom of expression and individuals' freedom to renounce their religion, or those seeking to internally reform, and not exit, their religious communities. The OIC's campaign in the UN HRC (referred to above) consistently focused solely upon Islamophobia and the expressed need to offer particular international legal protection to Islam. Many responded by pointing to the numerous Islamic republics in which defamation laws are used to oppress religious minorities or silence internal critics. Article 22(a) of the Cairo Declaration appears to confirm these kinds of concern by stating: 'everyone shall have the right to express his opinion freely in such manner as would not be contrary to the principles of the Shari'ah.' Limiting free expression in this way is clearly profoundly incompatible with the requirements of free expression in multi-faith, diverse environments, including those found within many of the states which have ratified the Declaration.

However, very few of those who have contributed to this area of concern are prepared to defend absolute freedom of expression. Particularly within human rights circles, most acknowledge that some people's human rights can be undermined by others' expressions of religious hatred and that instruments are required for providing sufficient protection. While I acknowledge the fact that group religious defamation laws are frequently used in ways which are systematically incompatible with human rights norms, I do not believe that such protections are necessarily incompatible with upholding human rights. Indeed, I believe (and shall argue in a moment) that the necessity of extending human rights thinking towards a relational account of agency (itself required by the need for human rights to more effectively respond to the challenges of identity-based claims) clearly requires a greater willingness to countenance the need for extending human rights protection beyond the individualist presumptions which much current thinking in this specific area are restricted by. A case can (and should) be made for a greater consideration of extending defamation protections to religious communities also.

Group defamation laws do exist within several European countries, such as Denmark, France and Norway. Section 130 of the German Penal Code exemplifies these laws by prohibiting 'attacks on human dignity by insulting, maliciously maligning, or defaming part of the population'.[3] The German law's emphasis upon human dignity is particularly pertinent and I shall return to it shortly. Like any legal prohibition upon hate speech or offence, these laws recognise that serious harm cannot be avoided by the intended victim simply turning the other cheek or choosing to 'change the channel', so to speak. Group-based, rather than more narrowly individualist-based, religious defamation laws also recognise the extent to which people's core interests can be deeply influenced, if not constituted, by their religious commitments and that these commitments must themselves be understood as communal goods, which resist disaggregating into separate, individual bundles. A legal acknowledgement of this can be found in a US Supreme Court ruling. Thus, in *Beauharnais v Illinois (1952)*, Justice Frankfurter writing for the Court stated:

> a man's job and his educational opportunities and the dignity accorded him may depend as much on the reputation of the racial and religious group to which he willy-nilly belongs, as to his own merits. This being so, we are precluded from saying that speech concededly punishable when immediately directed at individuals cannot be outlawed if directed at groups with whose position and esteem in society the affiliated individual may be inextricably involved. (*Beauharnais v Illinois, 1952*: 250)

While the protection offered remains steadfastly individualist, the ruling recognises the limitations of the long-standing distinction drawn between attacking ascribed characteristics and attacking the individuals who identify with these characteristics as part of their core identity.

Opponents to group-based forms of defamation laws and to the specific position I am outlining here will, doubtless, respond by suggesting that such concerns will result in wholesale interventions in civil society by overly sensitive judges seeking to protect groups of people with unduly 'thin skins'. They may also point to some of the manifest absurdities of so-called political correctness, whereby various self-appointed guardians of public morality attempt to ban an ever-expanding range of language terms which are deemed to be offensive to some group or other. Clearly, much of this is nonsense and little of it had any tangible effect upon improving the collective conditions of many of those groups who were the alleged victims of references to such things as 'blackboards'. However, we should avoid throwing out the proverbial 'baby with the bathwater' (at the risk of offending babies) in rightly dismissing the excesses of what Ravitch (2003) famously and provocatively referred to as the 'language police'. Concerted and systematic religious hatred does exist out there in many parts of the world. Many of those who perpetrate it do so precisely in order to seek to persuade others to join in their campaigns against those who profess a different faith or wear different clothing. Human rights exist, in part, precisely in order to counter such forms of hatred precisely because they have been shown to have direct effects upon the systematic violations of the human rights of those targeted. Individuals are targeted not on the basis of being abstract bearers of moral value (in a Kantian sense), but by virtue of their manifest identities and commitments, which they possess human rights to.

My position, whilst based upon existing IHRL in this area, draws upon the insights provided by the likes of Charles Taylor (1992) and Axel Honneth (1996) into the sheer extent to which fundamental human interests to, for example, leading a sufficiently dignified life can be systematically undermined by how others perceive and relate to us. For those for whom religious conviction provides a core source of their personal identity and commitments, others' persistent vilification of such religions will impact not simply that compartment of their lives some may be inclined to label as 'the merely religious', but their very sense of self and their capacity to lead a sufficiently dignified life. Group-based religious defamation laws offer a collective statement concerning the utterly unacceptable and intolerable character of seeking to deny the shared humanity of others through severely denigrating others' religious beliefs and practices.

To reiterate, this does not require the creation and robust policing of an entirely bland civil society and public space in which otherwise diverse communities of people are required to either ignore one another or refrain from any critical engagement with the core beliefs and practices of others. It does not require that cartoonists stop caricaturing others' idols, necessarily.[4] Nor does it license the violence of those whose often well-founded sense of long-term alienation leads to even worse forms of religious intolerance. It is based upon a principled insistence that multi-faith communities can peacefully co-exist only through recognising both the core capacity for acting in accordance with the ideal of humanity which we all share and an awareness of how this shared ideal allows for very diverse expressions of faith, which do not (and should not) develop in complete isolation from each other.[5] Along the second axis, groups and individual religious believers directly influence one another's opportunities to manifest their religious beliefs. This influence often occurs quite independently of any state action or intervention. In recognising our shared (although typically unequal) opportunities to help or hinder one another's religious freedom, we should also recognise the need for some forms of effective legal regulation of relations along this particular largely horizontal axis. This approach is not, I contend, incompatible with a human rights-based approach to religious freedom. Indeed, human rights can be indispensable to realising this objective. In this respect, I entirely share Jeremy Waldron's claim that group-based defamation laws are compatible with the objective of protecting forms of human dignity which are vulnerable to the actions and expressions of others. Like Waldron, I believe that upholding religious freedom within multi-faith societies requires the protection of a collective good, which we nevertheless all have a fundamental interest in supporting: public order. Waldron writes that laws of group defamation are:

> set up to vindicate public order, not just by pre-empting violence, but by upholding against attack a shared sense of the basic elements of each person's status, dignity, and reputation as a citizen or member of society in good standing – particularly against attacks predicated upon the characteristics of some particular social group. (Waldron 2012: 47)

Third axis – protecting the non-religious from the religious

I conclude my analysis with a brief discussion of a tension which has re-emerged recently in a number of developed and developing world societies: the complex relations between the non-religious and the religious. I focus particularly on the claims made by some amongst the latter that their religion either prevents them from interacting with or tolerating the primarily non-religious lifestyles of others, and the stronger claim that others' lifestyles should be legally proscribed because of their purported incompatibility with religious doctrine. As with other areas of concern, there is a potentially very wide range of examples to choose from. However, given the attention it has received recently and my omission of discussing sex to this point in the book, I shall restrict my analysis to the conflict between religious communities and sexual minorities, particularly so-called lesbian, gay, transgender and bisexual (LGTB) communities.

The human rights of sexual minorities are a developing and evolving field within IHRL. Clearly, all human beings are entitled to the enjoyment of all of their legally established human rights, irrespective of their sexual orientation. This was reaffirmed by the so-called *Yogakarta Principles* (2006), which outlined a set of principles covering the equal status of sexual minorities which member states of the UN are invited to endorse and actively support. As with other areas of human rights protection, the reality in many parts of the world falls far short of the legal standards. Indeed, in at least thirty-seven countries currently, homosexuality is illegal. In many of these countries, the criminalisation of sexual intimacy is ostensibly based upon overtly religious foundations. Thus, homosexuality carries a sentence of death in the Islamic Republic of Iran, multi-faith Nigeria, Sudan and Saudi Arabia. Other states in which there is a predominantly Christian population also inflict very harsh sentences upon those convicted of homosexuality, such as Uganda which passed the Anti-Homosexuality Act in 2014, which carries life imprisonment as a maximum punishment. In many other states across the world, sexual minorities are systematically persecuted on the grounds of the purportedly anti-religious nature of their lifestyles.

Clearly, any such laws are entirely incompatible with reconciling respect for human rights with that for diversity within a single country. Sexual minorities exist everywhere, regardless of state and religious repression. Everyone, regardless of their sexual orientation, is entitled to equal enjoyment of their fundamental human rights. No human right, such as the right of religious freedom, can be justifiably exercised in order to violate another's human right, such as choosing one's sexual partner or expressing one's identity through freedom of expression and association, for example. There can be no justification for the widespread persecution of others on the basis of their consensual lifestyles' failing to comply with the religious doctrines of others. Period.

However, a more complicated challenge has built up a head of steam in recent times within states which otherwise generally recognise the rights of sexual minorities. At the heart of this challenge is a recurring claim that an individual's religious faith justifies their acting in a discriminatory manner towards others on the grounds of these others' sexual orientation. Thus, in 2008 in Cornwall, England, the owners of a guest house refused to allow a gay couple to share a double-bed room on the grounds of their purported right to manifest their religious beliefs, which, they claimed, view homosexuality as sinful. In 2013 the UK Supreme Court ruled against the guest-house owners' right to exclude gay customers. The ruling in *Bull v Hall (2013)* argued that the guest-house owners violated equality law by directly discriminating on sexual grounds against gay couples. Lady Hale, writing for the Court, argued that sexual orientation was a core component of a person's identity, which could be directly harmed by others' discriminatory attitudes. Further, that manifesting one's religion does not extend to include actions which can have such a direct and harmful effect upon others. The United States appears to be currently experiencing an increasing number of similar such cases and challenges in which public servants and private providers are seeking exemption from anti-discrimination laws on the grounds that providing services to sexual minorities amounts to a violation of their rights to manifest their religious convictions. In June 2015, the US Supreme Court recognised same-sex marriage to be a basic, constitutional right in the landmark *Obergefell v Hodges* case. Suffice it to say, the Supreme Court's ruling has not been universally endorsed within the US. Indeed, the *Obergefell* ruling appears to have sparked something of a backlash across a number of particularly high-density Christian states in the southern United States. In September 2015 a Kentucky County Court official was jailed for refusing to issue marriage licences to gay couples on the grounds of her religious conviction. In April 2016 the Governor of Mississippi signed a law which enables business owners to deny services to gay couples. North Carolina has introduced a law which requires transgender people to use only those bathrooms which correspond with the gender listed on their birth certificates. Georgia sought to pass a so-called religious freedom bill which, like Mississippi, legalises business owners' refusal of services to gay couples. The bill was vetoed by the Governor. Most recently, a legal appeal is pending in Northern Ireland regarding an earlier ruling which held that it was unlawful for a bakery to refuse to bake a cake for a customer who requested the inclusion of a pro-gay marriage slogan on the cake (*Gareth Lee v Ashers Baking Co Ltd, 2015*). As I write (May 2016), what the UK media are referring to as the 'Gay Cake Row' has yet to be settled.

These cases raise complex challenges for human rights. Clearly, IHRL will typically resolve the conflict between religious conviction and others' lifestyles in favour of the latter in instances where claims to manifest one's religion result in the violation of others' fundamental rights. Some will doubtless continue to seek to limit their engagements with and exposure to those whose practices and beliefs they consider to be thoroughly unacceptable. This challenge certainly indicates the severe limitations to proposed forms of multicultural regulation which would accord a great deal of sovereignty to distinct communities, such as that advocated by Chandran Kukathas (2003) whose contribution to the area of legislating for diversity I considered in an earlier chapter. Within a genuinely diverse society, individuals are constantly interacting with other individuals and often these interactions raise precisely the kind of value conflicts I have discussed immediately above. A great many of our values and beliefs exert a profound influence on how we engage in the public domain, broadly defined. Simply seeking to afford individuals and communities the opportunity to imprison themselves within their own 'gated communities' avoids, rather than confronts, the challenge of diversity. Specifically, in respect of Christianity's view of sexual minorities, we are entitled to ask, as many gay Christians have asked, on whose authority do other Christians claim that a Christian God is necessarily homophobic? However, even if any mere mortal could ever determine that God was a homophobe, upholding a human rights-based defence of cultural diversity requires of all of us that, while we may continue to refuse to endorse the specific value commitments and choices of others, we nevertheless recognise the basic humanity we all share.

Conclusion

This chapter has attempted to chart a very rich and complex relationship. Human rights and religion have travelled along the same roads and, often, with the same intended destination: the salvation of humankind. They are not, however, identical, and the conceptual and practical differences between them have emerged to form potential and actual 'battlegrounds' upon which differing constituencies continue to seek to achieve the best for all of us. It is clear that religious communities (sometimes the same communities) can be the victims and the perpetrators of human rights violations and abuse. There would appear to be few grounds for imagining that this potential for conflict will be resolved any time soon. However, it should also be clear that religious

freedom and the opportunity of the vast majority of the world's population to profess their respective faiths does depend heavily upon human
rights and upholding the equal rights of all to their own particular
commitments.

Suggested reading

- Liam Gearon (ed.), *Human Rights and Religion: A Reader* (Brighton: Sussex Academic Press, 2002).
- Dominic McGoldrick, *Human Rights and Religion: The Islamic Headscarf Debate in Europe* (London: Hart Publishing, 2006).
- Jeremy Waldron, *The Harm in Hate Speech* (Cambridge, MA: Harvard University Press, 2012).
- John Witte Jr. and M. Christian Green (eds), *Religion and Human Rights: An Introduction* (Oxford: Oxford University Press, 2012).

Notes

1. See Berger (2015) for recent analysis of the complex relationship between state neutrality and religion.
2. See <http://www.musawah.org> (last accessed 27 July 2016).
3. Interestingly, section 130 was recently revised in order to comply with the EU Framework Decision on combatting Racism and Xenophobia. See Büro zur Umsetzung von Gleichbehandlung (2011).
4. I am specifically referring to the attacks on Charlie Hebdo and the issues this raises for considering the limits of critical engagement with others' religion. See Fourest (2015).
5. I return to explain this 'should not' phrase in the next, concluding chapter.

8

Working On a Dream?

I follow the longest chapter in the book with the shortest, which takes my analysis of human rights and cultural diversity to its conclusion. The preceding chapters have addressed a broad range of issues and challenges. I have sought to show how it is possible to continue to defend human rights as a universally valid doctrine whilst simultaneously espousing the value of cultural diversity. Despite the claims of some of its critics, the doctrine of human rights does not require that everyone must adapt and amend their prior cultural and religious commitments in order to comply with the allegedly censorious normative demands of human rights. An understanding of human rights based upon the continuing appeal of humanity does not seek to elevate the doctrine to the status of a new religion, nor does it require that all human beings convert to the cause of perfectionist liberalism. It does, however, stand opposed to those ways of being and believing which do, in effect, seek to deny the humanity of other human beings and of those who follow other ways of leading a humane life. The human rights doctrine must be capable of, on occasion, baring its proverbial teeth at those who, for example, seek to impose their partial 'truths' upon others, or who consider that maintaining their way of being and believing requires the denial of others' rights to be who they individually or collectively wish to be. Despite all of its many limitations, international human rights law is the most effective weapon the human rights community possesses.

Human rights continue to attract criticism from many different quarters. Much of this should be welcomed and embraced by the human rights community since it testifies to one of humanity's greatest successes: establishing and protecting the fundamental human rights of free expression and freedom of thought and conscience: the cornerstones of any sufficiently free society. Some of our critics are, in a sense, our most accomplished 'offspring', who are only practising what we have preached. However, not all critical engagements with human rights embrace or endorse the spirit of free expression and freedom of thought and conscience. Some of it, for a multitude of different reasons, aims to abandon the continuing pursuit of a global public ethic and replace it with a series of mutually incompatible, partial and conflicting 'truths' and jurisdictions. To borrow from Chandran Kukathas's (2003) metaphor of diverse societies comprising an archipelago of separate jurisdictions, this particular vision of how best to respond to the challenge of diversity evokes another, darker and more disturbing, metaphor: the Balkans. Seen in this light, cultural diversity is thereby envisaged as necessarily comprising distinct and separate communities, who are increasingly concerned to erect and maintain fences in order to keep *in* those who would have little real option but to remain and keep *out* those whose different expressions of humanity (through the idols they worship, the way they dress, or how and what they eat, for example) are interpreted as alien and hostile. It should be abundantly clear by now just how opposed I am to this unappetising vision of 'diversity'.

Many interpreted the fall of the Berlin Wall in 1989 as heralding the emergence of a new post-national, cosmopolitan age in which fences, boundaries, walls and all of the other solid paraphernalia of human division would be slowly demolished. The consequent expansion of the European Union and the development of other regional unions seemed only to confirm the optimistic hopes of many. Now, in 2017, current events seem to defy such cosmopolitan optimism. For many, the removal of barriers appears to have resulted only in increasing global and regional chaos and mayhem. Many now seem to consider the world to be increasingly anarchic and the understandable anxiety this raises offers a fertile ground for those who seek their own partial profit by stoking the fires of human vulnerability, rather than working collaboratively towards collective solutions and remedies. Fear causes people to close doors against others. Fear invokes in many a nostalgic yearning for allegedly simpler times in which difference was not so visible and proximate and no matter was, so to speak, quite so out of place.

A commitment to human rights entails rejecting counsels of despair. Claiming entitlement to a human right to manifest one's religion or creed, for example, entails an endorsement of the view that the same right can be exercised in a multitude of differing ways by a multitude of differing peoples. This, in part, is what I mean when I say that human rights rest upon an appeal to humanity. A human right is not a mutually exclusive commodity. We are all of us entitled to feel sufficiently safe and secure in familiar surroundings while so much of the world around us appears to be in turmoil. Some part of the appeal of a right to cultural identity speaks to this yearning to feel safe in one's own home. However, as I have argued throughout the preceding chapters, none of us becomes who we are in isolation from others. We are all of us as we are because of our relationships with others. My preferred approach to cultural diversity aims to acknowledge this and transform necessity into a virtue. After all, despite the growing impulses towards the contrary, we cannot collectively cleanse our actual and metaphorical neighbourhoods of those who differ from us. Walls and fences will not solve the challenge of how to manage diversity and have typically only fuelled what human rights also exist to combat: our collective propensity towards inhumanity. As some of us reach to close the door against others, human rights will continue to speak for those values and ideals which we should all be collectively proud of and will continue to lend a voice in support of humanity.

Bibliography

Books and articles

Adorno, T. W. (1973), *Negative Dialectics*, trans. E. E. Ashton, London: Routledge.

Anderson, B. (1991), *Imagined Communities: Reflections on the Origin and Spread of Nationalism*, London: Verso.

An-Na'im, A. A. (2008), *Islam and the Secular State: Negotiating the Future of Shari'a*, Cambridge, MA: Harvard University Press.

An-Na'im, A. A. (2009), 'Abdullahi An-Na'im', in F. Deng, A. An-Na'im, Y. Ghai and U. Baxi, *Human Rights, Southern Voices*, ed. W. Twining, Cambridge: Cambridge University Press, pp. 53–103.

An-Na'im, A. A. (2012), 'Islam and Human Rights', in J. Witte Jr. and M. C. Green (eds), *Religion and Human Rights: An Introduction*, Oxford: Oxford University Press, pp. 56–70.

Anthias, F. and N. Yuval-Davis (1989), *Racialized Boundaries*, London: Verso.

Appiah, K. A. (2005), *The Ethics of Identity*, Princeton: Princeton University Press.

Arendt, H. (1963), *Eichmann in Jerusalem: A Report on the Banality of Evil*, Harmondsworth: Penguin.

Baier, A. (1986), 'Trust and Antitrust', *Ethics*, 96: 2, 231–60.

Baier, A. (1991), *A Progress of Sentiments: Reflections on Hume's Treatise*, Cambridge, MA: Harvard University Press.

Barth, F. (1989), 'The Analysis of Culture in Complex Societies', *Ethnos*, 54: 3–4, 120–42.

Becker, G. (1996), *Accounting for Tastes*, Cambridge, MA: Harvard University Press.

Beetham, D. (1999), *Democracy and Human Rights*, Cambridge: Polity Press.

Beiner, R. (1992), 'The Moral Vocabulary of Liberalism', *Nomos*, 34, 145–84.

Beitz, C. (2009), *The Idea of Human Rights*, Oxford: Oxford University Press.

Benhabib, S. (2002), *The Claims of Culture: Equality and Diversity in the Golden Era*, Princeton: Princeton University Press.

Benhabib, S. (2008), 'L'Affaire du Foulard (The Scarf Affair)', *Yearbook of the National Society for the Study of Education*, 107: 1, 100–11.

Benson, P. (1994), 'Free Agency and Self-Worth', *Journal of Political Philosophy*, 9: 12, 650–8.Benhabib, S. (2011), *Dignity in Adversity: Human Rights in Troubled Times*, Cambridge: Polity Press.

Berger, B. (2015), *Law's Religion: Religious Difference and the Claims of Constitutionalism*, Toronto: University of Toronto Press.

Berlin, I. (1969), *Four Essays on Liberty*, Oxford: Oxford University Press.

Bielefeldt, H. (2000), '"Western" Versus "Islamic" Human Rights Conceptions?: A Critique of Cultural Essentialism in the Discussion on Human Rights', *Political Theory*, 28, 90–121.

Brems, E. (1997), 'Enemies or Allies? Feminism and Cultural Relativism as Dissident Voices in Human Rights Discourse', *Human Rights Quarterly*, 19: 1, 136–64.

Brown, G. W. and D. Held (eds) (2010), *The Cosmopolitanism Reader*, Cambridge: Polity Press.

Buchanan, A. (2013), *The Heart of Human Rights*, Oxford: Oxford University Press.

Büro zur Umsetzung von Gleichbehandlung (2011), 'Revising Section 130 of the Criminal Code in Accordance with the EU Framework Decision', <http://www.bug-ev.org/en/topics/focus-areas/dossiers/hate-crime/hate-crime-legislation/revising-section-130-of-the-criminal-code-in-accordance-with-the-eu-framework-decision.html> (last accessed 27 July 2016).

Caney, S. and P. Jones (eds) (2001), *Human Rights and Global Diversity*, London: Frank Cass.

Capotorti, F. (1991), *Study on the Rights of Persons Belonging to Ethnic, Religious and Linguistic Minorities*, New York: United Nations.

Charlesworth, H. (1995), 'Human Rights as Men's Rights', in J. Peters and A. Wolper (eds), *Women's Rights, Human Rights: International Feminist Perspectives*, New York: Routledge, pp. 103–13.

Cohen, J. (2004), 'Minimalism About Human Rights: The Most We Can Hope For?', *Journal of Political Philosophy*, 12: 2, 190–213.

Cover, R. (1983), 'The Supreme Court, 1982 Term – Foreword: *Nomos* and Narrative', *Harvard Law Review*, 97, 4–68.

Cranston, M. (1973), *What Are Human Rights?*, Oxford: Bodley Head.

Dacey, A. (2012), *The Future of Blasphemy: Speaking of the Sacred in an Age of Human Rights*, London: Continuum Press.

Donnelly, J. (2007), 'The Relative Universality of Human Rights', *Human Rights Quarterly*, 29: 2, 281–306.

Donnelly, J. (2013), *Universal Human Rights in Theory and Practice*, 3rd edn, Ithaca, NY: Cornell University Press.

Durkheim, E. and M. Mauss (1963), *Primitive Classification*, trans. R. Needham, Chicago: University of Chicago Press.

Dworkin, R. (1978), 'Liberalism', in S. Hampshire (ed.), *Public and Private Morality*, Cambridge: Cambridge University Press, pp. 113–43.

Dworkin, R. (1986), *Law's Empire*, Harvard: Harvard University Press.

Elster, J. (1983), *Sour Grapes: Studies in the Subversion of Rationality*, Cambridge: Cambridge University Press.

Elver, H. (2012), *The Headscarf Controversy: Secularism and Freedom of Religion*, Oxford: Oxford University Press.

Evans, C. (2012), 'Religion and Freedom of Expression', in J. Witte Jr. and M. C. Green (eds), *Religion and Human Rights: An Introduction*, Oxford: Oxford University Press, pp. 188–203.

Fagan, A. (2010), *The Atlas of Human Rights*, Berkeley: University of California Press.

Fagan, A. (forthcoming, 2017a), 'Unable to Leave: The Right of Exit & Multiculturalism', *Critical Review of International Social and Political Philosophy: Special Edition on Multiculturalism in Contemporary Britain*.

Fagan, A. (forthcoming, 2017b), 'Cultural Harm and Determining the Limits of a Right to Cultural Identity', *Human Rights Quarterly*, May.

Fagan, A. and H. Fridlund (2016), 'Relative Universality, Harmful Cultural Practices and the Human Rights Council', *Nordic Journal of Human Rights*, 34: 1, 1–19.

Ferrara, A. (2003), 'Two Notions of Humanity and the Judgment Argument for Human Rights', *Political Theory*, 31: 3, 392–420.

Fine, R. (2007), *Cosmopolitanism*, London: Routledge.

Finnis, J. (1980), *Natural Law and Natural Rights*, Oxford: Oxford University Press.

Fourest, C. (2015), *In Praise of Blasphemy: Why Charlie Hebdo Is Not Islamophobic*, Paris: Bernard Grasset.

Franck, T. M. (1999), *The Empowered Self: Law and Society in the Age of Individualism*, Oxford: Oxford University Press.

Freeman, M. A. (2009), *Reservations to CEDAW: An Analysis for UNICEF*, New York: United Nations Children's Fund, Division of Policy and Practice.

Friedman, M. (2000), 'Autonomy, Social Disruption, and Women', in C. Mackenzie and N. Stoljar (eds), *Relational Autonomy: Feminist Perspectives on Autonomy, Agency, and the Social Self*, Oxford: Oxford University Press, pp. 35–51.

Fukuyama, F. (1989), 'The End of History?', *The National Interest*, Summer, 3–18.

Gadd, D. (2012), 'Domestic Abuse Prevention after Raoul Moat', *Critical Social Policy*, 32: 4, 495–516.

Galston, W. (1995), 'Two Concepts of Liberalism', *Ethics*, 105: 3, 516–34.

Gauthier, D. (1986), *Morals by Agreement*, Oxford: Clarendon Press.

Geertz, C. (1973), *The Interpretation of Cultures*, New York: Basic Books.

Gellner, E. (1983), *Nations and Nationalism*, Ithaca, NY: Cornell University Press.

Ghanea, N. (2012), 'Religion, Equality and Non-discrimination', in J. Witte Jr. and M. C. Green (eds), *Religion and Human Rights: An Introduction*, Oxford: Oxford University Press, pp. 204–17.

Gould, C. (2004), *Globalizing Democracy and Human Rights*, Cambridge: Cambridge University Press.

Gray, J. (1989), 'Freedom, Slavery and Contentment', in *Liberalisms: Essays in Political Thought*, London: Routledge, pp. 69–88.

Gray, J. (1993), *Post-Liberalism: Studies in Political Thought*, New York: Routledge.

Gray, J. (2003), *Straw Dogs: Thoughts on Human and Other Animals*, Cambridge: Granta Press.

Green, L. (1995), 'Internal Minorities and Their Rights', in W. Kymlicka (ed.), *The Rights of Minority Cultures*, Oxford: Oxford University Press, pp. 256–74.

Griffin, J. (1986), *Well-being: Its Meaning, Measurement, and Moral Importance*, Oxford: Clarendon Press.

Griffin, J. (2008), *On Human Rights*, Oxford: Oxford University Press.

Gutmann, A. (ed.) (1998), *Freedom of Association*, Princeton: Princeton University Press.

Habermas, J. (1996), *Between Facts and Norms: Contributions to a Discourse Theory of Law and Democracy*, trans. W. Rehg, Cambridge, MA: MIT Press.

Habermas, J. (2001), *The Postnational Constellation: Political Essays*, trans. Max Pensky, Cambridge: Polity Press.

Haney, C., W. C. Banks and P. G. Zimbardo (1973), 'A Study of Prisoners and Guards in a Simulated Prison', *Naval Research Review*, 30, 4–17.

Hill, J. (1999), 'Note, Expressive Harms and Standing', *Harvard Law Review*, 112: 6, 1313–30.

Hobbes, T. [1651] (1962), *The Leviathan*, London: Fontana.

Holder, C. and David Reidy (eds) (2013), *Human Rights: The Hard Questions*, Cambridge: Cambridge University Press.

Hollis, M. (1999), 'Is Universalism Ethnocentric?', in C. Joppke and S. Lukes (eds), *Multicultural Questions*, Oxford: Oxford University Press, pp. 27–43.

Honig, B. (1993), *Political Theory and the Displacement of Politics*, Ithaca, NY: Cornell University Press.

Honneth, A. (1996), *The Struggle for Recognition: The Moral Grammar of Social Conflicts*, trans. J. Anderson, Cambridge: Polity Press.

Horowitz, D. L. (2001), *Ethnic Groups in Conflict*, 2nd edn, Berkeley: University of California Press.

Ignatieff, M. (2001), *Human Rights as Politics and Idolatry*, Princeton: Princeton University Press.

Ingram, D. (2000), *Group Rights: Reconciling Equality and Difference*, Lawrence: Kansas University Press.

Ingram, D. (2012), 'Group Rights: A Defense', in T. Cushman (ed.), *Handbook of Human Rights*, New York: Routledge, pp. 277–90.

Ishay, M. (2004), *The History of Human Rights: From Ancient Times to the Globalisation Era*, Berkeley: University of California Press.

Jones, P. (1999), 'Human Rights, Group Rights, and Peoples' Rights', *Human Rights Quarterly*, 21, 80–107.

Jones, P. (2001), 'Human Rights and Diverse Cultures: Continuity or Discontinuity', in S. Caney and P. Jones (eds), *Human Rights and Global Diversity*, London: Frank Cass, pp. 27–50.

Jovanović, M. A. (2005), 'Recognizing Minority Identities through Collective Rights', *Human Rights Quarterly*, 27: 2, 625–51.

Jovanović, M. A. (2012), *Collective Rights: A Legal Theory*, Belgrade: University of Belgrade.

Kant, I. (1970), 'Perpetual Peace: A Philosophical Sketch', in Hans Reiss (ed.), *Kant: Political Writings*, Cambridge: Cambridge University Press, pp. 93–130.

Kelsen, H. (1967), *Pure Theory of Law*, trans. M. Knight, Berkeley: University of California Press.

Kenny, M. (2004), *The Politics of Identity: Liberal Political Theory and the Dilemmas of Difference*, Oxford: Wiley.

Keown, D. (1992), *The Nature of Buddhist Ethics*, London: Macmillan.

Keown, D. (2012), 'Buddhism and Human Rights', in T. Cushman (ed.), *Handbook of Human Rights*, New York: Routledge, pp. 223–30.

Kernohan, A. (1998), *Liberalism, Equality, and Cultural Oppression*, Cambridge: Cambridge University Press.

King, S. B. (2012), 'Buddhism and Human Rights', in J. Witte Jr. and M. C. Green (eds), *Religion and Human Rights: An Introduction*, Oxford: Oxford University Press, pp. 103–18.

King, W. (1995), 'Religion', in Mircea Eliade (ed.), *Encyclopaedia of Religion*, vol. 12, New York: Simon and Shuster Macmillan, p. 282.

Kukathas, C. (1992), 'Are There Any Cultural Rights?', *Political Theory*, 20: 1, 105–39.

Kukathas, C. (2003), *The Liberal Archipelago: A Theory of Diversity and Freedom*, Oxford: Oxford University Press.

Kukathas, C. and P. Pettit (eds) (1990), *Rawls: A Theory of Justice and Its Critics*, Stanford: Stanford University Press.

Kymlicka, W. (1989), *Liberalism, Community and Culture*, Oxford: Clarendon Press.

Kymlicka, W. (ed.) (1995), *The Rights of Minority Cultures*, Oxford: Oxford University Press.

Kymlicka, W. (2001), *Politics in the Vernacular: Nationalism, Multiculturalism, and Citizenship*, Oxford: Oxford University Press.

Koenig, M. and P. de Guchteneire (eds) (2007), *Democracy and Human Rights in Multicultural Societies*, Aldershot: Ashgate.

Landman, T. and E. Carvalho (2009), *Measuring Human Rights*, London: Routledge.

Langlois, A. (2001), *The Politics of Justice and Human Rights: South East Asia and Universalist Theory*, Cambridge: Cambridge University Press.

Larmore, C. (1987), *Patterns of Moral Complexity*, Cambridge: Cambridge University Press.

Larmore, C. (1996), *The Morals of Modernity*, Cambridge: Cambridge University Press.

Lerner, M. (1980), *Belief in a Just World: A Fundamental Delusion*, New York: Springer.

Levey, G. B. (1997), 'Equality, Autonomy, and Cultural Rights', *Political Theory*, 25, 215–48.

Levy, J. (1997), 'Classifying Cultural Rights', in I. Shapiro and W. Kymlicka (eds), *Ethnicity and Group Rights: Nomos XXXIX*, New York: New York University Press, pp. 22–68.

Lewis, B. (2010), *Faith and Power: Religion and Politics in the Middle East*, Oxford: Oxford University Press.

Lukes, S. (1989), 'Making Sense of Moral Conflict', in N. L. Rosenblum (ed.), *Liberalism and the Moral Life*, Cambridge, MA: Harvard University Press, pp. 127–42.

Lukes, S. (2003), *Liberals and Cannibals: The Implications of Diversity*, London: Verso.

McColgan, A. (2000), *Women Under the Law: The False Promise of Human Rights*, Harlow: Longman.

MacCullum, G. (1972), 'Negative and Positive Freedom', in P. Laslett, W. G. Runciman and Q. Skinner (eds), *Philosophy, Politics and Society*, 4th Series, Oxford: Oxford University Press, pp. 174–93.

Mackenzie, C. (2000), 'Imagining Oneself Otherwise', in C. Mackenzie and N. Stoljar (eds), *Relational Autonomy: Feminist Perspectives on Autonomy, Agency, and the Social Self*, Oxford: Oxford University Press, pp. 124–50.

Mackenzie, C. and N. Stoljar (eds) (2000), *Relational Autonomy: Feminist Perspectives on Autonomy, Agency, and the Social Self*, Oxford: Oxford University Press.

Madison, J. [1785] (2010), *A memorial and remonstrance, presented to the General Assembly of the state of Virginia, at their session in 1785, in consequence of a bill brought . . . for the establishment of religion by law*, Farmington Hills, MI: Gale ECCO.

Mahoney, J. (2008), 'Liberalism and the Moral Basis for Human Rights', *Law and Philosophy*, 27: 2, 151–91.

Major, B. and T. Schmader (2001), 'Legitimacy and the Construal of Social Disadvantage', in J. Jost and B. Major (eds), *The Psychology of Legitimacy: Emerging Perspectives on Ideology, Justice and Inter-group Relationships*, New York: Cambridge University Press, pp. 174–204.

Margalit, A. and M. Halbertal (2004), 'Liberalism and the Right to Culture', *Social Research*, 71: 3, 529–48.

Margalit, A. and J. Raz (1990), 'National Self-Determination', *The Journal of Philosophy*, 87: 9, 439–61.

Maritain, J. [1961] (2015), *On the Use of Philosophy: Three Essays*, Princeton: Princeton University Press.

Martínez Cobo, J. (1986/7), *Study of the Problem of Discrimination against Indigenous Populations*, UN Doc. E/CN.4/Sub.2/1986/7, New York: United Nations.

Marx, K. (1978), *Das Kapital: Vol. 1* (1857), in R. C. Tucker (ed.), *The Marx-Engels Reader*, 2nd edn, New York: W. W. Norton, pp. 294–438.

Mayer, A. E. (1995), *Islam and Human Rights: Tradition and Politics*, Boulder, CO: Westview Press.

Menski, W. (2012), 'Hinduism and Human Rights', in J. Witte Jr. and M. C. Green (eds), *Religion and Human Rights: An Introduction*, Oxford: Oxford University Press, pp. 71–86.

Mernissi, F. (1975), *Beyond the Veil: Male–Female Dynamics in Muslim Society*, Cambridge, MA: Schenkman Press.

Mertus, J. (1994), '"Woman" in the Service of National Identity', *Hastings Women's Law Journal*, 5: 1, 5–23.

Mertus, J. (1995), 'State Discriminatory Family Law and Customary Abuses', in J. Peters and A. Wolper (eds), *Women's Rights, Human Rights: International Feminist Perspectives*, New York: Routledge, pp. 135–48.

Milgram, S. (1974), *Obedience to Authority: An Experimental View*, London: Tavistock.

Moller Okin, S. (1999), *Is Multiculturalism Bad for Women?*, Princeton: Princeton University Press.

Moyn, S. (2010), *The Last Utopia: Human Rights in History*, Cambridge, MA: Belknap Press.

Mullender, R. (2003), 'Hegel, Human Rights, and Particularism', *Journal of Law and Society*, 30: 4, 554–74.

Muslim Women's Network (2013), *Unheard Voices: The Sexual Exploitation of Asian Girls and Young Women*, <http://www.mwnuk.co.uk/go_files/resources/UnheardVoices.pdf> (last accessed 27 July 2016).

Mutua, M. (2002), *Human Rights: A Political and Cultural Critique*, Philadelphia: University of Pennsylvania Press.

Mutua, M. (2007), 'Standard Setting in Human Rights: Critique and Prognosis', *Human Rights Quarterly*, 29, 547–630.

Nickel, J. W. (1997), 'Group Agency and Group Rights', in I. Shapiro and W. Kymlicka (eds), *Ethnicity and Group Rights: Nomos XXXIX*, New York: New York University Press, New York, pp. 235–56.

Nickel, J. W. (2006), *Making Sense of Human Rights*, 2nd edn, Oxford: Wiley-Blackwell.

Nickel, J. (2014), 'Human Rights', in E. N. Zalta (ed.), *The Stanford Encyclopedia of Philosophy*, <http://plato.stanford.edu/entries/rights-human/> (last accessed 27 July 2016).

Novak, D. (2012), 'A Jewish Theory of Human Rights', in J. Witte Jr. and M. C. Green (eds), *Religion and Human Rights: An Introduction*, Oxford: Oxford University Press, pp. 27–41.

Nozick, R. (1974), *Anarchy, State and Utopia*, New York: Basic Books.

Nussbaum, M. C. (1990), 'Aristotelian Social Democracy', in R. B. Douglass, G. M. Mara and H. S. Richardson (eds), *Liberalism and the Good*, London: Routledge, pp. 203–52.

Nussbaum, M. C. (1997), 'Capabilities and Human Rights', *Fordham Law Review*, 66: 2, 273–300.

Nussbaum, M. C. and A. Sen (eds) (1993), *The Quality of Life*, Oxford: Oxford University Press.

Oh, I. (2012), 'Islamic Conceptions of Human Rights', in T. Cushman (ed.), *Handbook of Human Rights*, New York: Routledge, pp. 255–65.

O'Neill, O. (1993), 'Justice, Gender and International Boundaries', in M. C. Nussbaum and A. Sen (eds), *The Quality of Life*, Oxford: Oxford University Press, pp. 303–23.

Parekh, B. (2006), *Rethinking Multiculturalism: Cultural Diversity and Political Theory*, 2nd edn, Basingstoke: Palgrave Macmillan.

Parfit, D. (1986), *Reasons and Persons*, Oxford: Oxford University Press.

Pateman, C. (1988), *The Sexual Contract*, Oxford: Polity Press.

Paul, E. F., F. D. Miller and J. Paul (eds) (2003), *Autonomy*, Cambridge: Cambridge University Press.

Perry, M. J. (1998), *The Idea of Human Rights: Four Inquiries*, New York: Oxford University Press.

Pew Research Center (2012), 'Laws Against Blasphemy, Apostasy and Defamation of Religion Are Widespread', <http://www.pewresearch.org/daily-number/laws-against-blasphemy-apostasy-and-defamation-of-religion-are-widespread/> (last accessed 27 July 2016).

Pogge, T. W. (1997), 'Group Rights and Ethnicity', in I. Shapiro and W. Kymlicka (eds), *Ethnicity and Group Rights: Nomos XXXIX*, New York: New York University Press, pp. 187–222.

Pogge, T. W. (2002), *World Poverty and Human Rights*, Cambridge: Polity Press.

Pollis, A. and P. Schwab (1979), *Human Rights: Cultural and Ideological Perspectives*, Baltimore: Johns Hopkins Press.

Pollis, A. and P. Schwab (2000), *Human Rights: New Perspectives, New Realities*, Boulder, CO: Lynne Rienner.

Popper, K. (1962), *The Open Society and Its Enemies: Volume 1, Plato*, Princeton: Princeton University Press.

Posner, E. A. (2014), *The Twilight of Human Rights Law*, Oxford: Oxford University Press.

Putnam, H. (1987), *Representation and Reality*, Cambridge, MA: MIT Press.

Ramcharan, B. G. (2011), *The UN Human Rights Council*, Global Institutions Series, London: Routledge.

Rao, A. (1995), 'The Politics of Gender and Culture in International Human Rights Culture', in J. Peters and A. Wolper (eds), *Women's Rights, Human Rights: International Feminist Perspectives*, London: Routledge, pp. 167–93.

Ravitch, D. (2003), *The Language Police: How Pressure Groups Restrict What Students Learn*, New York: Vintage.

Rawls, J. (1971), *A Theory of Justice*, Cambridge, MA: Harvard University Press.

Rawls, J. (1993), *Political Liberalism*, New York: Columbia University Press.

Rawls, J. (1999), *The Law of Peoples*, Cambridge, MA: Harvard University Press.

Raz, J. (1986), *The Morality of Freedom*, Oxford: Clarendon Press.

Raz, J. (1990), 'Facing Diversity: The Case of Epistemic Abstinence', *Philosophy and Public Affairs*, 19: 1, 3–46.

Raz, J. (1994), *Ethics in the Public Domain: Essays in the Morality of Law and Politics*, Oxford: Clarendon Press.

Reed, E. D. (2012), 'Christianity and Human Rights', in T. Cushman (ed.), *Handbook of Human Rights*, New York: Routledge, pp. 231–43.

Rehal, M. and S. Macguire (2014), *The Price of Honour: Exploring the Issues of Sexual Violence within South Asian Communities*, Coventry: Coventry Rape and Sexual Abuse Centre.

Reich, W. (1971), *The Mass Psychology of Fascism*, 3rd edn, trans. Vincent Carfango, New York: Farrar, Straus and Giroux.

Renteln, A. D. (1988), 'The Concept of Human Rights', *Anthropos*, 83: 4/6, 343–64.

Ruggie, J. (2014), *Just Business: Multinational Corporations and Human Rights*, New York: W. W. Norton.

Saghal, G. (1992), 'Secular Spaces: The Experiences of Asian Women Organizing', in G. Saghal and N. Yuval-Davis (eds), *Refusing Holy Orders: Women and Fundamentalism in Britain*, London: Virago Press, pp. 163–97.

Sahlins, M. (1972), *Stone Age Economics*, London: Routledge.

Said, E. (1985), *Orientalism*, Harmondsworth: Penguin.

Said, E. (2000), 'The Clash of Definitions', in *Reflections on Exile and Other Literary and Cultural Essays*, London: Granta, pp. 569–90.

Sandel, M. (1982), *Liberalism and the Limits of Justice*, Cambridge: Cambridge University Press.

Sanders, D. (1991), 'Collective Rights', *Human Rights Quarterly*, 13: 3, 368–86.

Scanlon, T. M. (1998), *What We Owe to Each Other*, Cambridge MA: Harvard University Press.

Schacter, O. (1983), 'Human Dignity as a Normative Concept', *American Journal of International Law*, 77: 4, 848–54.

Sen, A. (1981), *Poverty and Famines: An Essay in Entitlement and Deprivation*, Oxford: Oxford University Press.

Sen, A. (2005), 'Human Rights and Capabilities', *Journal of Human Development*, 6: 2, 151–66.

Seton-Watson, H. (1977), *Nations and States*, London: Methuen.

Shachar, A. (2001), *Multicultural Jurisdictions: Cultural Differences and Women's Rights*, Cambridge: Cambridge University Press.

Shapiro, I. and W. Kymlicka (eds) (1997), *Ethnicity and Group Rights: Nomos XXXIX*, New York: New York University Press.

Sharma, A. (2004), *Hinduism and Human Rights: A Conceptual Approach*, New Delhi: Oxford University Press.

Shklar, J. N. (1989), 'The Liberalism of Fear', in N. L. Rosenblum (ed.), *Liberalism and the Moral Life*, Cambridge, MA: Harvard University Press, pp. 31–8.

Smith, A. D. (1986), *The Ethnic Origins of Nations*, Oxford: Blackwell.

Smith, A. D. (1996), 'Culture, Community and Territory: The Politics of Ethnicity and Nationalism', *International Affairs*, 72: 3, 445–58.

Soroush, A. (2000), *Reason, Freedom and Democracy in Islam*, trans. M. Sadri and A. Sadri, Oxford: Oxford University Press.

Sullivan, D. (1988), 'Advancing the Freedom of Religion or Belief through the UN Declaration of the Elimination of Religious Intolerance and Discrimination', *American Journal of International Law*, 82, 487–520.

Sullivan, D. (1995), 'The Public/Private Distinction in International Human Rights Law', in J. Peters and A. Wolper (eds), *Women's Rights, Human Rights: International Feminist Perspectives*, New York: Routledge, pp. 126–34.

Sunder, M. (2001), 'Cultural Dissent', *Stanford Law Review*, 54, 495–567.

Sunder, M. (2012), 'Keeping Faith: Reconciling Women's Human Rights and Religion', in J. Witte Jr. and M. C. Green (eds), *Religion and Human Rights: An Introduction*, Oxford: Oxford University Press, pp. 281–98.

Sunstein, C. R. (1991), 'Preferences and Politics', *Philosophy and Public Affairs*, 20: 1, 3–34.

Tajfel, H. (1975), 'The Exit of Social Mobility and the Voice of Social Change: Notes on the Social Psychology of Inter-group Relations', *Social Science Information*, 14: 2, 101–18.

Tamir, Y. (1993), *Liberal Nationalism*, Princeton: Princeton University Press.

Taylor, C. (1981), *The Sources of the Self*, Cambridge: Cambridge University Press.

Taylor, C. (1985), *Philosophical Papers, Volume 2: Philosophy and the Human Sciences*, Cambridge: Cambridge University Press.

Taylor, C. (1992), 'The Politics of Recognition', in *Multiculturalism and 'The Politics of Recognition'*, A. Gutmann (ed.), Princeton: Princeton University Press, pp. 25–73.

Thompson, R. H. (1997), 'Ethnic Minorities and the Case for Collective Rights', *American Anthropologist*, 99: 4, 786–98.

Thornberry, P. (1991), *International Law and the Rights of Minorities*, Oxford: Clarendon Press.

Tillich, P. (1948), *The Shaking of the Foundations*, London: Charles Scribner and Sons.

Tully, J. (1991), *Strange Multiplicity: Constitutionalism in an Age of Diversity*, Cambridge: Cambridge University Press.

UN Division for the Advancement of Women (2009), 'Good Practices in Legislation on "Harmful Practices" Against Women', Report of the expert group meeting, New York: United Nations, <http://www.un.org/womenwatch/daw/egm/vaw_legislation_2009/Report%20EGM%20harmful%20practices.pdf> (last accessed 18 August 2016).

Van der Vyer, J. D. (2012), 'The Right to Self-determination of Religious Communities', in J. Witte Jr. and M. C. Green (eds), *Religion and Human Rights: An Introduction*, Oxford: Oxford University Press, pp. 236–53.

Van Dyke, V. (1985), *Human Rights, Ethnicity, and Discrimination*, Westport, CT: Greenwood Press.

Van Dyke, V. (1995), 'The Individual, the State, and Ethnic Communities in Political Theory', in W. Kymlicka (ed.), *The Rights of Minority Cultures*, Oxford: Oxford University Press, pp. 31–56.

Waldron, J. (1995), 'Minority Cultures and the Cosmopolitan Alternative', in W. Kymlicka (ed.), *The Rights of Minority Cultures*, Oxford: Oxford University Press, pp. 93–119.

Waldron, J. (2012), *The Harm in Hate Speech*, Cambridge, MA: Harvard University Press.

Walker, G. (1997), 'The Idea of Nonliberal Constitutionalism', in I. Shapiro and W. Kymlicka (eds), *Ethnicity and Group Rights: Nomos XXXIX*, New York: New York University Press, pp. 154–86.

Walker, L. (2009), *The Battered Woman Syndrome*, 3rd edn, New York: Springer.

Walzer, M. (1989), 'Nation and Universe', *The Tanner Lectures on Human Values, Delivered at Brasenose College, Oxford University, May 1 and 8, 1989*, <http://tannerlectures.utah.edu/_documents/a-to-z/w/walzer90.pdf> (last accessed 27 July 2016).

Walzer, M. (1994), *Thick and Thin: Moral Argument at Home and Abroad*, Notre Dame, IN: University of Notre Dame Press.

Walzer, M. (1998), 'On Involuntary Association', in A. Gutmann (ed.), *Freedom of Association*, Princeton: Princeton University Press, pp. 64–74.

Witte Jr., J. and M. C. Green (eds) (2012), *Religion and Human Rights: An Introduction*, Oxford: Oxford University Press.

Wolterstorff, N. P. (2008), *Justice: Rights and Wrongs*, Princeton: Princeton University Press.

Wolterstorff, N. P. (2012), 'Christianity and Human Rights', in J. Witte Jr. and M. C. Green (eds), *Religion and Human Rights: An Introduction*, Oxford: Oxford University Press, pp. 42–55.

Wong, D. (1991), 'Relativism', in P. Singer (ed.), *A Companion to Ethics*, Oxford: Blackwell, pp. 442–50.

Young, I. M. (1990), *Justice and the Politics of Difference*, Chicago: Chicago University Press.

Zimbardo, P. (2007), *The Lucifer Effect: How Good People Turn Evil*, New York: Random House.

Legal instruments

African (Banjul) Charter on Human and Peoples' Rights, adopted 27 June 1981, OAU Doc. CAB/LEG/67/3 rev. 5, 21 ILM 58 (1982).

ASEAN Charter (2007), <http://www.mfa.go.th/asean/contents/files/other-20121217-165728-100439.pdf> (last accessed 27 August 2016).

Charter of the United Nations, 26 June 1945, 59 Stat. 1031.

Convention against Torture and Other Cruel, Inhuman, or Degrading Treatment or Punishment, New York, 10 December 1984, 1465 UNTS 85.

Convention Concerning Indigenous and Tribal Peoples in Independent Countries (ILO No. 169), 72 ILO Official Bull. 59, 28 ILM (1989) 1382.

Convention on Biological Diversity 1992, 818 ILM (1992).

Convention on the Prevention and Punishment of the Crime of Genocide, New York, 9 December 1948, 78 UNTS 277.

Convention on the Rights of the Child, New York, 20 November 1989, 1557 UNTS 3.

Convention on the Rights of Persons with Disabilities, New York, 13 December 2006, UN Doc. A/61/611.

Council of Europe Convention for the Protection of Human Rights and Fundamental Freedoms, Strasbourg, 1994, ETS No. 005, 213, UNTS 222, as amended by Protocols Nos 3, 5 and 8.

Council of Europe Framework Convention on the Protection of National Minorities, ETS No. 157, 34, ILM (1995) 351.

Council of the European Union, Council Framework Decision 2008/913/JHA of 28 November 2008 on Combating Certain Forms and Expressions of Racism and Xenophobia by Means of Criminal Law.

Indigenous and Tribal Populations Convention, 1957, (ILO No. 107), 328, UNTS 247; Cmnd 328.
International Convention on the Elimination of All Forms of Discrimination against Women, New York, 18 December 1979, 1249 UNTS 13.
International Convention on the Elimination of All Forms of Racial Discrimination, New York, 7 March 1966, 660 UNTS 195.
International Covenant on Civil and Political Rights, New York, 16 December 1966, 999 UNTS 195.
International Covenant on Economic, Social and Cultural Rights, New York, 16 December 1966, 993 UNTS 3; 6 ILM (1967) 360.
League of Arab States Revised Arab Charter on Human Rights, 22 May 2004, reprinted in *International Human Rights Report*, 12, 893 (2005).
Organization of American States American Convention on Human Rights 'Pact of San Jose, Costa Rica' (B-32), OAS Treaty Series No. 36, 1144 UNTS 123.
Organization for Security and Cooperation in Europe, Document of the Copenhagen Meeting of the Conference on the Human Dimension of the CSCE (June 1990).
Uganda, Anti-Homosexuality Act (2014), <http://www.refworld.org/pdfid/530c4bc64.pdf> (last accessed 27 August 2016).
United Kingdom, Racial and Religious Hatred Act (2006), <http://www.legislation.gov.uk/ukpga/2006/1/contents> (last accessed 27 July 2016).
United Nations, Beijing Declaration and Platform of Action, adopted at the Fourth World Conference on Women (27 October 1995).
Vienna Convention on the Law of Treaties, 1155 UNTS 331.

Non-legally binding documents

Beijing Declaration and Platform for Action, Fourth World Conference on Women, 15 September 1995, A/CONF.177/20 (1995).
Cairo Declaration on Human Rights in Islam, 5 August 1990, UN GAOR, World Conf. on Hum. Rts., 4th Sess., Agenda Item 5, UN Doc. A/CONF.157/PC/62/Add. 18 (1993).
Declaration on Religious Freedom *Dignitatis Humanae* on the Right of the Person and of Communities to Social and Civil Freedom in Matters Religious Promulgated by His Holiness Pope Paul VI on December 7, 1965.
Inter-American Development Bank, *Operational Policy 7-65 on Indigenous Peoples*, adopted 22 February 2006.
UN Commission on Human Rights, *Indigenous Issues: Human rights and indigenous issues, Report of the Special Rapporteur on the situation of human rights and fundamental freedoms of indigenous people, Rodolfo Stavenhagen, Addendum*, E/CN.4/2006/78/Add.5 (17 January 2006).

UN Declaration on the Elimination of All Forms of Intolerance and of Discrimination Based on Religion or Belief, adopted 25 November 1981, GA Res. 55, UN GAOR, 36 Sess., Supp. 51 at 171, UN Doc. A/36/684.

UN Declaration on the Elimination of Violence against Women, General Assembly, UN Doc. A/RES/48/104 (1993).

UN Declaration on the Rights of Indigenous Peoples, UN Doc. A/RES/61/295 (2007).

UN Declaration on the Rights of Persons Belonging to National or Ethnic, Religious and Linguistic Minorities, UN Doc. A/Res/47/135 (1992).

UN General Assembly, *Promotion of human rights: human rights questions, including alternative approaches for improving the effective enjoyment of human rights and fundamental freedoms*, UN Doc. A/67/287 (2012).

UN Human Rights Council, *Report of the Special Rapporteur on the situation of human rights and fundamental freedoms of indigenous people, Rodolfo Stavenhagen*, UN Doc. A/HRC/4/32 (2007).

UN Human Rights Council, *Report of the Special Rapporteur on the rights of indigenous peoples, Victoria Tauli Corpuz*, UN Doc. A/HRC/30/41 (2015).

UN Human Rights Council, Resolution 16/3 *Promoting human rights and fundamental freedoms through a better understanding of traditional values of human kind*, A/HRC/RES/16/3 (2011).

UN Human Rights Council, Resolution 16/18 *On the issue of religious defamation*, A/HRC/RES/16/18 (2011), <http://www2.ohchr.org/english/bodies/hrcouncil/docs/16session/A.HRC.RES.16.18_en.pdf> (last accessed 27 July 2016).

UN Vienna Declaration and Programme of Action adopted by the World Conference of Human Rights, UN Doc. A/CONF.157/23 (1993).

UNESCO Convention on the Protection and Promotion of the Diversity of Cultural Expressions (2005), <http://portal.unesco.org/en/ev.php-URL_ID=31038&URL_DO=DO_TOPIC&URL_SECTION=201.html> (last accessed 27 July 2016).

UNESCO Universal Declaration on Cultural Diversity (2001), <http://portal.unesco.org/en/ev.php-URL_ID=13179&URL_DO=DO_TOPIC&URL_SECTION=201.html> (last accessed 27 July 2016).

United States Commission on International Religious Freedom, Annual Report 2015, <http://www.uscirf.gov/sites/default/files/USCIRF%20Annual%20Report%202015%20%282%29.pdf> (last accessed 27 August 2016).

Universal Declaration of Human Rights, GA Res. 217A (III), UN Doc. A/810 at 71 (1948).

Treaty monitoring body general comments

United Nations Economic, Social and Cultural Rights Committee, General Comment No. 21, Article 15 (Forty-third session, 2009), E/C.12/GC/21.

United Nations Human Rights Committee, General Comment No. 12, Article 1 (Twenty-first session, 1984), Compilation of General Comments and General Recommendations Adopted by Human Rights Treaty Bodies, UN Doc. HRI/GEN/1/Rev.1.
United Nations Human Rights Committee, General Comment No. 22, Article 18 (Forty-eighth session, 1993), UN Doc. CCPR/C/21/Rev.1/Add.4.
United Nations Human Rights Committee, General Comment No. 23, Article 27 (Fiftieth session, 1994), Compilation of General Comments and General Recommendations Adopted by Human Rights Treaty Bodies, UN Doc. HRI/GEN/1/Rev.1.

Legal cases

Advisory Opinion, *Western Sahara*, Advisory Opinion 16 October 1975 (1975) ICJ Reports 12.
Beauharnais v Illinois 343 US (1952).
Bull v Hall (2013), <https://www.supremecourt.uk/cases/docs/uksc-2012-0065-judgment.pdf> (last accessed 27 July 2016).
Calder v British Columbia (AG) SCR 313 (1973) 4 WWR 1.
Centre for Minority Rights Development (Kenya) and Minority Rights Group International (on behalf of Endorois Welfare Council) v Kenya, Comm 276/2003, 25 November 2009.
Christian Education, South Africa v Minister of Education, 2000 (4) SA 757; 2000 (10) BCLR 1051 (CC).
Dogru v France 49 EHRR 8 (2009).
Hodkin v Registrar (2013), <https://www.supremecourt.uk/cases/docs/uksc-2013-0030-judgment.pdf> (last accessed 27 July 2016).
Gareth Lee v Ashers Baking Co Ltd (2015), <http://www.equalityni.org/ECNI/media/ECNI/Cases%20and%20Settlements/2015/Lee-v-Ashers_Judgement.pdf> (last accessed 27 July 2016).
Mabo v Queensland (No 2) [1992] HCA 23; (1992) 175 CLR 1.
Obergefell v Hodges 576 US (2015), <http://www.supremecourt.gov/opinions/14pdf/14-556_3204.pdf> (last accessed 27 July 2016).
Sahin v Turkey (2007) 44 EHRR 5.
Santa Clara Pueblo v Martinez 436 US 49 (1978).
S.A.S. v France (2014), <https://strasbourgobservers.com/2013/11/29/s-a-s-v-france-a-short-summary-of-an-interesting-hearing/> (last accessed 27 August 2016).
Sesana and Others v Attorney-General (2006) AHRLR 183 (BwHC 2006).
The Church of the Holy Trinity v United States 143 US 457 (1895).
Torcaso v Watkins 367 US 488 (1961).
United States v Kauten 133 F.2d 703 (2d Cir. 1943).

United States v Seeger 380 US 163 (1965).
Wisconsin v Yoder 406 US 205 (1972).

Other sources

Invisible Girl Project, <http://invisiblegirlproject.org/the-issue/> (last accessed 27 July 2016).
Musawah Women's Movement, <http://www.musawah.org> (last accessed 27 July 2016).
Yogakarta Principles (2006), <http://www.yogyakartaprinciples.org> (last accessed 27 July 2016).

Index